MOZART'S
DON GIOVANNI

Da Capo Press Music Reprint Series
GENERAL EDITOR
FREDERICK FREEDMAN
VASSAR COLLEGE

MOZART'S
DON GIOVANNI

A Commentary by
CHARLES GOUNOD

Translated from the Third French Edition by
Windeyer Clark and J. T. Hutchinson

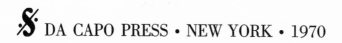 DA CAPO PRESS • NEW YORK • 1970

A Da Capo Press Reprint Edition

This Da Capo Press edition of
Mozart's Don Giovanni
is an unabridged republication of the
first English edition published in London
in 1895.

Library of Congress Catalog Card Number 78-125050

SBN 306-70015-8

Published by Da Capo Press
A Division of Plenum Publishing Corporation
227 West 17th Street
New York, N.Y. 10011

MOZART'S
DON GIOVANNI.

—

CHARLES GOUNOD.

THE translators beg to thank Messrs. Novello for their courteous permission to quote from Lady Macfarren's English version of the Operatic text.

MOZART'S
DON GIOVANNI;

A COMMENTARY

BY

CHARLES GOUNOD.

TRANSLATED FROM THE THIRD FRENCH EDITION

BY

WINDEYER CLARK,

Licentiate of the Royal Academy of Music,

AND

J. T. HUTCHINSON,

Professor of Singing and Associate Royal Academy of Music.

(COPYRIGHT. AUTHORISED TRANSLATION.)

ROBERT COCKS & Co.,

6, NEW BURLINGTON STREET, LONDON, W.

BY SPECIAL APPOINTMENT

Music Publishers to H.M. The Queen and H.R.H. The Prince of Wales.

1895.

PREFACE.

DON GIOVANNI, that unequalled and immortal masterpiece, that apogee of the lyrical drama, has attained a hundred years of existence and of fame*; it is popular, universally accepted, and consecrated for ever. Is it understood? This wondrous example of truth of expression, beauty of form, appropriateness of characterisation, deep insight into the drama, purity of style, richness and restraint in the instrumentation, charm and tenderness in the love passages, loftiness and power in pathos—in one word, this finished model of dramatic music—is it admired, is it loved as it should be? I may be permitted to doubt it.

The score of *Don Giovanni* has exercised the influence of a revelation

---

* It was first performed at Prague, Oct. 29, 1787.

upon the whole of my life; it has been and remains for me a kind of incarnation of dramatic and musical infallibility. I regard it as a work without blemish, of uninterrupted perfection, and this commentary is but the humble testimony of my veneration and gratitude for the genius to whom I owe the purest and most permanent joys of my life as a musician.

There are in history certain men who seem destined to mark, in their own sphere, a pinnacle beyond which it is impossible to advance. Such was Phidias in the art of sculpture, and Molière in that of comedy. Mozart is one of these men; *Don Giovanni* is such a pinnacle.

One word as to the aim of this book. I dedicate it especially to young composers, and to those who take part in the interpretation of *Don Giovanni.* It is not here my intention to teach either the one or the other, but I have thought that in presence of beauties so profound and delicate, distributed with such profusion in this imperishable masterpiece, it would not be use-

less to make known and to record the
impressions and emotions of a musician
who has loved it unswervingly and
admired it unreservedly.

DON GIOVANNI.

Intuition, the spontaneous penetrating insight of genius, is nothing but
an unconscious philosophy; it is reason
perceived by feeling, which is, in man,
the first phase of creative power,
Hence the infallibility of genius; it
sees, we *reason*. I shall endeavour to
point out what Mozart has seen.

A COMMENTARY

ON

DON GIOVANNI.

THE OVERTURE.

FROM the beginning of the Overture, Mozart is completely in the spirit of the drama, of which it is an epitome. The first chords, so powerful and solemn with their syncopated rhythm, establish at once the majestic and formidable authority of Divine justice, the avenger of crime. After the first four bars (which are rendered yet more terrible by the silence which completes the second and the fourth) there commences a harmonic progression, the sinister character of which freezes one with terror, as would the appearance of a spectre. We shall find this same passage recur in the last scene of the drama, when, in response to the invitation to supper, the statue of the Commandant arrives at the house of the assassin. There is nothing to equal the tragic tranquility of this series of chords, the linking together of which is one of the innumerable inspirations of this unique musician. They are sustained by a rhythm whose fatal persistence suggests that mercy is no longer possible for this impenitent being, who has defied the world by his crimes and heaven by his blasphemies. Everything in this tremendous introduction breathes terror and inspires awe : the persistent and unfathomable rhythm of the strings, the sepulchral timbre of the wind instruments, wherein the intervals of an octave from bar to bar resemble the steps of a stone giant, the minister of Death ; the syncopations of the first violins, which, starting at the eleventh bar, probe the innermost recesses of this dark conscience ; the figure of the second violins, which entwines like an immense reptile around the culprit, whose stubborn resistance struggles blindly and insultingly to the end ; the scales, those affrighting scales, ascending and descending, which manifest themselves like the billows of a tempestuous sea; the menace suspended over the head of the criminal by the solemnity of this impressive opening; everything, in fact, in this prodigious page is of the highest tragical inspiration—the force of terror could go no further.

But suddenly, and with feverish audacity, the *Allegro* breaks out in the major key : an *Allegro* full of passion and delirium, deaf to the warnings of Heaven, regardless of remorse, enraptured of pleasure, madly inconstant and daring, rapid and impetuous as a torrent, flashing and swift as a sword, overleaping all obstacles, scaling balconies and bewildering the alguazils. With regard to rhythm, there are to be met with here two kinds of accent that Mozart specially affected. The first, which is to be found in the third and fourth bars, is the dwelling upon the second beat of the bar (which in ₵ time is a weak beat, but which has the effect of syncopation on the half

of the first beat in 𝄵, duple time).
This gives to the rhythm, especially
in a quick movement, an air of eagerness, of impatience, of breathlessness,
which well expresses the dissolute
career of Don Giovanni among those
pleasures so quickly forgotten, so constantly renewed.   The other accent
is the *sforzando*, which gives much
energy to the first beat, from which
the rest of the musical phrase springs
with such flexibility and lightness.
Examples :

But how many salient points and
piquant incidents there are to admire
in this overture, the dazzling fancy of
which, it has been said, only cost its

author the labour of a night ! From
the first, what sonority is obtained
with so few notes and by such simple
means ! What youthfulness of manner and what lordly magnificence are
there in bars 8 and 9 of the *Allegro* !
What brightness in the tone and the
rhythm of the wind instruments which
succeed the delicate and refined sonority of the strings ! What impetuosity in the quaver figure, which, starting at bar 16, leads through such a
vivid and fiery *crescendo* ! What
coaxing charm in the 3rds of the
hautboys and clarionets in the 32nd
bar ! What vigour in the unison of
bars 47 and 48 against the sustained
notes of two trumpets and two horns !
And how tumultuous, yet still clear, is
the effect of the double imitation in
canon, commencing at the 55th bar !
What ingenious counterpoint appears at
bar 102 in that marvellous conjunction
of wind instruments in imitation, and the
figure of the violins, full of roguishness
and gaiety ! Finally, what grace and
unexpected freshness in the modulation
to F, which links the Overture to the—

RISING OF THE CURTAIN.

ACT I.—No. 1.*

LEPORELLO, Don Giovanni's valet, or, more exactly, his beast of burden, is alone in the open air, awaiting his master, who has penetrated by night into the palace of the Commandant, in order to carry off the noble and beautiful Donna Anna. Instantly, from the first notes of the symphony, the orchestra shivers with Leporello (chicken-heart!) who is benumbed more by fear than cold, and starts at the slightest sound. In two bars Mozart has depicted his man:

> "Rest I've none by night or day,
> Scanty fare and doubtful pay,
> Every whim I must fulfil;
> Take my place whoever will!"

After the complaints so ludicrously emphasised by the employment of the

---

* I adopt here, for the division into numbers, the order of the Italian score, which is in two acts.

same form of passage four times, Leporello grows bold :

> "I myself will go a-courting,
> I the gentleman will play,
> But with him no more I'll stay."

Thereupon, observe the air of resolution and gallantry assumed by the orchestra. And then

> " Gaily he within is sporting,
> I must keep off all intrusion,
> For his lordship needs seclusion,
> I myself will go a-courting."

He has made up his mind.

> "But I think I hear him coming,
> I'll keep safe out of his way."

Again the orchestra depicts new fears, and Leporello prudently steps aside, while a tumultuous passage introduces the desperate struggle between Donna Anna and her would-be ravisher. What a hand-to-hand encounter, what energy in her despairing cry,

> "Help, oh heaven, will none befriend me?"

What a marvellous painting is given by the orchestra of this breathless contest! Remark also the utterances of the poltroon Leporello. In the presence of such truthful expression the eyes might be closed ; the music renders the drama visible.

Awakened by the cries of his daughter, the Commandant appears, sword in hand, and demands satisfaction for the outrage. Swords are crossed, and after some rapid passes, which the scales in the violins and basses seem to make scintillate in the obscurity, the Commandant falls, mortally wounded.

Here occurs a short Trio of incomparable majesty, a masterpiece of tragic expression, and one of the most imposing pages of musical drama that it is possible to conceive. As usual, the situation is defined from the first note. There is no hesitation, no useless preamble ; the lugubrious gravity of the movement, the rhythmical uniformity of the violin triplets over the holding-notes of the wind instruments, the basses—abashed, as it were, by the murder—marking with icy regularity the first and third beats of the bar, the appropriate employment (with prodigious ease and freedom) of the three bass voices, each according to its character, all of these bestow upon this never-to-be-forgotten scene an impression of awe and astonishment that has not been surpassed by the pen of Dante or the chisel of Michael Angelo. This Trio concludes with five bars for orchestra, so striking that they deserve to be the object of special analysis—yes, five bars have been sufficient for Mozart to manifest the power of his genius, as one instant sufficed for the " Let there be light " of the Creator. The reason is that genius expresses by a single word what it sees at a single glance, and that this word is the *exact name* for the thing seen. This absolute accuracy of expression never relaxes for a moment in this master of masters, the truest and most beautiful, the most human and the most divine of all.

What can be more mournful than the chromatic phrase which descends slowly, as if exhausted by the blood which oozes from the wound ! How the eyelids droop over that look which will soon be extinguished for ever! How life struggles to re-assert itself, by a last effort (at the third bar), only to relapse finally upon that terrifying chord which announces the departure of the soul, and the commencement of the rigidity of death.

Thus terminates this powerful Introduction, the most beautiful exposition of the lyrical drama known to me.

No. 2.

MEANWHILE, Donna Anna, who has escaped from the hands of her assailant, re-enters with her betrothed, Don Ottavio. Let us follow, step by step, note by note, this scene of sustained and inexpressible beauty. First, what anxiety, what bewilderment of restlessness in the four bars which precede the recitative, "*Ma qual mai s'offre, oh Dei, spettacolo funesto agli occhi miei!*" ("What is this I behold ; can I believe my senses !") At sight of the body extended upon the ground, the poor agitated girl has instinctively divined that it is her father. With what forebodings does she hasten, panting and maddened by terror. Alas! it is he ; it is indeed he! "*Il padre, padre mio, mio caro padre!*" What a tender and at the same time distracting sob is that which occurs at the resolution of the dominant 7th chord in the key of A flat. What union of

grief and indignation in the declamation of the following words : " *Ah!
l'assassino mel trucidò!* " And then there is a flood of tears, which, where everything is so admirable, must be specially admired : this touching plaint of the voice in dialogue with that of the orchestra, and the ascending progression of chords which affects everything with ghastly reality. " *Quel sangue—quella piaga—quel volto tinto e coperto del color di morte.*" Oh! the sad harmony following upon the last words " *di morte* "; how mournful and gloomy it is ! And that which succeeds it—the measured and palpitating rhythm of the four crotchets. " *Ei non respira più! fredde le membra!* " How the trembling hands of the poor girl long to restore this adored parent to life. At last she is overpowered by despair, at the return of those three exclamations, still more poignant than the first time, " *Il padre, padre mio, mio caro padre!* " This last cry, and the chord which accompanies it, cause her to burst into tears ; it is the climax of grief.

But that which one cannot too often remark, nor too often endeavour to make understood, that which renders Mozart an absolutely unique genius, is the constant and indissoluble union of *beauty of form* with *truth of expression.* By this *truth* he is *human*, by this *beauty* he is *divine*. By truth he touches us, he moves us, we recognise each other in him, and we proclaim thereby that he indeed knows human nature thoroughly, not only in its different passions, but also in the varieties of form and character that those passions may assume. By beauty the real is transfigured, although at the same time it is left entirely recognisable ; he elevates it by the magic of a superior language, and transports it to that region of serenity and light which constitutes Art, wherein Intelligence repeats, with the tranquility of Vision, what the heart has experienced in the trouble of Passion.

Now the union of truth with beauty is Art itself.

Let us return, however, to the analysis of this admirable scene.

After that last despairing cry :
"*Padre amato !*" Donna Anna again
falls prostrate beside the corpse : "*Io
manco, io moro !*"

What perfection, and at the same
time what nobility of expression are
found in the two bars for orchestra
which precede the words "*Io manco*"
and which are reproduced, with still
more enfeebled effect before the words
"*Io moro!*" Suddenly Don Ottavio
addresses the servitors of Donna Anna,
who have hastily assembled in response to the cries of their mistress.
"*Ah, soccorete, amici, il mio tesoro.*"
What eagerness and solicitude is
there in the broken rhythm of the
orchestra! And he, the unfortunate
lover, what sufferings does he endure
for the sake of her whom he loves, and
with what anxiety does he watch her
slightest movements! "*Il duolo es-
tremo la meschinelli uccide!* ("Her
grief extreme hath cruelly overwhelmed her!") But no. "*Già rin-
viene*" ("She awakens"). "*Date-
le nouvi ajuti*" ("Newly revives
her sorrow"). At last Donna Anna

regains consciousness and murmurs
feebly "*Padre mio!*" "*Celate*," exclaims Don Ottavio, "*allontanate agli
occhi suoi quell' ogetto d'orrore.*"
(" Hasten, and bear away ere she
perceive it this memorial of terror.")
Then turning towards Donna Anna:
"Look up, my dearest, oh, turn to me."
But she rises, and in a superb burst of
indignation, exclaims—

> " Cruel, why art thou near me?
> Leave me alone to perish,
> Since he I most did cherish
> Is lost for evermore!"

What resolute energy in the opening
attack of the voice, which precedes the
orchestra, upon the words "*Fuggi,
crudele, fuggi*," to return almost
immediately to an expression of grief
at the words: "*Lascia, che mora
anch' io.*"
What is so marvellous in Mozart is
the ease with which he, so to speak,
gives to each word its exact value and
meaning in the sentence, without de-
tracting in the least from the unity of
style and character of the musical
phrase. Every idea flows from the

fountain-head with such abundance
that nothing seems to lack spontaneity,
although each detail satisfies the
most rigorous demands of thoughtful reflection. This is because true
genius is the highest form of judgment,
whose privilege it is to attain its end
with directness and infallibility, as
common sense reaches its aim without
having need to climb the successive
degrees of logical reasoning: genius
is an authority both on account of its
evident truth, and its captivating
beauty.

At the sight of Donna Anna's tears,
Don Ottavio responds, accompanied
by a most caressing violin figure,
displaying a tender compassion at
the words : " *Senti, cor mio deh
senti, guardami un solo istante, ti
parla il caro amante, che vive sol per
te.*"

"Listen to me, oh, listen,
Turn but thine eyes upon me,
I know thou'lt not disown me,
Who love thee evermore."

There is much charm and touching
grace in Donna Anna's reply ; great

dignity and noble simplicity in this very natural conflict between her grief as a daughter and her tenderness as a lover! Each note in the stifled voice, in the subdued and restrained emotion of the orchestra, translates faithfully the reserve that is momentarily imposed upon love by grief. "*Tu sei—perdon, mio bene, l'affano mio, le pene. Ah, il padre mio dov'è*"?

> " 'Tis thou—forgive, oh dearest,
> Of all now left me the nearest.
> My father I would see ! "

What could be more noble and more purely sympathetic than the arpeggios of the first and second violins, which seem for a moment to pour the balm of pity upon the open wound of grief! Don Ottavio responds : "*Lascia, o cara, la rimembranza amara, hai sposo e padre in me!*"

> "Hush, oh, dearest,
> Breathe not the word thou fearest;
> Thou'st husband and father in me ! "

There could be nothing more loyal, more generous or more protecting than the intonation of the interval of the 7th upon the words "*Hai sposo, hai padre,"* nothing firmer or more re-assuring than the last two bars : " *Hai sposo e padre in me."*

Beneath such accents are revealed a heart and an arm which can be relied upon without fear.

After this touching dialogue, the re-petition of which gives greater breadth to the phrase and more intensity to the expression, Donna Anna yields herself entirely to the desire for vengeance. " Ah ! " she exclaims proudly, " if thou canst, avenge him, swear it by heaven above." " I swear it ! " Don Ottavio replies resolutely, " I swear it by our love." Immediately bursts forth the magnificent perora-tion, full of both decision and anguish, " *Che giuramento, oh Dei ! "*

The two lovers retire. Don Gio-vanni reappears with Leporello, and a rapid dialogue in recitative ensues between master and servant.

The *recitativo secco*, which is to be met with for some time after Mozart in the Italian masters of the early part of this century (among others in the operas of Rossini), is no longer in use. It was called "*recitativo al cembalo*," because it was accompanied (by the conductor himself) upon a small *clavecin* placed in front of him and backing upon the prompter's box.

This kind of recitative had great advantages. Apart from the fact that it permitted the composer to glide rapidly over all those parts of the dialogue which were not to be set as musical numbers, it gave rest to the attention, and displayed so much better the worth of the pieces really devoted to the expression and the development of the interesting scenes.

Nowadays, in lyrical works everything is treated with almost equal importance, which occasions not only great length of performance, but also a monotony which promptly becomes fatiguing to the auditor. Recitative,

pure and simple, answered ingeniously
by its vivacious style and by a kind
of musical familiarity for all those
minute stage details which enter much
more into the domain of conversation
than into that of the musical drama.

Don Giovanni succeeds in imposing
silence upon his valet, whose admoni-
tions bore him, by remarking that he
perceives a woman coming. " Let us
watch this fair lady ; step aside here
with me."

No. 3.

ELVIRA appears, Elvira the despised
love, the slighted wife, the exasperated
spouse, always searching for her unfaithful husband, and vowing to avenge
herself if she should find him. Indignation, jealousy, rage, all of these are
expressed by the orchestra from the
first bar of the symphony which precedes this marvellous number.

" Where shall I find a token to guide my steps
     to thee?
My heart is nearly broken, the world is dark
     to me!"

In Mozart the expression is always
so perfectly and so absolutely accurate
that the musical phrase depicts even
the gestures and attitudes of the personages speaking ; it really portrays
them, both in mind and body. This
is especially apparent ten bars after the
entry of the voice, where one almost
seems to be in the clutches of jealousy,
described by the darting passages of
the violins, violas, and basses which
occur in this piece of instrumentation,

so restrained and yet vibrating with
truth of expression, upon the words :—

> "Ah! if he stood before me,
> Fiercely his vows I'd spurn!"

What a delightful "aside," at once
caressing and voluptuous, is that of
Don Giovanni :—

> "Look yonder, 'tis a damsel
> Who's by her swain forsaken!"

Observe the cooings of a libertine
compassion upon the words "*Poverina,
poverina!*" and the enchanting cajolery
of the orchestra at " *Cerchiam di con-
solare il suo tormento.*" (" I think I'll
go and try just to console her.")
Thereupon Leporello ventures to remark pertinently :—" No doubt, like
many others you'll cajole her."

Don Giovanni approaches and recognises Elvira.

Here the recitative re-appears.
After several embarrassed—and em-
barrassing explanations, Don Giovanni
escapes, leaving Donna Elvira with
Leporello. "Pray, Ma'am, be com-
forted," says he, " for you are not, nor
have been, and neither will be, or the

first or last of them. Look here now,
see this not small volume, 'tis almost
full of the names of his fair ones;
town and village, distant countries,
yes, foreign nations, can witness bear
to his infatuations."

No. 4.

WE must follow, step by step, this masterly air, so justly celebrated, which abounds with points of humour and raillery.

What delicacy and what sobriety of instrumentation is here ! At the beginning, though only the stringed instruments are employed, there is always completeness in the harmony of the second violins and violas which accompany the alternate phrases of the first violins and of the basses.

At the 16th bar the horns appear; their fanfare, mingled with the laughter of the flutes and bassoons, emphasises with an air of braggadocio this list of fair ones who have been deceived. At the same time the descending staccato scales of the first violins reappear after the recital of each series of conquests by this indefatigable but inconstant lover : six hundred and forty here, two hundred and thirty there, a hundred in France,

ninety-one in Turkey; but in Spain,
ah! in Spain, a thousand and three!
In the orchestra there is immediately
an ostentatious display of boastfulness, and an accumulation of nuances
accompany the recital of this fabulous
enumeration of countesses, waiting-
maids, rustic beauties, courtly dames
and maidens — in short, women of
every rank and of every age.

Observe the snarling mockery of
the wind instruments during this inexhaustible recapitulation, the bantering summing-up of all his successes
in the palaces or in the streets; notice
how the face of this chattering servant
is brightened with a trivial joy, and
yet the music never loses its air of
distinction while depicting this trivi-
ality.

Then follows an *Andante* full of
grace and cajolery attendant upon
another kind of description, that of
the different attractions needed by
the noble gallant in order to vary his
pleasures and re-awaken his desires.

With what admirable art (I have
already spoken of it, and shall often

have to do so again), with what admirable art does Mozart reconcile the delineation of each detail and the necessary structure of the whole musical phrase in its logical unity.

There is here, it seems to me, a striking analogy between that perfection and that facility of craftsmanship which are met with in the masterpieces of painting and sculpture; every detail is most scrupulously observed, and nothing disturbs the tranquil balance of the work as a whole.

This second part of the air is an impressive and sustained example of the innate delicacy and instinctive scrupulousness with which the innocence of genius abounds, and that sure instinct that spontaneously fashions every detail (however transient it may be) in each one of the features that compose the interest and mobility of life, the ensemble of which would escape the most sustained efforts of scrutinising observation.

Let us analyse minutely this fidelity to details, united to so much tranquility and freedom in the general contour of the piece.

"Is a maiden fair and slender,
  He will praise her for modest sweetness,
Then the dark ones are so tender!
  Lint-white tresses shew discreetness."

Sixteen bars are sufficient for Mozart to make a finished portrait of these three kinds of beauties.

What flexibility and grace there is in the first eight bars, so calmly proceeding upon a tonic pedal, and how charming is the momentary diversion to the chord of the sub-dominant, at the end of the sixth bar, returning at once (and with what ease!) by the chord of the dominant in the seventh bar, to the conclusion upon the tonic in bar eight. Eight bars for a phrase perfect and complete in harmony and melody, perfect and complete as a portrait also! What a privilege, among so many others, is that rapidity of glance and conciseness of language which permits genius to say so many things in so few words without omitting anything essential to the perfection of the picture. In the four bars that follow, which are devoted to "the brunette," there is great decision of attitude, we see that this "brunette" is resolute and determined. In the other four bars, dedicated to "the fair one," the phrase becomes caressing, and inclines with a graceful inflexion towards the expression of sweetness.

Next follows the recital of the Don's preferences according to the seasons:—

"When 'tis cold he likes her portly,
In the summer, slim and courtly";

then on a pompous ascending passage, the majestic presence of the "tall and haughty"; a figure in the contrary direction describes the gracefulness of the "tiny one," so well expressed by the rapid articulation of the syllables in a phrase descending through the vocal compass, just as one lowers the hand towards the ground in describing anyone of small stature. However, all these youthful varieties are not sufficient for Don Giovanni. He must even have those of mature age, if only as *specimens* in the collection.

Nevertheless, it is the young, the uninitiated, for whom he has a predominant passion. No matter to him if a woman be rich, beautiful, or ugly: provided it be a petticoat he asks nothing more.

There is, in the conclusion of this number, starting at the words " *delle vecchie jà conquista*," a crowd of details, each one finer and more piquant than the preceding. Thus, at the words, " That their names may grace these pages," there is an interrupted cadence upon the chord of B flat, which seems to say :—" Even the old ladies, isn't it shameful ? "

At the phrase, " *Non si picca, se sia ricca*,"—(" poor or wealthy, wan or healthy," — the inspiration of Mozart produces an almost unheard-of accuracy of expression ; it is the succession of trills which, after being heard on the first beat for five bars, heightens the effect still more at the sixth bar by marking each one of the three beats with great spirit.

It would be impossible to render in more felicitous style the cynical indifference with which this man, steeped in sensuality, consigns one after the

other, his innumerable and unhappy
victims, to the region of forgetfulness.

One point which deserves particular mention is the touch of musical
comedy by which this lengthy enumeration is terminated at the words
*" Pur che porti la gonella, voi sapete
quel che fà."*

"He to win them makes his duty
And, you know it, not in vain."

There is upon the words *" voi sapete "* such an astounding aggregation
of details, so full of significance in the
choice of rhythm and timbre, that, in
spite of its apparent reticence, we fully
understand what is in question at *" voi
sapete."* There is not a note, not a
rest, not a sound which does not contribute its clear though subdued share
to this coarse diagnosis, which the
divine hands of genius alone could
attempt without raising a blush, so
completely do they purify everything
they touch.

First we must notice the expressive
reserve of the basses, playing softly
by themselves on the first beat of the
bar (*Andante*, bar 63), the notes be-

ing quitted immediately as if they were embarrassed at what is going to be said, and the comical *sotto voce* of the strings, whose bashful reticence is so pleasantly and so unostentatiously scoffed at by the two hautboys and the bassoon; then the detached notes of the solo bassoon mingling its mocking " ha ha's " with the fresh and youthful laughter of the flute : all of this is so absolutely perfect in discernment and so powerful in portrayal that I cannot find its equal in the dramatic music of any other composer.

Observe the treatment of the orchestra here ; observe it, with its exact balance between what is *necessary* and what is *sufficient*, fulfilling its true mission, that of participation, not self-assertion, reconciling, with as much reserve as precision, the thousand nuances of a character with its undisturbed unity ; abiding, with the wise economy of real power, in the exact medium of intensity and length in the dramatic situations, neither overpowering nor feeble, never having anything too much, yet having all

that is necessary. Ah! how far removed are we from that ponderous
and pretentious bombast that is supposed to be touching when it is really
overwhelming, and which mistakes
heaviness for richness, and bathos for
grandeur! But to proceed.

No. 5.

WE are now in the midst of country revels. Two young peasants who are betrothed, Zerlina and Masetto, come upon the scene, all bedecked with flowers and ribbons, as gay as larks, and are followed by their companions, assembled to celebrate the wedding. Here the colouring of the artist, always true and accurate in expression, changes as if by enchantment. There is a freshness of tone, a sprightliness of rhythm, a heartiness of mirth, redolent of country life. A short duet, full of laughter and freedom, is interrupted here and there by the joyous acclamations of the peasants : it is like a flight of butterflies across an atmosphere of sunshine.

No. 6.

Don Giovanni and Leporello enter.
Mozart here resumes the brisk and
familiar form of simple recitative which
enables him to glide rapidly over the
facetious words and compliments offered by Don Giovanni to all these
pretty maidens, and especially to Zerlina, with whom he is longing to be
alone. Accordingly he enjoins Leporello to entice her betrothed (Masetto)
away,* and then begins the celebrated
and delightful duettino " *Là ci darem
la mano.*"
It is marvellous to see here,
as everywhere in the Opera, how
exact Mozart's taste is in the
just proportion of accent and expression. There is neither weakness nor exaggeration. No useless
developments, yet nothing lacking.
The proportions of the piece, por-

---

* No mention is made by M. Gounod of the song
for Masetto, which here follows in the original, but
which is frequently omitted in performance.—(*Translators.*)

trayal of the characters, combination of instruments, and blending of the various tone-colours, all reveal that certainty of insight which is the mark and secret of authority. Can there be anything more coaxing, more enticing, than the opening phrase uttered by Don Giovanni :—

"Give me thy hand, oh fairest,
Whisper a gentle 'Yes,'
Come, if for me thou carest,
With joy my life to bless."

Are not impatience and ardour of sensual desire hidden under the mask of this gentle persuasion? And the response of Zerlina (repeating the same musical phrase), is it not stamped by that languor of resistance which is already a weakness, and which is emphasised by the addition of two bars before the full close (bars 16, 17). Then the gallant is more and more pressing. The dialogue becomes very animated, each singing but two bars :

"Come, dearest, let me guide thee."

Accompanying this *Mezzo-forte* by the wind instruments, Mozart at once

gives prominence to the longings of
the singer ; Zerlina, in two bars also,
and with timid grace, replies :—

"Masetto sure will chide me."

Don Giovanni responds in a two-bar
phrase :—

"I'll change thy fortune."

Zerlina, her will becoming weaker and
weaker, says :—

"Ah, that I could deny thee."

Then the opening subject reappears,
but now broken, divided between the
two voices, which thus continue the
contest up to the moment when Zerlina finally yields, repeating three
times a melodic progression, which
grows fainter by each repetition being
a third lower than the preceding :

presto non son più   for - te,non son   più

for - te, non son più   for - te

" Let us go," urges the Don, and
" Let us go," cries she in her turn
with resolute gaiety.

Then this charming duet is completed by a joyous peroration in $\frac{6}{8}$ time, characterised by the sprightliness of childhood and the heedlessness of youth.

No. 7.

DONNA ELVIRA, the indignant wife, now appears, and surprises her faithless husband in the very act of abduction. Recitative, " Leave her, thou vile seducer," &c., &c. Here follows an air, characterised by great hauteur and dignity.

" The traitor means deceit,
His flattery heed thou not."

says Elvira to Zerlina. Nothing could better express the resentment of a woman outraged in her love. It might be thought that this air makes useless repetition of the sentiments of jealousy and rage which are found in the commencement of the Terzetto, No. 3, and which is in reality nothing but an air for Donna Elvira interrupted by the "asides" of Don Giovanni and Leporello. But, apart from the fact that the situation is different, the sentiment is of another shade. Here one feels that Elvira is dominated by a sentiment of contempt, and that

she seeks above all to cast shame
upon the revolting conduct of her husband, who is not only unfaithful, but
also an ungovernable libertine. The
rhythm of this fine piece depicts admirably that revulsion of feeling which
causes the blood to rush to the face
in an outburst of indignation. However, it is not impossible that Mozart
may have written it at the solicitation
of the singer in order to give a little
more importance to the part of Elvira.
Composers are occasionally obliged to
yield to the demands of those who in-
terpret their works, under penalty of
discontenting them and making them
dissatisfied with their rôles.

In the score of "Don Giovanni"
there are two or three other numbers
upon which I shall have occasion to
make the same remark, that, notwithstanding their intrinsic value (which
cannot be disputed), do not, perhaps,
owe their situation in the work solely
to dramatic considerations.

No. 8.

THE quartet "*Non ti fidar, o misera*" is a faultless model of dramatic music. The characters and the situations are here treated with that unerring instinct which one cannot cease to admire, so entirely does it satisfy at one and the same time the demands of the most rigorous analysis and the requirements of the most complete synthesis. Donna Elvira's opening phrase is full of dignity and unwavering accusation :

> "Oh, ere thou trust in him, beware!
> His heart is cold as stone;
> Know that his vows are writ in air,
> I their deceit have known."

Mozart gives to his characters a musical contour of such striking accuracy that it is impossible to be deceived about the qualities of each ; he draws them and paints them so that they stand out bodily before our eyes. Be it a "*grand seigneur*," like Don Giovanni, a nobleman like

Don Ottavio, a "*grande dame*," like
Donna Anna or Donna Elvira, rustics
such as Zerlina or Masetto, a digni-
tary like the Commandant, or a valet
like Leporello, the musical form is
always a faithful, distinct, and striking reflexion of the personage; it reproduces the character, the language,
the rank, the manner—noble or ple-
beian; and that not by the convenient
and commonplace process of artificial
unity, which consists of fastening a
phrase, like a label, upon an individual
—a formula which, once adopted, is
reproduced with obstinate persistence.
Unity, with Mozart, is identity, not
monotony; he shows us the same
individual under a variety of circumstances: it is analogous to the character of a handwriting, which is always apparent, notwithstanding that
it is composed of different letters.
The "asides" of Donna Anna and
Don Ottavio, starting from bar 10,

"Heaven! a noble lady this!"

are marked by a feeling of respect, of
sympathy, I was almost going to say
of favourable prepossession for the

plaint uttered in such accents of truth.
Don Giovanni interposes, with affected
and ironical compassion :—

> "Poor girl, she's quite demented,
> I sorely do lament it!
> The fit may be prevented
> If she's by me besought."

There is in this thought a disdain,
a superciliousness, a lack of heart and
of pity expressed with marvellous simplicity of means. Nothing could render more appropriately the phrase :
" Poor girl, she's quite demented."
But Elvira protests : " The traitor, oh
believe him not ! " (bar 28). What
energy is there in thus giving him the
lie, as she draws herself up proudly !
How well the intonation expresses the
sudden gesture ! As to the two wit-
nesses of this altercation, one feels
that they are confused ; their hesita-
ting accents contrast with the impetuous outbursts on the part of Donna
Elvira (bar 36). The doubt and uncertainty are accentuated again from
bars 40 to 49. At bar 50 indecision
is at its height : they question and
consult each other. What is happen-

ing; who is the dupe here? What is
one to believe?

DON OTTAVIO (*aside*).
    Is she injured or deceiving?
    Ere we part from her I'd know!

DONNA ANNA (*aside*).
    Great her sorrow, past relieving,
    But no madness doth she show.

DON GIOVANNI.
    While they scan me, unbelieving,
    From their presence I'll not go.

DONNA ELVIRA.
    Friends, his wiles are past conceiving,
    Falsehood he will ne'er forego.

Underlying these four "asides"
there is an instrumental phrase of
twelve bars (three for each character),
which represents in a most striking
manner stupefaction, anxiety, and astonishment, and is one of those inspirations that immediately arrest the
attention and imprint themselves in the
memory, so vividly do they picture
the situation. It is the gift of ethi-
cal resemblance carried to its highest
point. Where can there be found
among the works of Mozart any form
which does not reveal consummate
powers of portrayal. A few bars

farther on (bar 68), in a subdued
voice and with rapid articulation, Don
Giovanni murmurs prudent advice into
the ear of Donna Elvira.

> " *Zitto, zitto, che la gente,*
>   *Si raduna a noi d'intorno ;*
> *Siate un poco più prudente,*
>   *Vi farete criticar.*"

> (Hush, be still, thy silly raving
>   Will a rabble gather round us ;
> Thy unwomanly behaving
>   Makes me quite of thee ashamed.)

She responds :

> " *Non sperarlo, o scellerato.*
>   *Ho perduto la prudenza,*
> *Le tue colpe ed il mio stato*
>   *Voglio a tutti palesar !*

> (Villain, darest thou to blame me ?
>   Through the world I will pursue thee,
> As a traitor I'll proclaim thee,
>   For by thee I am defam'd !)

At this point an impetuous passage
occurs, alternating between the voice
and the orchestra, with such skill
displayed in the gradations of sonority that the accompaniment never
smothers the vocal part. What a
masterpiece is this quartet, and what

a lesson of powerful expression combined with economy of means !

Donna Elvira withdraws, and in a
short recitative Don Giovanni makes
his excuses and takes leave. Donna
Anna and Don Ottavio are left alone,
and then bursts forth one of the finest
instances of musical and dramatic eloquence that it is possible to conceive.

No. 9.

BY the inflexion of his voice and the accent of his words, Donna Anna recognises her betrayer : her looks follow him, and, no longer in doubt, she exclaims : "*Don Ottavio! son morta!*" Nothing can equal the impression of agitation produced by this forcible entrance of the orchestra ; it is the letting loose of a wild flood of instrumental declamation ; a turmoil of terror and bewilderment. *In one bar* the thunderbolt falls upon the unhappy Donna Anna. One bar of the orchestra ! And with what power is it reproduced, increasing throughout the course of this prodigious recitative, of which not a note must be lost. The climax is reached at the affrighted cry "*O Dei! quegli è il carnefice del padre mio!*" ("Oh, Heaven! that was the murderer of my dear father!") Breathlessly she relates the occurrences of that fearful night. "No

longer can I doubt—his words at part-
ing, his soft and honey'd voice, all
bring before me, past the chance of
a doubt—the vile intruder who dared
into my chamber." The subsequent
narration is prefaced by a single bar
for the strings, which is in itself a
stroke of genius. With two chords
Mozart conveys instantly the impression of darkness by passing, through
a chord of the dominant 7th, from the
key of G minor to that of E flat minor.
This sudden appearance of a new key
suffices to suggest the night : we feel
that we are in darkness. But listen
to the sequel, starting at the words
" *Tacito a me s'appressa.*" ("Silently
he drew near me.") The whole of
this passage is rendered with an extraordinary animation and sense of confusion. At the words " *Io grido !* "
the initial bar reappears, upon which
rests the expression of all this pertur-
bation. There is not a single note
which does not captivate and retain
our attention. " *Alfine,*" resumes
Donna Anna, " *il duol, l'orrore dell'
infame attentato accrebbe sì la lena*

*mia, che a forza di svincolarmi, tor-
cermi e piegarmi, da lui mi sciolsi."*
(" At last my dread, my horror of the
dastardly ruffian lent strength un-
wonted for the moment ; I struggled
with tortuous writhings ; fearfully, with
an effort, I flung him from me.")
Here, again, this desperate struggle
is visibly portrayed to us ; we *see* it,
thanks to the employment of syncopation and the wild bowing of the violins,
which seems to tear the strings.   But
this is not all.   " *Allora rinforzo i
stridi miei, chiamo soccorso ; fugge il
fellon, arditamente il seguo fin nella
strada per fermarlo, e sono assalitrice
d'assalita.   Il padre v'accorre, vuol
conoscerlo, e l'iniquo che del povero
vecchio era più forte, compie il misfatto
suo, col dargli morte !* "   (" Aloud,
then, I clamoured for assistance, called
on the household ; he sought to fly,
but boldly I pursued him into the
street, that we might trace him, becoming of my assailant the assailer.
'Twas there that my father straight-
way challenged him, and the villain,
by whose strength he was easily over-

powered, stayed not his guilty madness, gave him the death-blow.")
This narration, the poignancy and truth of which cause a shudder, is linked to one of the highest inspirations that ever flowed from the pen of a musician. In a paroxysm of avenging fury Donna Anna turns to Don Ottavio:

> " *Or sai, chi l'onore*
> *Rapire a me volse,*
> *Che fù il traditore*
> *Che il padre mi tolse.*
> *Vendetta ti chieggio,*
> *La chiede il tuo cor.*
> *Rammenta la piaga*
> *Del misero seno,*
> *Rimira di sangue,*
> *Coperto il terreno,*
> *Se l'ira in te langue*
> *D'un giusto furor.*"

> (" The wretch now thou knowest
> Who sought my betraying,
> And vengeance thou owest
> My father's foul slaying.
> For justice I sue thee;
> I ask of thy troth.
> Remember, when wounded,
> His life-blood was flowing;
> Unsolaced, unshriven,
> He heard not my crying;
> My heart will be riven
> If thou break thy oath.")

Boldness of style, nobility of form, authoritative accent, inconsolable grief, all contribute to the sublimity of this immortal page. From the first bar the style is dignified and majestic, the injunction resolute and irresistible. The orchestral basses emphasise energetically the imperious character of the gesture, indicated by a single stroke of this infallible master's pencil. There is nothing more natural or more touching than the tears that gush out (bar 7) at the words " *Che il padre mi tolsi*," and after them the imprecation reappears with new power, induced by the imitation of the voice by the basses at the words " *Vendetta ti chieggio.*" And then the sobbing recommences (bar 17), breathless and suffocating, to give place (bar 33) to the return of the cry for vengeance, at the recapitulation of the first phrase : " *Or sai, chi l'onore.*"

One must thoroughly appreciate the wonderful science of Mozart to understand with what an incredible restraint in the employment of the instruments

he should have attained such richness
of colouring combined with such power
of expression. We remain astonished
that by such simple means, and with so
few notes, his instrumentation should
be always so full and sonorous. That
is, and it cannot be said too often, the
result of that profound and unfailing
judgment which never goes beyond
the limits of necessity. Anything that
is superfluous encumbers the score,
and makes it heavy instead of enrich-
ing it. It is so with the art of Michael
Angelo, wherein the muscular function
is not impeded by the presence of
those obstructions, those redundancies
which detract from the play and the
elasticity of the tissues, and only produce a diminution of energy. Hence,
so much perspicuity of plan, elegance
of form, flexibility and animation of
movement. Mozart combines the
perfection of plastic beauty with truth
of pathos. Like that head of Niobe
that is rendered so profoundly sorrow-
ful by a slight deflection of the eye-
brow, the most poignant anguish never
interferes in the works of Mozart

with the serene tranquility of the form.*

---

* In the original, Donna Anna now makes her exit, and a recitative for Don Ottavio leads to his Aria " *Dalla sua pace,*" of which there is here no description by M. Gounod.—(*Translators.*)

No. 10.

STILL trembling at the crime of his master and the tragic end of the Commandant, Leporello appears hurriedly. " I'll stay with him no longer," says he, " I will not have this madman for a master! See, there he comes; look at him, so cool, just as if nothing e'er had happened."

Don Giovanni, quite bewitched by the pretty faces of the rustic beauties, exclaims : " These country girls with their gay sports invite me; we will return to them." All this is in rapid recitative, which leads to the vivacious Aria "*Fin ch'han dal vino.*" It may be said that in this song " care is thrown to the winds." Its animation is as that of one possessed, and its dizzy progress never halts for a moment. The movement indicated by the master is *Presto*, $\frac{2}{4}$ time, which is evidently only meant to have one beat in the bar. It is clear that Mozart has wished to avoid the impression of a second beat (the weak beat), which would have taken away from the rhythm its power and impetuosity. There is, then, to the listener, only the effect of the strong accent, and it is this which gives to the air such a striking character of energy and ardour. In addition, the four quavers, throbbing without intermission all through the accompaniment, depict perfectly the breathless excitement of this votary of pleasure.

No. 11.

MASETTO re-enters, followed by Zerlina, with whom he is having a lover's quarrel. "Faithless girl! no longer I'll bear your caprices," &c. Zerlina makes the best excuses she can. This little outburst of vexation, rapidly rendered in simple recitative, leads to the charming cantilena "*Batti, batti, O bel Masetto.*"

The score of Don Giovanni is truly a great work, for there is not one of its numbers that is not in itself a masterpiece. I think there can be no doubt— as I have before remarked—that certain numbers, or at least, certain portions of them, have been written in deference to the wishes of those who played the various characters. This compliance (which, though not always indispensable, may be sometimes inevitable), is not carried so far as to introduce in the work anything that might be regarded as a blemish. The exquisite taste of Mozart sufficed to remove the

reproach of vulgarity even from that
which was unnecessary; and it follows
that, in Don Giovanni, all which is
required musically for the situations or
the characters is absolutely irreproachable and perfect.

Let us return to this delightful inspiration, "*Batti, batti.*" One is
tempted to ask if Mozart ever had to
seek for the musical form of his
characters. That form suits so perfectly that they seem themselves to
have suggested the music which represents them.

Can one imagine anything more
coaxing, more pacifying, more submis-
sive than the opening: "Canst thou
see me unforgiven?" &c. Notice first
the voice part, which is doubled in the
octave by the violins in a most caressing manner; then observe the persistent accompaniment of the violoncello solo, in a figure which streams
uninterrupted throughout the piece;
all of this is characterised by a per-
suasiveness in the smile, look, and
attitude that is irresistible. The first
sixteen bars establish at once the

melodic form with the repose of tonality that reveals the strength of inspiration, and which, moreover, is most enchanting to the ear and the mind of the listener. It is, too often, the absence or poverty of ideas which leads to that abuse of modulation so frequent in a multitude of modern compositions. Tonal unity is dreaded as a weakness, and composers launch out into endless harmonic digressions, the inevitable result being most wearisome monotony. Another charm of Mozart's music is the intimate relationship which binds together the different phrases of the musical sentence, giving it that logical character the secret of which belongs to him more than any other composer. The strain which commences at the 17th bar is a striking example of this. It seems as if nothing else could have been there but what *is* there, so natural and entirely satisfactory is the progression. This period of eight bars, or rather of four bars repeated, expresses with rare felicity the submission of Zerlina, ready to endure anything.

And then, starting at bar 25, what touching resignation is indicated in the responsive figure of the voice and violoncello—a figure which is repeated four times consecutively, leading to the charming *sforzando*, *piano*, which is the climax of the suppliant expression in bars 29 and 30, and which takes a still stronger character of self-accusation in bars 31 and 32, leading through bars 33 and 34 to the exquisite close of this delightful melodic period ! Then ensues a beautiful re-entry of the initial theme (bars 35 to 52), this time varied by a graceful embroidery that gives it new charm. The eight succeeding bars (53 to 60) have a delicacy of expression, an accuracy of portrayal that is truly marvellous. " Ah ! " says Zerlina, assured of her conquest, " confess it, thou no longer canst withstand me." Only the unfailing instinct of Mozart could have conceived and expressed the thousand nuances of coaxing, the dove-like cooings, the lamb-like gentleness, the seductive glances—in one word, the whole array of fascinations of which a woman is so complete a mistress when she wishes to effect a reconciliation.

These qualities abound in the eight bars which terminate the *andante.* Starting at bar 52, how happily the shakes of the first and second violins in octaves express poor Masetto's bursts of sulkiness! He tries not to give way, but finally yields, as is ever the case. The violoncello passages seem to insinuate her roguish glances at the bumpkin, while the triple repetition of the music in bars 53 and 54 is full of persuasive entreaty. Finally, bars 59 and 60, wherein the syncopations of the voice part are blended so archly with the quicker notes of the violoncello, show us the triumph of Zerlina.

At last she is victorious. " *Pace, pace, o vita mia !* " she exclaims. A delightful *allegro* (or rather *allegretto*) in $\frac{6}{8}$ time, full of frolic, celebrates this happy reconciliation, while a most delicious solo for the violoncello ripples an accompaniment.

Mozart, divine Mozart! To know thee is to worship thee. Thou art the personification of perpetual truth, perfect beauty, inexhaustible charm; always profound, yet always clear; combining the entire knowledge of humanity with the simplicity of childhood! Thou hast experienced all things, and expressed them in a musical language that never has, and never will be, surpassed.

"'Tis no use my resisting," says Masetto; "little witch, you've cajol'd me." Suddenly the voice of Don Giovanni is heard from within, giving orders for the preparation of the *fête*. Terror of Zerlina. "Ah, Masetto! Hark! 'tis his lordship; how his voice makes me tremble!" "Why do you thus change countenance?" responds Masetto. "Ah! there is something between you, and you dread I should know it."

This little scene is in rapid recitative.

No. 12.

HERE begins the grand Finale of the first act. It is a striking commencement. " Quickly, quickly," sings Masetto, " I'll outwit him; in some nook I'll creep and watch him. None will see me, here in safety I can wait." From the first bar the listener is aware that this is to be a Finale of vast proportions. And, as a matter of fact, its various movements are throughout of the highest order of beauty. The first fifty bars reveal the feverish agitation of the unhappy Masetto, once more doubting the fidelity of Zerlina. His restlessness is depicted by the first notes of the orchestra—a tremolo which is at once both comical and impressive. Bars 6, 7, 8, 9, 10, and 11 express particularly his mistrust and suspicion.

At bar 51, accompanied by a brilliant fanfare for the full orchestra, Don Giovanni appears, followed by the peasants, who are about to cele-

brate the *fête* to which he has invited
them. Upon a charming *decrescendo*
of the voices and orchestra the rustics
withdraw ; Zerlina endeavours to hide
herself by mingling with them, but
Don Giovanni, who has never lost
sight of her, bars the way. Then fol-
lows an *andante* in $\frac{3}{4}$ time, a marvel of
grace and captivation, accompanied
by the gentle whisperings of the
orchestra.

ZERLINA.
> In this arbour I will hide me,
> None my presence here perceiving.

DON GIOVANNI.
> Sweet Zerlina, I'm beside thee (*detains her*).
> To escape a lover's glance will ne'er
> succeed.

Does not one seem to see the precaution with which the little Zerlina
goes upon tip-toe during the exquisite
dialogue of the voice and the first
violins in the first five bars ? And
with what cat-like dexterity does Don
Giovanni extend his claw over Zerlina
(bars 8 and 9) in order to seize her as
she passes ! " If thou'rt kind," says
she, with languid resistance, " I pray

thee leave me." His only reply is a caressing entreaty to stay.

From bar 10 to bar 29 we are enveloped by an ineffable charm, and I do not believe that the trembling of the tender passion could be expressed in language more delightful and captivating.

I know no one but Mozart that could have discovered, with a certainty as unfailing as it is complete, the musical form of all emotions, and of all their nuances of passion and character. Passions and characters constitute the whole of the human drama, and therein Mozart is without a rival.

Don Giovanni is a heartless libertine. Therefore it is not the tenderness of love but the longings of desire that Mozart has so marvellously rendered in this inimitable dialogue between the Don and Zerlina ; in it we find again, perhaps with heightened expression, the sentiment of the duet " *La ci darem la mano.*"

Can anything be imagined more suave, more pleading, than this little phrase of two bars, short, yet so fully expressive of Zerlina—" *Ah ! lasciate mi andar via !* " the music of which is exactly repeated by Don Giovanni at the words " *Nò, nò, resta, gioja mia !* " The four bars which follow are of the same style. Zerlina renews her supplications : " *Se pietade avete in core !* " (If thou'rt kind, I pray thee leave me ! ") " *Si ben mio,* " responds Don Giovanni, " *son tutto amore !* " (" All my heart's thine own, believe me ! ") Here the expression of his caresses and of the intoxicating atmosphere reaches a climax ; everything seems to breathe danger. To the enchanting vocal melody, doubled by the flute, the hautboy, and the bassoon, is added the sustaining figure of the basses, *and, above all,* the inexpressible cajolery of the first violins seems to envelop the whole with an air of voluptuous magnetism.

Don Giovanni is about to carry away the faltering Zerlina, but he has reckoned without Masetto, who stands erect before him. " Masetto ! " he exclaims. " Yes, Masetto," is the

response. " So surly, wherefore,
pray ?

> " Zerlina here is sighing
> Because the hours are flying,
> And thou from her away,"

replies the Don.

These eighteen bars teem with
comicalities of great ingenuity. " Ha,
ha ! you are caught," say the horns,
with their four clear notes, the last of
them being sustained into the following bar, while the strings express the
surprise and embarrassment of Zerlina.
As to Don Giovanni, nothing discon-
certs him ; he is too accomplished a
roué to lack assurance. Accordingly
he treats the matter lightly, as is testi-
fied by the laughter of the flutes alternating with that of the first violins,
whilst the bantering distinct notes of
the horns reply to the bassoons, leading to a phrase of the most perfect
irony, which this simpleton of a
Masetto understands as a very
flattering profession of civility.

Here ensues an instrumental combination, which, if I am not mistaken,
Mozart was the first to introduce in

dramatic music. Ignoring for eight bars the regular orchestra, he employs a small supplementary band placed on the stage for the *fête* that Don Giovanni has prepared for the worthy peasants. This band will be utilised a little later on to show an ingenious example of counterpoint during the ball. Don Giovanni, Zerlina, and Masetto advance gaily towards the scene of the festivities. At the same moment Donna Anna, Donna Elvira, and Don Ottavio, all three masked, enter at the opposite side of the stage, still pursuing their relentless search for the guilty one. In a single bar, Mozart, with his own incredible promptitude of transition, establishes the new situation. The orchestra suddenly assumes a sombre and mysterious tone ; it envelops itself with prudence and precaution, like the characters which it introduces. After two simple bars, which depict the grave and severe attitude of the new arrivals, the first and second violins commence a figure of staccato notes in octaves, which suggest, with marvellous penetration, the mystery which these personages assume. It might be said that the orchestra also, like them, is concealing itself under a mask. Donna Elvira is the first to speak :

"We come in night and darkness,
    By just resentment guided,
    To Heaven we have confided
Our trust this woe to end."

Don Ottavio, who shares Elvira's feelings, is accompanied by the same figure of the orchestra, and beseeches Donna Anna to banish all fear. But she is dreading, for her lover's sake, the issue of this enterprise. "Our path is full of danger," says she with an anxiety that is faithfully delineated by the succession of sixths in the orchestra. This movement leads to a minuet played by the band on the stage.

Leporello opens the window, and, perceiving the three unknown maskers, draws his master's attention to them :

" Sir, see those charming maskers,
    Here standing just below us ! "

Don Giovanni, appearing at the window, replies :

> " Hoping they may not know us,
> Ask will they please ascend."

> " That voice and manner, surely
> 'Tis he whom we are seeking ! "

utter the three, aside. Leporello succeeds in attracting their attention. " What is your pleasure ? " inquires Don Ottavio.

> " My master sends to invite you
> An hour with him to spend,"

answers Leporello, to which Don Ottavio responds :

> " Thanks, we accept with pleasure."

Here occurs the celebrated and admirable trio, known generally as the " Trio of Masks."

This piece is one of the innumerable jewels which compose the diadem of the prince of music. It is marked *Adagio*, but the time-signature is ₵, which indicates that there should be but two beats in the bar.

The indications of a Mozart are not to be questioned, but accepted. That is a first principle. And then we must

endeavour to understand them. Now
it is well known that in many an instance a bar of *adagio*, be it in
duple, triple, or quadruple time, is
composed of such a considerable
number of short notes that it becomes
necessary to sub-divide each beat into
two or three, according to whether the
time is simple or compound. This
is a delicate question from the conductor's point of view, which I propose to consider in the Appendix to
this book, wherein I shall speak of
those concerned in the interpretation
of the work, be they conductors or
singers. In the present instance (the
Trio of Masks) it seems to me that
the imposing and solemn character of
the piece *does not necessitate two beats
only in the bar*, and that the altera-
tion of ₵ into ₵ is more favourable
than prejudicial to amplitude and nobility of execution. Beating two in
the bar would, I believe, increase
fatally the risk of dropping into a rate
of movement that would be too quick to
render faithfully the elevated inspiration
of this piece, so majestic in its beauty.

The first two bars, with their notes detached from each other by rests, already forbode something solemn, demanding attention and contemplation.

This trio is, in effect, an invocation.

"Thou Power above, be near us,
    Our hopes on Thee depend,"

say Donna Anna and Don Ottavio; and Donna Elvira, a prey to the violence of her resentment, cries:

"Thou wilt avenge and hear us,
    To me Thou'lt justice send!"

Upon these few words Mozart has constructed an ensemble of such interest in the expression, such marvellous and appropriate vocal combination of the tenor and two soprano voices, such charm of melody, harmony, and instrumentation, that to hear it is truly to be enraptured. But it demands a rendering as perfect as the master's inspiration.

The entry of the two voices without accompaniment exacts irreproachable accuracy of intonation, the absence of which might compromise the whole effect of this piece, which is only supported by a few subdued chords for the wind instruments, allowing the voice parts to manifest all their importance and clearness.

The engraved full score that I have before me is that of J. Frey, who was a publisher of 5, Place des Victoires. Unfortunately it is full of mistakes and misprints. Four important errors at least can be discovered in this trio alone.

I advise composers to impress upon their minds the flexibility of form and the purity of style with which the voices proceed and are combined in this admirable trio, so full and so noble that, notwithstanding its brevity, it gives the listener the impression of a movement of large proportions. One experiences an analogous feeling before Raphael's "Vision of Ezekiel," that celebrated picture, which, after the inspection of a few moments, appears gigantic, in spite of the smallness of its dimensions.

A brisk movement, *Allegro*, $\frac{6}{8}$, heralds the return of Don Giovanni, already quite excited over this rural escapade. This brief *allegro* is full of heedless gaiety, which has no suspicion of the impending danger.

" Pretty maidens," says Don Giovanni, " now rest from your dancing." " Cooling drinks ye all want to refresh ye," adds Leporello. " Zerlina, be prudent ! " implores Masetto. This dialogue, so full of freedom and animation, leads to a *Maestoso* in $\frac{2}{4}$ time.

Upon a lofty and dignified opening, wherein the brilliant sonority of the trumpets predominates, Leporello addresses the three masks, who have remained discreetly in the background :

" Ye maskers fair, to greet you
My master is advancing ; "

to which the Don adds :

" Come nearer, I entreat you,
Welcome I say to all ! "

They respond :

" We thank your kindly greeting,
We join your festive ball."

This reply, the music of which expresses the most exquisite politeness, leads to the beautiful ensemble " *Viva la libertà*," so noble and of such sumptuous sonority that its amplitude conceals the absence of development.

"Go thou," says Don Giovanni to Leporello, "and place the dancers," and again we hear the minuet that was previously played by the band upon the stage whilst Leporello was conveying his master's invitation to the three masks.

This time the minuet is assigned to the principal orchestra, while the members of the stage band divide into two groups. The first group play the strains of a new dance in $\frac{2}{4}$ time, the second group perform yet another *motif* in $\frac{3}{8}$ time—one of those contrapuntal combinations which were but child's play for the ingenuity of Mozart. The different dance rhythms of the three orchestras, the voices of the performers, the vigilant "asides" of Donna Anna, Donna Elvira, and Don Ottavio, the bad temper of Masetto, the trouble of Zerlina—all of these are expressed simultaneously, without the least confusion, and with consummate ease and dexterity. Don Giovanni is just disappearing with

Zerlina, while Leporello imprisons poor Masetto in a circle of dancers. Suddenly a cry is heard from behind the scenes. It is Zerlina, who, terrified by the advances of Don Giovanni, appeals for aid. At this moment the grandiose peroration of the important Finale to the first act commences.

Donna Anna, Donna Elvira, and Don Ottavio, who have not for a moment lost sight of the villain whom they are pursuing, appeal to the indignation of the surrounding throng. " Let us help this poor innocent ! " exclaim all three. " Her cries come from this side," shriek the peasants; " force the door open ! " Immediately the voices and the orchestra, in a unison that is like the surging of a furious sea, attack this door precipitately, crying, " We are near, thou art protected." At last the door is broken open, Zerlina reappears, distracted and affrighted, while Don Giovanni leads the terrified Leporello forward by the ear. " Here's the scoundrel," exclaims the Don, " just detected ! Now receive thy just reward. Wretch, thou diest!" This shameless ruffian, this brazen libertine, who, however, fears nothing, pretends to draw his sword and threaten his poltroon of a valet, who dares not murmur a word. The rhythm of the orchestra at this entry of Don Giovanni depicts the most consummate combination of insolence, audacity, and effrontery. After five bars there occurs an instrumental effect astonishing in its power of expression. The energetic chords of the strings, expressing the tyrant's brutality, are followed by a few notes of the wind instruments, which suggest by their timbre and arrangement the cold perspiration of Leporello. At the eleventh bar, accompanied by an orchestral figure full of determination and resolution, the authoritative tone of which is accentuated still more by the imitative passages to which it gives rise, the three masks exclaim successively :

Don Ottavio : Get you gone, sir !

Donna Elvira : Falsehood here will not avail thee.

Donna Anna : Thou thyself art now ensnared.

Then they unmask, and Don Giovanni recognises all three. It is now his turn to be confused, intimidated, and abandoned by the orchestra, which only leaves to him the feeble chords of the wind instruments that have served to show the cowardice of Leporello. " Traitor ! " they all exclaim, " nought can now thy fate retard." Don Giovanni is speechless, confounded by this universal execration. And then the terrible and scathing final period commences—full of threats of vengeance. It is a conflict, a tumult, a volcano of voices and orchestra, of incomparable power, although at the same time of miraculous brilliancy and simplicity. It proves that distinctness and truth of inspiration constitute a power which dispenses with prodigality or extravagance.

However, Don Giovanni takes courage again. The coda of the Finale shows him defying fortune, and still holding his head erect. " Not my custom 'tis to tremble," he cries defiantly, and upon a haughty outburst from the orchestra he draws his sword and forces his way through the crowd, who dare not bar his progress.

Thus terminates the Finale of the first act—a truly extraordinary conception, as beautiful as it is powerful, as symphonic as it is dramatic, in which every element has its exact and complete part, wherein there is nothing lacking and nothing superfluous. It bears the impress of genius.

ACT II.—No. 13.

THE charming duet which opens this act consists of an altercation between Don Giovanni and Leporello. The latter, disgusted at the life led by his master, and which his master compels him to lead, tired of the indignities which he has to endure every day, declares that his patience is exhausted and that he is determined to leave.

" I'll not believe thee,"

says the Don,

" Whate'er thou say ; "

to which Leporello responds :

" I would not grieve ye,
But I'll not stay."

The strings, with two hautboys and two horns, constitute the whole of the accompaniment, but every note has a meaning—nothing is unnecessary, and the sonority, though rich, is not over-powering. From a dramatic point of view it would be impossible for music to express this dispute between master and man with greater accuracy of rhythm and intonation.

Then follows a brisk recitative, in which they endeavour to arrive at an understanding :

DON GIOVANNI: Leporello!

LEPORELLO: I hear, sir.

DON GIOVANNI: Come here; this will make peace between us.

LEPORELLO: What, sir?

DON GIOVANNI: Four gold pieces.

LEPORELLO: Oh! now listen. This is the last time I'll take such compensation. You'll find yourself mistaken if you think to soothe a man of my mettle, like those poor women, by coin and empty phrases.

DON GIOVANNI: There's enough on that score. Say, are you ready to do me a small service?

LEPORELLO: So you give up the women.

DON GIOVANNI: They're my first necessity of life, &c.

LEPORELLO: But what is your small service?

DON GIOVANNI: Have you seen the pretty damsel of Donna Elvira?

LEPORELLO: Not I.

DON GIOVANNI: It is your loss, then. I would fain try my fortune, and it has struck me, as evening is upon us, 'twould make the jest new and more diverting if I put on thy cloak in this adventure.

LEPORELLO : I can see no occasion for this strange masquerading.

DON GIOVANNI : Delay me not. Delays in love are treasons.

No. 14.

I DO not think that there exists any piece of music more perfect than this trio.

Is it because I have a particular weakness for the constant and inexpressible charm which pervades it? I cannot say.

I seek in vain for any passage that is not of the most perfect beauty. I cannot find one. Musical art is displayed here in such perfection that were this the only specimen in existence, we should still possess the very essence of music. I know nothing in the world more exquisite.

Elvira is alone on the balcony. She is thinking, with the persistent fondness of true love, of him who returns her devotion by scandalous neglect.

> "Oh! hush, sad heart, from grieving!
>   Thy days of joy are over;
> The traitor with wiles deceiving,
>   Hath broke my heart in twain.

Such is the sentiment which fills the

first thirteen bars. Elvira accuses her heart; she reproaches it (bars 3, 4, 7, and 8) that it still beats for him who is unworthy ; she resolves (bars 9, 10, and 11) to banish him from her memory ; she is ashamed of her weakness (bars 12 and 13).

The varying phases of feeling could not be rendered more faithfully than is done here by means of rhythm, turn of the melody, accents, nuances, musical punctuation, harmony, and the different instrumental combinations.

The following phrase, comprising bars 14, 15, 16, 17, and 18, is an appeal to prudence and precaution :

" Softly," says Leporello, " 'tis Donna Elvira ; perchance you might regain her."

"Thou here awhile detain her," replies the Don ; " I'll soon come back again."

The expression of these five bars is so striking that it would seem impossible to imagine anything more true. It is the absolute agreement of sound with sense.

The syncopation on the second

quaver of the bar, the figure of the bassoons imitated by the basses, and then reproduced by the flutes and clarionets, finally the mysterious accent of bar 18, all represent with marvellous accuracy the demeanour of people who seek to escape observation.

At bar 19 the figure of the first subject reappears. "Elvira, hear my sighing," murmurs Don Giovanni from beneath the balcony. The instinct of genius makes no mistake here. It is in the very phrases of Elvira that Don Giovanni finds the insolent expression of his false tenderness. This borrowing is an abuse of confidence, a musical forgery, which Don Giovanni perpetrates, uttering as his own the sincere language of his wife in order to deceive her the better. At bar 27 Elvira shudders.

"Ah! is it thou, ungrateful?"

And also in bars 27 and 28 the indignant accent of bars 9 and 10 is reproduced. But Don Giovanni appeases this transient resentment immediately. "'Tis

I," he exclaims, with an exaggerated affectation of sweetness.

> " 'Tis I, and fondly relying,
>   My love thou'lt not disdain."
>
> " Strangely his words affect me,"

says Elvira, while Leporello mutters :

> " She must be of the maddest
>   In him to trust again."

(Bars 32 to 36). An imitative passage of extreme elegance reproduces here the piquant and mischievous figure of bars 14 and 15. At bar 37 occurs a melodic phrase of a most caressing style, which is a foretaste of the famous serenade which Don Giovanni is about to warble to Elvira's waiting maid.

Bars 47, 48, 49, and 50 emphasise by the tremolo of the strings Elvira's resistance, whilst the wind instruments protest against the hypocritical tenderness of the voluptuary, who sings :

> " Ah ! do believe, I conjure thee."

While this proceeds, Leporello whispers to his master (bars 51 to 54),

> " I cannot keep from laughing."

The syllabic descent of the voice part

has an extraordinary effect, and leads in a marvellous manner to the re-appearance of the opening subject, wherein the three voices are combined with incredible grace of form and harmony. But what is really remark-able is the manner in which Mozart has developed the figure

The first imitation begins in the octave above, then it appears in thirds, next in contrary motion, fol-lowed by a *crescendo* which leads to the *forte* at bar 72, succeeded by a *piano* staccato (bar 73) which depicts with extreme ingenuity Elvira's hesita-tion, Don Giovanni's snares, and Lepo-rello's uncertainty as to the result of the shameful deception.

The ensemble terminates at the re-capitulation of the music in bars 63, 64, 65, 66, and 67, followed by a coda of six bars founded upon the music of bar 12.

In the meantime Elvira descends from the balcony. The obscurity of the night has hindered her from recognising Leporello, who, favoured by his disguise, begins to like the situation, and prepares to embrace Elvira.

Don Giovanni addresses and frightens them ; then they fly.   Once master of the place, he flirts with the waiting maid, singing a delightful serenade.

No. 15.

THIS serenade is a pearl of inspiration, alike in the elegance of its melody, harmony, and rhythm. Over the continuous accompaniments of the orchestra is heard a melodious figure assigned to the mandoline, the rhythmical division of which into six semiquavers and three quavers is most happy. The song itself is a masterpiece of grace and gallantry. In bars 15, 16, 17, and 18 there is a most enchanting harmonic progression; bars 20 and 21 express an intensity of longing and marvellous captivation—but someone comes. It is Masetto, who, accompanied by his friends, is seeking Don Giovanni in order to kill him.

" Who goes there ? " " The servant am I of Don Giovanni." " The servant of that villain ! These friends and I are seeking to kill him." " Very pleasant," says the Don ; " I'll do my best to help you."

No. 16.

"Go half to left and half to right," &c.

This air, so little appreciated, is full of mischievous fun. Observe among other points the syncopated passage for all the strings at the words "*ferite, ferite!*" which is quite a stroke of genius. The comrades separate, according to the instructions of the sham Leporello, during which time Don Giovanni retains Masetto, in order to whisper a few words to him. "Masetto, show your weapons." "They're good ones," he responds. "Look here, I have a musket ; besides, there is this pistol." Thereupon Don Giovanni possesses himself of Masetto's weapons, and belabours him soundly. During the desperate cries of Masetto, who writhes with pain, Don Giovanni escapes and Zerlina appears. "Did I hear someone speaking? I thought it was Masetto. What has happened ?" Masetto, groaning meanwhile, relates the circum-

stances. " Come, come," says Zerlina ;
" if that's the worst, there's no great
harm done. Come with me home to
supper, and give your faithful promise
you'll never more be jealous; those
bruises can be cured where love is
zealous."

No. 17.—AIR.

THIS number is a veritable masterpiece, of most penetrating charm and
absolute beauty of form.   The symphony is in itself perfection; it deserves
particular examination.   The listener
is enraptured by the caressing figure
of the violas and violoncellos

in bars 3 and 4.   Bars 7 and 8 are of
exquisite grace, and the repetition
(upon the first beat of bar 8) of the
dominant 7th chord which concludes
the preceding bar produces a positively
enchanting impression.   Bars 17 and
18, with the shake of the first violins
over the chords of the wind instruments,
represent to us a coaxing and pretty
smile, as does also the answer of the
voice (bars 19 and 20) against the tranquil accompaniment of the strings.
What could be more tender than the
subject comprised in bars 24 to 32,

which leads in such a charming and simple way to the resumption of the initial phrase ? And what persuasive power is displayed in the uniformity of bars 47, 48, and 49, followed by the delightful captivating glances of bars 50 and 51 !

" Ah, well," says Zerlina, " the remedy for thy sufferings, dost thou know where it is ?   Place thy hand there upon my heart. Dost thou hear it beat ? " Bars 62, 63, and 64, with the figure of the violins in octaves over the detached notes of the wind instruments, are absolutely delightful. Mozart alone possesses grace and charm in such a marvellous degree ; he is irresistible.   Masetto has been led away by Zerlina.   Then Leporello enters, still clad in the garb of Don Giovanni, and much distressed at having to drag Madam Elvira everywhere, of whom he wishes to rid himself.

The scene changes.   We are in a forest.*   " It seems to me," says

---

* In the score of Bernhard Zugler the direction is— " A dark courtyard, with three doors, in front of Donna Anna's house."—(*Translators.*)

Leporello, "that I perceive the light of torches, which are advancing from this side." He trembles like a leaf.

"What fearest thou, my beloved ? " says Elvira. "Oh, do not leave me ; in mercy leave me not ! "

And then commences the admirable sextet.

No. 18.

THIS stupendous piece, composed
of successive episodes of the highest
interest, is a model of dramatic music.
From the first notes of the orchestra,
in two bars only, Mozart makes us
feel the terrors of the misguided Elvira
in this solitary and sombre spot. The
succession of thirds at the commencement seem already to spread an alarm-
ing shadow over Elvira; she has to
grope her way. The whole of her
phrase is accompanied by sudden
starts in the orchestra, which are a
striking representation of the palpita-
tion of her heart.

Quite different is the trembling fear
of Leporello. From the third bar one
feels that he is only thinking of making his escape without a care as to
what may happen to his unfortunate
companion.

The orchestra depicts him prying
into every corner, and bruising himself
at every step, before he finds an out-

let. At last he succeeds, and it is
marvellous to see how all of a sudden
the voice and the orchestra glide
away, as it were, on tip-toe. Here,
again, the resemblance of the musical
idea to the action on the stage is absolutely accurate.

At this point Donna Anna and Don
Ottavio appear. The two instrumental
bars which accompany their entrance
are of sovereign beauty. There is,
perhaps, no one but Mozart whose
genius could concentrate with such
power, yet with such slight means, the
true and complete character of the
personage who is to speak or act. At
the entrance of Donna Anna and Don
Ottavio the music assumes an incomparable nobility of expression and
loftiness of accent.

The entire phrase of Don Ottavio,
" *Tergi il ciglio* " (" Cease from griev-
ing "), is of exquisite tenderness, combined with touching reserve and delicacy. It is not the accent of passion,
but that of a profound and enduring
love. Donna Anna's reply, " *Lascia
almen alla mia pena*," is characterised

by superb dignity and elevation of sentiment; it is an inconsolable fidelity to that sorrow which speaks to her constantly of the father she has vowed to avenge. This phrase and that of Don Ottavio are accompanied by a continuous figure for the second violins, which seems to express the indissoluble bond that unites these two souls alike in tenderness and in sorrow. Suddenly a new and characteristic rhythm appears in the orchestra. The groping in the obscurity of the night is again indicated. Elvira and Leporello reappear on different sides of the stage.

"Oh! my husband, I have lost thee!"

sighs Elvira, in the utmost anxiety.

"Not for worlds I'd have her find me,"

says Leporello, in a transport of fear.

At last they both perceive an outlet, but at the moment of flight they are forced back on to the stage by the unexpected arrival of Donna Anna and Don Ottavio, Masetto and Zerlina, who take Leporello for Don Giovanni.

"Wretch! now we hold thee! Whither art going?" exclaim Zerlina and Masetto, barring the way, while the poor devil pulls his hat over his eyes and turns up his collar to avoid recognition. The orchestra here adopts a firmly marked rhythm of thrilling energy. We feel that Leporello's arrest is imminent.

"Nought now can save thee!"

exclaim Donna Anna and Don Ottavio.

"Die thou perfidious one"

is the cry of all except Elvira, who, in supplicating tones, seeks to pacify their wrath.

"Oh, heaven, forbear ye,"

she pleads, and in the orchestra there reappears the panting rhythm that accompanied her terror and anxiety when she was seeking to recover her husband in the gloom of night. But they all indignantly reject the idea of pity. "No, no; he dies!"

Elvira implores earnestly, but in vain. The stubborn conflict between the two contrasted rhythms is strikingly expressive. In the midst of this turmoil Leporello gives himself up for lost. With face still hidden in his cloak, he laments his fate in a tone of indescribable misery. The voice part, the strings, the wind instruments all portray him crawling at the feet of his accusers, pale with fright, a chicken-hearted poltroon with chatter-ing teeth, while the basses of the orchestra are immovable as though paralysed. We cannot help admiring here, as elsewhere, the remarkable certainty and promptitude with which, without losing a moment, Mozart en-ters completely into the spirit of the characters and situation.

Leporello's whining, accompanied by the piteous supplication of the hautboys, is ended by an interrupted cadence, to which succeeds a new rhythm. Leporello makes himself known, to the stupefaction of all around. Eight bars are devoted to the expression of their surprise, then the abrupt rhythm reappears, showing the uncertainty in which each one is plunged. Finally there is a powerful *Allegro*, which forms the last section and the climax of this masterly sextet.

This *Allegro* is of colossal strength. Although there is no new time signature in the score, yet it seems to me without doubt that this movement should be beaten as ₵—that is to say, two in the bar, not four as in the preceding. A few words only are sufficient to furnish the material for this vigorous page.

"Fear and doubting quite distract me;
All my head is in confusion."

The piece is treated with the science of a consummate symphonist. We find, at the same time, the dazzling *verve* and radiant transparence which characterise the Italian genius of a Cimarosa or a Rossini.

Although Salzburg was his birthplace, Mozart was more Italian than German. Through his early travels in Italy he had assimilated its sunny temperament, imbibed its sunshine, and breathed the atmosphere of that enchanting country, which, second only to Greece, might have been the land of the gods.

In two strokes of the bow, as if by a magical transformation, the style of the piece is completely changed. Leporello, who was a moment before crushed by a weight of terror, begins to recover himself, and contemplates the possibility of safety by flight. The agitated movement of the orchestra suggests that he has still a buzzing in his ears, and that at the first opportunity he will scuttle off as fast as his legs will carry him. His syllabic utterances, full of bewilderment, show us exactly what is passing in his mind (bars 17, 18, 19, and 20 of the *Allegro*), and especially from 27 to 35, when the unhappy servitor's confusion reaches a climax, and drives him distracted to the conclusion of his phrase, which is of irresistible effect. Sixty years after the day when I heard this immortal work for the first time I can still remember the frantic enthusiasm that was excited in the public by the powerful voice of Lablache—that actor of genius, that inimitable singer, who fired his audience with enthusiasm. But then what flashes of genius at every moment illumine the work of the master! What a thunderbolt is that

tremendous outburst of the bass voice,
which splits open, so to speak, the terrible unison of the orchestra! Finally I
must point out the superb vocal peroration that commences 27 bars before
the end—a marvel of counterpoint and
of harmonic combination.

No. 19.

LEPORELLO'S submission to the humiliating wishes of his master threatens to cost him dear, for each of the characters demands the privilege of being the first to make him expiate his faults. This unanimity furnishes material for Leporello to sing a characteristic air. It may be, speaking from a theatrical point of view, that this piece conduces to tedium in the sense that it is only a repetition of those fears of which Leporello has given such a complete exposition in the preceding sextet. Therefore it is generally omitted in the performance of the work. Finally Leporello succeeds in making his escape. Don Ottavio addresses those around him.

"Friends," says he, "this confirms me," &c.

No. 20.—AIR.

THOSE who have never heard the celebrated tenor Rubini, the contemporary of Lablache and Mme. Malibran, can form no idea of the acclamations with which this famous air, "*Il mio tesoro intanto*," was received. The audience were in a frenzy of delight, and the illustrious *virtuoso* always received an encore. It must be admitted that he was an incomparable singer, and I shall never forget the religious silence with which he was listened to. Anyone who dared to breathe a word would have been remorselessly silenced. Ah! in those times people went to the theatre, not to gossip, but to listen to delightful music rendered in magnificent style by singers who were great musicians.

I should not be surprised if this air had been written at the request, or at least for the express use, of a favourite *virtuoso* in Mozart's day. Not only are the expression and the design delightful, breathing all the freedom of a real inspiration, but the middle and the end of the song present vocal passages that can only be explained by the desire to display the singer's accomplishments. The song is, nevertheless, of exquisite sentiment and unequalled charm. The progression from bar 18 to bar 19 by the melodic figure of the voice part over the sustained notes of the horns is a genuine inspiration.

The scene now changes, and represents a cemetery. On an elevated pedestal is the marble statue of the Commandant. Don Giovanni enters, to escape, doubtless, from some pursuer, or to rid himself of the importunities of some damsel. He has scaled the cemetery wall, bursting with laughter.

" Ha, ha! most amusing," he chuckles ; " they will not seek me here. What splendid moonlight ; 'tis as light as in daytime! This is just such a night as suits for the chase of pretty damsels ! . . . . I wish now I knew how the droll encounter ended between that poor Elvira and Leporello." Leporello appears. "Ah!" he exclaims, "on your account I have almost been murdered."

A moment after, when the Don has made a laughing reply, a sepulchral voice, accompanied by lugubrious chords, resounds through the cemetery. "Your jest will turn to woe ere it is morning."

From this point to the end of the work every incident is highly dramatic. "Who was speaking?" inquires Don Giovanni. "Oh," replies Leporello," some soul tormented, from the land of spirits, pays homage to your merits." The sepulchral voice continues: "Misguided, perverted; anger not the departed!"

These two utterances of the statue freeze us with terror.

To the chanting of this voice, funereal in itself, and still more so by the harmonies which sustain it, is added a particularly sinister sonority due to the appearance of the trombones, which Mozart here introduces for the first time in the opera. Combined with the

hautboys, the clarionets, and the bassoons, they produce an awe-inspiring
impression.

"It must be someone hiding by
yon wall laughing at us," observes the
imperturbable Don. Then, raising his
eyes: "Say, can that hideous structure be the Commandant's statue ?
That inscription I'd like to hear."
The stammering Leporello reads: "I
here await the vengeance decreed by
Heaven upon a base assassin." "An
exquisite buffoonery!" says Don Giovanni; "Tell the old man I ask him to
sup with me this evening!"

No. 21.—DUET.

THIS duet, although presenting a comic aspect, is profoundly tragical, not alone by reason of the surrounding circumstances, but by the powerful and terrible contrast between the sceptical insolence of Don Giovanni and the reverent silence which should reign in the cemetery. Even the fright of Leporello ceases to be ludicrous, so much is it mingled with the dread of sacrilege. But we must enter into a detailed examination of this number to see with what marvellous intelligence Mozart has seized upon the slightest incidents of this tragi-comic scene.

In the first two bars Leporello salutes the statue of the Commandant with affected assurance. Then he respectfully delivers his master's invitation, which costs him unheard-of efforts, as may be divined by the sudden start of the violins in bar 4. At the 6th bar he has no longer strength to continue, and shrinks with fright. At bar 9 he trembles in every limb. In bars 10, 11, 12, and 13 Don Giovanni sharply addresses him : " Proceed at once or I'll spear thee ; I'll kill thee at a blow." These four bars evince the sceptical braggadocio that is amused by the valet's dismay. At bar 20 there is the same attempt at civility from Leporello as at the beginning of the duet. Bar 28, a new threat from Don Giovanni : " Die, then ! " " No, no ! " ejaculates Leporello ; " wait a moment, wait a moment ! " and he continues politely. Here commences an orchestral dialogue of marvellous penetration, which analyses the physical and the inmost details of fear. In bars 32 and 33 Leporello places himself on guard against the blow which threatens his life ; he seems to call to his aid the first and second violins, who respond with prudence. But in bars 34 and 35 danger is announced by the flutes and bassoons. Greater vigilance becomes necessary (bars 36 and 37), and at bars 38 and 39 the danger becomes more acute, causing him to redouble his precautions (bars 40, 41,

42, and 43). But, alas! his efforts are
in vain. The disaster is complete, in
spite of all the obstacles opposed to
the course of events by the dissonances
of 2nds which regularly succeed one
another here. The whole of this
period, from bar 32 to 43, occurs over
a persistent throbbing of the violas
that suggests a fixed and stupefied
look which makes one die with laughter
until the modulation at bar 44 reveals
the catastrophe. And then, upon the
tremolo of the violins and a disconso-
late progression for the basses, the
misery of the poor wretch is at its
height ; he speaks no more, but quakes
and whines and bleats. " Thou fool,"
says Don Giovanni ; " what's there to
scare thee ? " " O master," responds
the other, " look yourself and spare
me ! See, with his head of marble
he nods." And, in a rhythm that
expresses his stupefaction with astonishing veracity, the voice and the
orchestra imitate the nodding of the
statue. " Give answer," demands Don
Giovanni resolutely of the marble
figure, " if thou hear'st me. Wilt thou

come to supper?" "Yea!" replies
the statue, with an inclination of the
head. A sustained note of the horn
accompanies this answer with frigid
effect, and its prolongation after the
entry of the rest of the orchestra is
like a funeral knell. This time Leporello is overcome, overwhelmed; from
the orchestra is heard only a nervous
tremour and chattering of teeth. As
for Don Giovanni, he bears himself
blithely, singing:

"He hath accepted duly ;
Come, let us go make ready
To meet this stony guest."

Upon a rapid *decrescendo*, full of the
boastfulness of Don Giovanni and of
relief for Leporello, they hasten away.
Thus terminates this wonderful duet,
one of the most extraordinary delinea-
tions of character and of sensations
that has ever existed in dramatic music.

No. 22.—SCENA AND AIR.

THE scene changes and now represents the apartment of Donna Anna. Don Ottavio is beside her, and implores her to hasten their union. "Ah!" he exclaims, "since faithful love or prayers cannot move thee, too well I see that thou dost not love me." "Not love thee?" she answers; "Ah! ne'er believe it. Could I accept, while my tears yet freshly flow, the blest fulfilment of my heart's dearest wishes? . . . . Seek not to persuade me till my grief is assuaged."

This recitative of Donna Anna and the *Cantabile* which succeeds it are of the most elevated sentiment, in which all the scruples of grief and all the duties of a mourner are united to the noblest expressions of tenderness. The charming *Allegretto* which follows contains several florid vocal passages (bars 20-28) that were probably introduced by Mozart to display the virtuosity of the singer, as he already

had done in the air for Don Ottavio
(No. 20). What grace and feeling
are shown from bar 30 to the end of
the air! What ardent hope (starting
from bar 35) when the dwelling upon
the second beat is so passionately
marked! What secret and faithful
tears, what stifled sighs, in bars 40
and 41, so expressive and so tender!

No. 23.—Finale.

WE have arrived at the last tableau of this grand and noble drama. It comprises three important scenes, which are so closely linked together that Mozart has thought proper to group them under the one word— Finale, following the plan of the Finale to the first act. The scene represents Don Giovanni's banqueting hall, and he awaits the coming of the Commandant. A band of musicians occupy the back of the stage. Don Giovanni enters, richly dressed, accompanied by a joyous and careless orchestral fanfare.

> " Ah ! I see the table's ready,
> Play a gay and festive measure ;
> Costly is my cup of pleasure,
> And I'll drain it to the end."

Immediately the musicians on the stage strike up a series of pieces in different rhythms, whilst Leporello brings in the dishes and the choice wines which compose the repast, all the while freely making observations on his master's gluttonous appetite. The whole of this scene is treated with gaiety, freedom, and charming grace, and is accompanied by very varied combinations of wind instruments. Suddenly Donna Elvira appears. She makes a last effort to bring her husband to a better mode of life, and hastens, not to re-awaken any tenderness in that fickle heart, but for the purpose of saving him, should it not be too late.

The entire movement is full of tender solicitude and earnest pleading. Don Giovanni, cruel and unmoved, only replies to her grief by bitter and humiliating raillery. Elvira, her courage exhausted, yet more brokenhearted than indignant, departs, leaving him to his impenitence. She has scarcely disappeared when she utters a cry of fear. She finds herself face to face with the *man of stone*, faithful to his appointment.

"A scream! What means it?" says Don Giovanni.

"Go and see what is the matter."

Leporello goes towards the door, and immediately reappears, pale as death. The rhythm and instrumentation of this passage strike terror to the heart.

" Oh, good sir, for Heaven's sake,
    Not a step do that way take," &c.
" Coward,"

says Don Giovanni.

" If I would be enlightened I must go myself."

He seizes a torch, advances to the door, and then recedes terrified. The statue is before him. Then commences that formidable interview, than which there is perhaps nothing more imposing in dramatic music.

The appearance of the spectre is accompanied by the sinister chords which occur at the opening of the Overture. I will not repeat here what I said at the commencement of this study as to the majesty of these terrible harmonies. They reappear in this formidable scene, and are rendered, if possible, still more imposing by being heard in the presence of the mysterious being whom they portray with so much power. Obstinately

incredulous, insolently impious and
sacrilegious as he is, Don Giovanni
begins to comprehend that this is no
laughing matter, and that Divine justice
is not a subject for sport. Nevertheless
he endeavours to maintain a bold front
until the end. " Ah, ah!" he says,

> " Truly I did not expect it,
> But anew I'll sup with thee.
> Leporello, serve the table;
> For my guest another cover."

" Halt!" interposes the Commandant.

> " Earthly food he no longer desireth
> Who of heavenly food hath partaken;
> Cast away from thee now all such trifling,
> Heed the sentence I hither have brought."

And, whilst the beads of cold perspiration stand on Leporello's forehead,
Don Giovanni addresses his visitor:

> " Well, what wouldst thou? I listen."

A harmonic progression of terrible
import begins here, before which one
can understand that the most resolute
heart trembles with fright. Lugubrious harmonies, overwhelming rhythm,
fantastic and sinister instrumentation
all contribute to give this relentless

accuser an inexpressible authority.
The Statue says:

> " Thou didst thyself invite me,
> For that I must requite thee ;
> Then answer me,
> As my guest when shall I claim thee ? "

At the words " thou didst thyself
invite me," the orchestra proceeds by
a series of four-bar phrases, the effect
of the whole progression resembling
the upheaval of immense waves, which
mount, mount, mount always, ready to
engulf the guilty one. By a powerful
sforzando on the first chord of each
phrase, Mozart has given the impression of a raging sea, the waves of
which swell in a majestic *crescendo*,
breaking into foam on the shore with
a solemn sound. We see that this
tempest will terminate the blasphemer's
career, flight being no longer possible.

> " My heart is firm within me ;
> I have no fear ; I'll come,"

says Don Giovanni.

> " Give me thy hand in token,"

replies the Statue.

> " Take it then,"

adds the Don.

Immediately, as if by an electric shock, the orchestra is agitated, and writhes in frightful convulsions, announcing that the catastrophe is near.

" There's time yet for repentance," says the Statue.

" For me there's no repentance," ejaculates Don Giovanni.

This grievous struggle, this horrible agony, is a sublime and heartrending painting ; it is the despair of the damned in the clutches of inexorable justice. Foaming with rage, spent with fatigue, Don Giovanni falls at last, as though crushed, at the feet of the statue, who pronounces with tragic slowness the supreme sentence:

" *Alas ! It is too late.*"

At the same instant dreadful spectres emerge as from a flaming crater, and inclose Don Giovanni in an infernal circle. The doomed man cries in the height of fear :

" Is Hell let loose to torture me ? "

And the phantom choir reply :

" Torments eternal await thee."

Don Giovanni expires at last in the

midst of a veritable musical conflagration, a double apotheosis of heavenly justice and human genius. Here ends, at least on the stage, this colossal work, the score of which contains several more very beautiful numbers which complete the immense Finale of the last act as it flowed from the pen of Mozart, but which, after the overwhelming effect of the scene which precedes them, are superfluous from a dramatic point of view, and offer an interest that is purely musical.

It is from Leporello, the only eye-witness, that the other characters in the drama learn the tragic end of Don Giovanni.   Don Ottavio beseeches Donna Anna to consent to their union.   She asks for a delay of another year, as she stills mourns the loss of her father.   As to Leporello, whom the death of his master has left without employment, he dreams of finding a place in some hotel.   All is finished by a moral reflection, in fugal form, " Such is the end of the evil-doer."

This is evidently very cold after the

deep impression which has been made, and the exigencies of the drama here outweigh the musical beauties, however striking they may be. A genius so vast and at the same time so delicate as that of Mozart would do justice even to these superfluities. It must be borne in mind that in his time the public wanted a moral ending, explicitly setting forth the facts themselves, and that they were perhaps also desirous of knowing what became of the other characters in the piece, once delivered from him who had been the cause of all their troubles. Be that as it may, the interest gradually decreased, for, as regards the drama, justice had been done, and from this no appeal could be made.

An Appendix printed at the end of the score contains several pieces added by Mozart after the first representations of his work. One might venture to say that these additions have been demanded by those interpreters whose parts appeared somewhat meagre, for they relate principally to the three less important *rôles*—

those of Donna Elvira, Don Ottavio,
and Masetto.   Amongst these additions it is necessary to cite a very
beautiful air for Donna Elvira,* which
still maintains its place on the stage,
and, above all, the admirable recitative
which precedes it, a true masterpiece
of declamation and accompaniment.
Also there is Don Ottavio's delicious
cantilene, " *Dalla sua pace*," which is
charmingly graceful and refined.

---

* " *Mi tradi.*"

APPENDIX.

MOZART'S music, so clear, true, natural, and penetrating, is, notwithstanding, seldom perfectly performed. What is the reason ?

This is the question I propose to examine, and, if possible, to make comprehensible to my readers in this Appendix. In the execution of the works of Mozart, it is necessary, before everything, to avoid *seeking for effect*. I mean here by the word *effect*, not the impression produced on the listener by the work itself, an impression of charm, grace, tenderness, terror—in a word, all the feelings which the musical text offers, or, at least, should offer, *by itself* in the form and portrayal—but that *exaggeration* of accent, light and shade, and time which too often lead the executants to substitute their own ideas for those of the author, and to distort the nature of his thoughts instead of reproducing them simply and faithfully. When a great musician has written a work, and such a musician as Mozart, the least that one can do him the honour to suppose is that he has *wished* to write *what* he has written, and there are very strong presumptive reasons for saying that in trying to express *more* than Mozart has done they would express *less*.

What would be thought of an engraver who should replace by outlines and figures of his own those of a picture by Raphael?

Does an actor dare to introduce a phrase, a verse, a word of his own invention in a work of Racine or Molière?

Why should the language of *sounds* be treated with less respect than that of words?

Is the truth of expression less an obligation in one than the other?

What remains of a musical thought if executants distort accents, nuances, and the respective values of notes? Absolutely nothing. Many singers do not give the least thought to these matters. Preoccupied as they too often are with the idea of gaining admiration for their voices, they sacrifice without scruple *the demands of expression to the success of the virtuoso,* and the lasting triumph of truth to the empty and evanescent gratification of vanity.

It is hardly necessary to say that in thus permitting personal whims to replace obedience to the text, a gulf is created between the author and the auditor. What meaning is there, for example, in a prolonged pause on certain notes, to the detriment of the rhythm and the balance of the musical phrase ? Do they reflect for an instant on the perpetual irritation caused to the listener — to say nothing of the insupportable monotony of the proceeding itself. And then what becomes of the orchestral design in this constant subordination to the singer's caprice ? It is impossible to draw up a complete catalogue of abuses and licences of all sorts which in the execution alter the nature of the sense and compromise the impression of a musical phrase.

One may be permitted to remind musicians that want of attention to the following points causes nearly all the usual infractions of the rules of art and of good taste :

The rate of movement.
The light and shade.
The breathing.
The pronunciation.
The conductor.

I.—THE RATE OF MOVEMENT.

WHENEVER the real expression, the
true character, the just sentiment of a
piece depends upon the ensemble, the
most important, the most indispensable condition is, undoubtedly, the
exact and scrupulous observance of
the time in which the composer has
conceived it. The speed determines
its general *character*, and, as this
character is an essential part of the
idea, to alter the time is to alter
the idea itself to such a degree as to
destroy sometimes the sense and expression. It cannot be denied that a musical
phrase may be absolutely travestied
and disfigured by an excess of slowness or rapidity of the time in which it
is performed. I could quote many
examples. Here is one which I shall
never forget, it shocked me so much.
At a ball given by the Minister of
State during the winter of 1854-55,
if I mistake not, the old *contredanse*

(quadrille) was still in existence, or, rather, was just dying out. All of a sudden I heard the orchestra strike up the first figure. Horror! abomination! sacrilege! It was the sublime air of the High Priest of Isis in Mozart's "Il Flauto Magico" falling from the height of its solemn and sacred rhythm into the grotesque stamping of satin shoes and patent leather boots. I fled as if I had the devil at my heels!

However, a very incomplete idea of the importance of the musical movement would be formed if it were considered purely from a mathematical point of view only, and I shall now endeavour to consider the circumstances which might cause mathematical differences in the time, the music nevertheless retaining its identity of character and expression.

1st. The size of the building in which the performance is held. This is a question of acoustics and proportion. In a very large hall, a movement would bear to be taken less quickly than if executed in a smaller one.

2nd. The style of the executant, the amplitude of delivery, and the production of the voice.

I will cite here two famous examples—Duprez and Faure. When Duprez came to the Opera and filled the place which Nourrit had occupied with so much brilliancy and distinction for fifteen years, it was a complete revolution in lyrical declamation. Nourrit was a great artist; the dignity of his character, the culture of his intelligence, a constant care of truth in his varied and numerous *rôles* of the *répertoire* of that period—these qualities obtained for him not only the favour and esteem of the public, but an influence at the theatre which was felt by all around him. With rare talent as an artist he played the principal parts in all the grand operas, from " La Vestale," " Masaniello," and " Guillaume Tell," to " Robert le Diable," " La Juive," and " Les Huguenots," in the last of which he created the part of Raoul de Nangis, stamping it with an ineffaceable impression. His powerful acting so held

his audience, that he succeeded in
making them forget that his voice
was a little thin and guttural, and that
he used the falsetto register too frequently. The coming of Duprez took
everybody by storm. I was present at
his *début*, which took place in the part
of Arnold (" Guillaume Tell"). Duprez
returned from Italy preceded by a great
reputation and the well-known story of
the chest C, which was to raise a
tempest of applause at the end of
the celebrated air of the last act. It
was unnecessary to wait till then to
know that the success of the great
singer was assured. In two bars it
was made. From the first verse of
the recitative, " Il me parle d'hymen !
Jamais, jamais le mien!" one felt
that this was a transformation in the
art of singing, and when Duprez
finished the phrase of the duet in the
second act, " Oh, Mathilde! idole
de mon âme," there was a frenzy of
enthusiasm throughout the house. He
had a breadth of declamation and
volume of tone which captivated the
hearer, and the admirable melodies of

the great Italian master shone with a new lustre owing to the marvellous notes of his voice. The use of the chest voice and the amplitude of his declamation, permitted Duprez to take the time slower than his illustrious predecessor had done without appearing to alter it, so well did he know how to captivate the ear by the fulness of his voice, and to move the audience by his dramatic powers. Faure in our day has been a new and striking example of the same thing. He produces the sounds with such richness and fulness, he gives them such interest by a continual modulation of the tone (and occasionally, perhaps, a little more than is necessary), that one forgets the duration which he gives them, and which is hidden under his admirable method and his unrivalled pronunciation. To these illustrious names must be added those of Pauline Viardot, Miolan Carvalho, Gabrielle Krauss, the brothers De Reszke, Lassalle, and others who have understood the importance of declamation. But the preceding remarks on time have nothing to do with the accent, which is also, from an entirely different point of view, a matter of great importance. Unfortunately, many singers of to-day do not sufficiently consider this subject, great detriment being thus caused to the music and considerable annoyance to both composer and conductor.

Much might be said upon this topic. I must be satisfied to touch lightly upon it, as this is not the place to set forth a complete course of musical education.

II.—The Bar (*La Mésure*).

DISREGARD of the accent is one of the
modern faults, it entirely destroys the
musical equilibrium. Many singers
regard the bar as an insupportable yoke,
and as an obstacle to feeling and expression. They think that it makes
machines of them, and that it takes
away all grace, charm, warmth, and
freedom in performance. Now it is
exactly the reverse. The bar, instead
of being the enemy to the musical
phrase, gives protection and freedom
to it. It is not difficult to demonstrate
this. Let us consider it first as a
principle of unanimity of performance.
The essential character of the bar is
the equality of the duration of the
beats which compose it. If, then,
inequality is introduced, the unity
which is essential to the phrase, and
which alone permits one to feel it, is
destroyed.

2nd. If the misrepresentation of the bar is injurious to such an extent upon an isolated phrase, what confusion will it not bring in the execution of an ensemble ? The effect would be indescribable.

3rd. There is still the orchestra to be considered. It presents a multitude of figures of accompaniment subjected to the laws of accent, and from which laws there can be no deviation under penalty of abominable confusion. Sixty or eighty musicians cannot be left in a state of constant uncertainty. Deprived of the word of command, they will not know what to do in order to avoid disorder and cacophony.

But the bar, which is a principle of order with regard to the rhythm, is no less essential to the expression. The idea of the bar includes that of rhythm, which is its characteristic sub-division.

To neglect the bar and its regulating influence injures the rhythm and the prosody.

These few reflections are sufficient to give an idea of the detrimental effects which disregard of the accent may cause to musical works. Another question of extreme importance in the matter of musical expression is that of light and shade.

III.—THE NUANCES.

WE understand by the word "nu-ance" the degree of intensity of any sound, whether it be produced by a voice or instrument. That is to say, the gradations of tone play in musical art a part analogous to that of pro-portion in the art of painting.

We see by this how the true obser-vation of the nuances is indispensable to the faithful rendering of a musical phrase, and to what degree the thought-less caprice of the executant can alter the sense and character to such an extent as to make it unrecognisable by substituting for the author's intentions and indications the nuances and accents of pure fancy. It is here that the independence of the singer most frequently finds the opportunity of giving free scope to his imagination, and Heaven knows how he uses it.

It matters little whether the accent be neglected, whether the prosody be sacrificed, whether the melodic figure be altered, or whether affectation destroys the logical and natural movement of the musical phrase, provided that the *sound* be noticed and applauded *for itself.* These performers are entirely mistaken as to the function and *rôle* of the *voice.* They take the *means* for the *end*, and the servant for the master. They forget that fundamentally there is but one art, *the word*, and one function, *to express*, and that consequently a great singer ought to be first of all a great *orator*, and that is utterly impossible without absolutely truthful accent. When singers, especially on the stage, think only of displaying the voice, they should be reminded that that is a sure and infallible means of falling into *monotony ;* truth alone has the privilege of infinite and inexhaustible variety.

IV.—The Breathing.

This important question of the breathing may be regarded under two distinct aspects—the one purely physical, the other purely expressive. Under the first it devolves upon the composer to write in such a way as not to exceed the power of the respiratory organs, under the penalty of seeing his musical phrase divided into fragments, which would disfigure it. But, as regards the expression, it is another thing. Here it is prosody and punctuation which determine and regulate the expression. Unfortunately this rule is seldom observed. A singer does not scruple to divide a section of a phrase, often even a word, in order to take breath, for the sake of a sound to which they wish to give exaggerated power and duration, to the detriment of the musical sense and the prosody, which ought to be the first consideration. It is ridiculous to introduce, for example, a respiration between " my " and "love" in the phrase

"To thee I give my love "

—a respiration which nothing can justify; but then the singer has had the pleasure of showing off on a short syllable until all the breath has been used, just for the sake of gaining a noisy demonstration of conventional applause. Such licences simply disfigure the form of the musical idea, and are revolting to common sense.

V.—The Pronunciation.

There are two special points to observe in the pronunciation.

1st. It should be clear, neat, distinct, exact; that is to say, the ear ought not to be left in any uncertainty as to the word pronounced.

2nd. It should be expressive; that is to say, *to paint in the mind the feeling* enunciated by the word itself. All that concerns clearness, neatness, and exactness may be more properly classed as *articulation*. Articulation relates to the due formation of every sound in the word. Everything else may be described as *pronunciation*. It is by the latter that we make the word picture the thought, the feeling, the passion which it envelops. In short, the function of articulation is to form the material sounds of a word, whereas that of pronunciation is to reveal its inner meaning. Articulation gives clearness to the word; pronunciation gives it eloquence. True instinct, though lacking culture, can make all these distinctions apparent. One cannot insist too much upon the value and interest which clear articulation and expressive pronunciation give to singing, so important are they. By the force of expression, they exercise such a power over the listener that they make him forget the insufficiency or the mediocrity of the vocal organ; whilst the absence of these qualities, though the voice may be the most beautiful in the world, leaves him unmoved.

The foregoing considerations show how much depends upon simplicity, sincerity, and freedom from all preoccupation as to personal success.

Can there be a higher ambition for a performer than to be an artist capable and worthy of interpreting Mozart's music, so pure and so true; or a more noble dream than to inspire love for the works of such a master, and thus contribute to the sacred and salutary devotion to the true and the beautiful? But, alas! in art, as in everything else, the abnegation of self is rare, although it is the condition of all true greatness.

It remains only to speak now of the conductor, who plays such an important part in the performance.

VI.—THE CONDUCTOR.

THE conductor is the *centre* of the musical performance. This word, in itself, shows the importance and responsibility of his functions.

First of all, the unity of the movement, without which there is no possible ensemble, is in the hands of the conductor. That is self-evident, and does not need demonstration. It is on this point most necessary, and at the same time most easy, for the conductor to make his authority felt ; his *bâton* is one of command.

But, apart from the ensembles, how often does this command degenerate into servitude ? What compliance there is to the caprices of the singers, and what fatal neglect of the interests of art and the real value of the works performed !

However, it is not necessary that the rule of the conductor should amount to an unyielding and mechanical rigidity, which would be the absurd triumph of the *letter* over the *spirit*.

A conductor who would be like an

inflexible metronome throughout a musical composition would be guilty of an excess of strictness as unbearable as an excess of laxity.

The great art of the conductor is that power which may be called suggestive, and which elicits from the singer an unconscious obedience, whilst making him believe that it is his own will that he follows. In short, the singer must be persuaded and not constrained. Power is not in the will, but in the intelligence; it is not questioned, but it is felt. It behoves the conductor, then, to understand, and to make others understand, how much he will concede to them in the matter of time without altering the character of the movement. It is his duty to seize upon the difference between elasticity and stiffness, and to atone, without abruptness, for any momentary retardation by an imperceptible return to the normal and regular time.

It is also essential that the conductor should not mistake precipitation for warmth—the result would be to sacrifice the rhythmical power of the declamation and the fulness of tone. It is commonly imagined that a *crescendo* ought to be *hurried*, and a *diminuendo* gradually slackened. Now, it is precisely the contrary which is nearly always the case. It stands to reason that one feels inclined to lengthen a sound in augmenting its intensity, and *vice versâ*. But this is not all.

It is an error to think that the conductor can make himself entirely understood by means of the *bâton* or the bow which he holds in his hand. His whole demeanour should instruct and animate those who obey him. His attitude, his physiognomy, his glance should prepare the singers for that which is demanded of them; his expression should cause them to anticipate his intentions, and should enlighten the executants.

Yet it is not necessary for him to indulge in wild gesticulations. True power is calm, and when the poet of antiquity wished to express the might of Jupiter, he represented him as making the whole of Olympus tremble at his nod. In short, the conductor is the ambassador of the master's thought ; he is responsible for it to the artists and to the public, and *ought to be* the living expression, the faithful mirror, the incorruptible depositary of it. One could write volumes upon the important duties of a conductor, and I certainly hold that these duties should be made the object of a regular course of lectures, the plan for which might be clearly indicated in the general musical education given by our conservatoires. Here is a want which I hope may be supplied in the future. Besides the considerable benefit which would accrue to the musical works, this would be an opening offered to a whole group of special aptitudes, which are as rare as they are necessary ; it would also be a serious guarantee of authority to the artists.

And now, having written this book in all sincerity, I rely upon that of the reader to form an opinion of it. My only wish and hope has been to serve the interests of an art to which I have consecrated my life.

Printed by Horace Cox, Windsor House, Bream's Buildings, E.C.

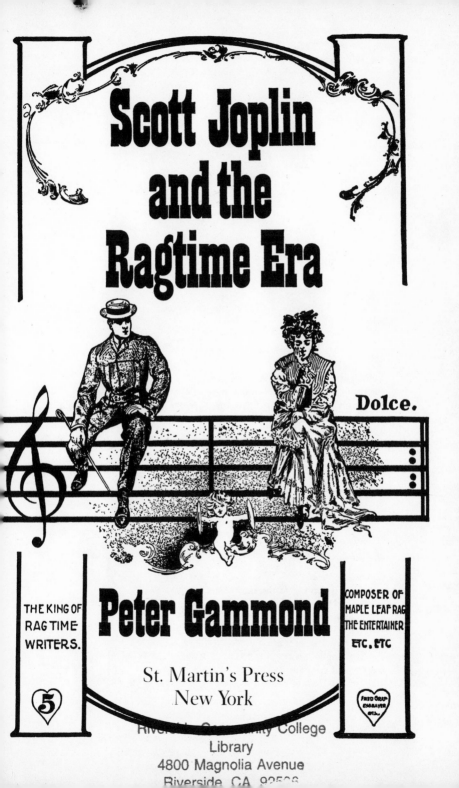

Scott Joplin and the Ragtime Era

Dolce.

THE KING OF RAGTIME WRITERS.

COMPOSER OF MAPLE LEAF RAG THE ENTERTAINER ETC. ETC

Peter Gammond

St. Martin's Press
New York

Library of Congress Cataloging in Publication Data

Gammond, Peter.
      Scott Joplin and the ragtime era.

      Bibliography: p.
      Discography: p.
      "Checklist of music by Scott Joplin": p.
      1. Joplin, Scott, 1868-1917. 2. Ragtime music —
History and criticism. I. Title.
ML410. J75G35   786.1'092'4   75-25758

Contents

5

Acknowledgments

The author and publisher would like to thank the following for supplying photographs or for giving permission for their reproduction. The Mansell Collection, 1, 2, 3, 5, 6, 8, 16, 17, 33, 34, 45, 49; Radio Times Hulton Picture Library, 4, 7, 11, 14, 19, 20, 35, 36, 40, 44; Mary Evans Picture Library, 9, 10; Virginia State Library, 12; John Hall, 15, 24, 25; Len Sirman Press, 18, 46; John R. Freeman & Co., 21, 23, 38, 39, 43; Decca Records, 22; Fisk University Library, Tennessee, 26, 29, 32, 37; State Historical Society of Missouri, 27, 28; Chicago Historical Society, 30; Historical Pictures Service – Chicago, 31; The British Piano Museum, 41; Crown copyright, Science Museum, London, 42; Melody Maker, 47, 48, 50, 51, 52; National Broadcasting Company, Inc., 53; Anthony Crickmay, 54, 55; The National Film Archive, 56; The Associated Press Ltd, 57; BBC, 58.

Picture research by Annette Brown

Foreword by Eubie Blake

Ragtime was considered out of fashion and now, all of a sudden, I'm amazed that after fifty years of neglect it's become the craze of the world. I knew all the time that it was good music because rhythm is the most contagious thing there is. You just play that rhythm and people in the audience feel happier. Scott Joplin's kind of ragtime was melodic too, and the bass is so important. Some people wrote anything and called it ragtime. But the real ragtime is popular again because it had all the best things in music: rhythm, melody and syncopation.

Anything that is syncopated is basically ragtime. I don't care whether it's Liszt's *Hungarian Rhapsody* or Tchaikovsky (my favourite composer) in his *Waltz Of The Flowers*.

When I was a boy in Baltimore I heard nothing but ragtime all around me. Folk from New Orleans say that it started there; I don't know about that, but I heard it all my life. Whenever Negroes played, it was ragtime. At a funeral they would play the Chopin *Funeral March* on the way there, and on the way back they'd play it in ragtime. I really don't know where it all started but it was around when I was five or six.[1]

I started playing what I heard about me. My mother was very religious and hated ragtime like all the high-class Negroes. I was sorry that they didn't understand it. The purists said it was not art because it came from backroom bars. I played it in houses of ill-repute when I was fifteen. I had to put on long pants to play there. I played at Aggi Shelton's where they sat on beer kegs and there was sawdust in the floor.

People ask me where ragtime originated. Rudi Blesh, in his

1 Eubie Blake was born on 7 February 1883.

7

book, said that when they were having a hen party they put out a white flag which they called the white rag, and the name came from that. I don't know. It was always called ragtime as far back as I remember. When I played it at home my mother would yell, 'Take that ragtime out of my house. As long as I'm here, you don't play ragtime in this house!' I had to go somewhere else to practise. *She* knew where it came from. She'd play things like *Jesus Knows All About My Struggles* – and that wasn't ragtime.

On 14 May 1915 I met Noble Sissle. Later, with F. E. Miller and Aubrey Lyle, we wrote *Shuffle On*. They wrote the book, we wrote the songs. James Reese Europe got Sissle to bring me to New York, and the first ragtime number I wrote was called *Charleston Rag* – one of the things I play to this very day. I learned from players like Jimmy Green and Big-Head Wilber. I only saw Scott Joplin once in 1907, 8 or 9 it would be. He was in Washington trying to negotiate a production of his *Treemonisha*. He played at a party on Pennsylvania Avenue, but he was very ill at the time. He played *Maple Leaf Rag* but a child of five could have played it better. He was dead but he was breathing. I went to see him after but he could hardly speak he was so ill.

Scott Joplin's music was classical ragtime. Other players played it differently. None of them sounded like Joplin but it was the same idea. My knowledge of ragtime came from hearing it all my life. I don't play it better than Earl Hines, but I play it differently. Once, to try to show I could be like those clever guys, I wrote a modern syncopated piece called *Novelty Rag* – and I wish I'd never written it. I don't mind how people play my things; I like them to play them the way they feel. Music like the blues will always be around because of its soulful melody, and ragtime will always be around because of its rhythm. I really think ragtime's going to stick this time.

Introduction

The fascination of popular music of past times is the way it brings us a sense of the life-style, the colour, the pre-occupations, the tastes and the pace of its particular period. Ragtime, in its original form, could only have come from the 1890s. It has the unself-conscious charm and good manners of late-Victorianism. But because it grew up in America it also has the boisterous quality of a music that had its roots in folk song and dance going back to the hard pioneering days of American history. Because it is a black American music it has the supple rhythmic grace and the under-lying melancholy that these warm-hearted but frustrated people have always offered to the world.

Ragtime found its feet before jazz had given popular music a new brash vulgarity and vitality. It had a certain primness about it that could be found in Victorian drawing-room ballads. But it also had a fund of rich and direct melody and infectious rhythmic qualities that Tin Pan Alley could not resist. Ragtime was not only the spirit of the 1890s but also of the frivolous 1920s. They are both flavours that today, in the otherwise serious 1970s, we look back to with a certain amount of envy. We are wise enough to know that all was far from well in many areas of society in those days, but somehow it all seemed more settled and sane.

Like all the best popular music, ragtime had somewhat seedy and shady beginnings. Because its exponents were poor and mainly without an academic background, they practised their art and wrote their music in the lowliest and bawdiest of saloons and bars, brothels and cafés; any place where song and dance, wine and women, could liven up an otherwise drab and hard-working life. But it was a forward-looking time in America, a time of rapid expansion, and ragtime soon became a commercial prospect as the means of spreading it became cheaper and accessible to many. You might think of the early 1900s as the real beginning of the pop boom with sheet music and player piano rolls starting to sell in substantial quantities and the gramophone and phonograph making professional entertainment in the home a clear possibility.

In this hurly burly of social upheaval and musical mayhem, the lonely figure of Scott Joplin emerges as one of those inexplicable geniuses who occur once or twice in a generation. He was a quiet, introverted person who had to learn his art in places that were probably not all that much to his liking or easy to work in. He left his family in boyhood and worked his way around the country. His father had been a slave a few years before Joplin was born and there was no wealth or academic training to help him on his road. His first marriage was a failure. He died in a mental home, a frustrated and pathetic figure. He had his musical successes like the immortal *Maple Leaf Rag*, but his dreams went far beyond being a popular tunesmith. His ambition was to distil from the bubbling life of Negro folksong an art music that would be acceptable to both the black and white worlds of classical music.

Instead, he simply achieved a personal collection of compositions of great distinction and beauty; and then saw his achievement by-passed as that which he had helped to give birth to went back to its lowly beginnings, becoming once again a music of the people. As such it gave pleasure to millions and has its own sturdy worth. But it was not what Joplin intended or hoped for. The opera on which his sights had always been set and which took years of effort to produce had only a single rehearsal performance in Harlem in 1915. Nobody was interested, at that time, in thinking of ragtime in anything but vulgar and strictly commercial terms; except Joplin and a few like him.

Nevertheless it is not strictly accurate to suggest, as Rudi Blesh said in his preface to the fourth edition of *They All Played Ragtime*, that it has taken seventy years for ragtime to be remembered again. As a musical phenomenon with a very special flavour it has always been treasured and held in deep affection by the few; as an ingredient of most subsequent jazz and popular music it has been with us ever since the 1890s whether the world realised it or not. Blesh was also a little unfair to himself as the man who wrote (with Harriet Janis) a truly magnificent and detailed book on the subject way back in 1950 with very little practical help from other books or historians. Obviously he was listening intently to ragtime long before then, as were many writers and collectors who tried in vain to bring this delightful music to the world's attention. I flatter myself that I had a ready and inquisitive ear tuned in its direction as far back as 1944 without, as I realise now, being one hundred per cent sure of what I was really listening to. Years after that, in common with many other critics, I was still praising performances that only half caught the true essence of ragtime – in spite of being warned off them by wiser and more discerning acquaintances. Yet perhaps even the experts were just a little surprised when they at last heard ragtime played in a clear and unadorned style by an academically trained musician like Joshua Rifkin, without the accumulated flavours of jazz which had hidden its true grace and beauty for so long. We were even more surprised when, more or less used in its pure and original form, it caught the imagination of a wide public – many of whom weren't even jazz lovers – through its use in a very good film, set in the 1930s, called 'The Sting'.

Ragtime never actually disappeared; but it had been so much changed, adulterated, perverted, absorbed into jazz and popular song, and so distorted in the hands of uncomprehending 'serious' composers, that the world at large had forgotten what the real thing was like. After all the first ragtime craze was around 1900 before most of our parents were even married. In fact, there are plenty of precedents in musical history for the 'real thing' coming back with an impact that its imitations had long enjoyed. For once, true justice has been done in that it was Scott Joplin – unquestionably the greatest writer if not the actual inventor of ragtime – who got the first credit. He had died, with a heavy heart, as long ago as 1917, feeling that his true merits had largely been ignored and that his efforts to make ragtime universally respected had been a failure. If only he could see now how he has been vindicated; how his own music is respected and loved; and what an immense influence it has had on the language of popular music. Joplin's partial success in his lifetime, his subsequent neglect, the final acclamation by posterity, is a pattern not uncommon in the arts. In music there is an almost parallel case in the career and reputation of Gustav Mahler (1860–1911) [Joplin 1868–1917] whose works suffered almost complete neglect before receiving their due acclamation.

Two first-rate books on ragtime already exist; and from which, of necessity, I must borrow half my facts. These books are the basic *They All Played Ragtime* by Rudi Blesh and Harriet Janis (5th edition: Oak Publications, New York, 1971) which did all the spadework; and *The Art of Ragtime* by William J. Schafer and Johannes Riedel (Louisiana State University Press, Baton Rouge, 1973) which is a wide-ranging scholarly assessment of the subject, itself making sincere acknowledgment to the earlier work. Both of them are long and thorough academic books, well researched – and the deeply committed ragtime enthusiast need look no further. But like most books written for the specialist, they make no concessions to the beginner and, while both are eminently readable, give so much fact and detail and throw so many names around with gay abandon that they make your head whirl. That leaves room for a fairly straightforward, unbiased account of ragtime, which I hope might be read with some comprehension and pleasure by the thousands of people who have just made a casual acquaintance with ragtime and Joplin – probably through the charmingly insinuating strains of *The Entertainer* by way of a screen soundtrack or an LP recording about seventy-five years after it was written.

Most writing on music, and especially on jazz (to which ragtime is related) tends to get too involved, too technical, and usually very much on an offensive tack – on the principle that attack is the best means of defence. For instance, the early apologies made because jazz was a black music were quickly replaced by fiery attacks on white intrusion into the field and assertions of the beauty of its blackness. These racial overtones are even more complex and delicate today than ever before; but they are impossible to avoid. Because I don't have partisan feelings on these matters and because I can write about jazz and ragtime as one never exclusively committed to their protection and enshrinement – being equally in love with Mozart, Schubert, Mahler, Offenbach and Gershwin, to mention but a few – I hope I can look at the whole subject in a fairly balanced and sane manner. I find I cannot resist following a scholastic, musicological trail of sorts when we begin to look at the influence and subsequent history of ragtime; but I can assure everyone who cares to follow that it is an interesting route to ramble. What really matters, I think, is that I share a growing opinion that ragtime is an extremely beautiful and long underrated music and that Joplin at last has got his due recognition. Let's try to sort out the story in as uncomplicated a way as possible.

Shepperton, England, October 1974

Hullo Ragtime!
A Broad Definition

Magnetic Rag

BY

SCOTT JOPLIN

Composer of
MAPLE LEAF RAG
EUPHONIC SOUNDS
Etc.

❦ 5 ❧

SCOTT JOPLIN MUSIC PUBLISHING CO.
NEW YORK, N.Y.

Scott Joplin is the pivot of this book and he will take up a major part of it although, to be honest, there is not a great deal of intimate detail known about his daily life or background. Who, in America in the late nineteenth century, thought it worth documenting the life of an obscure Negro ragtime composer – let alone the details of his family – on his father's side of slave descent. Most of what we know about Joplin is by way of verbal reminiscence caught, just in time, from the lips of a few of his contemporaries who survived him. He died in 1917 before either jazz or ragtime were considered of academic interest.

As for ragtime – nothing ever comes completely out of the blue and it must have been created from existing materials . . . but, firstly, to begin at the beginning, let's try to define ragtime. Here it is best to step warily because so many definers in the past have tried to put things in a nutshell and ended up with a half-truth. It is wiser to avoid trying to make a neat, epigrammatic, comprehensive definition and to approach the subject from various angles.

Basically, ragtime, that is the 'classic' ragtime (which covers a period beginning with the first published rags of 1897 to about 1915), is a written piano music. During its heyday it was transcribed for other instruments and published in orchestral form; but it was originally written as piano music, partly as being eminently suited to the instrument, partly for the purely practical reason that the piano was the popular instrument of the day, gracing even the poorest front parlours of America as it did in England and elsewhere. It was the 'sheet-music era' with most music being either piano solo or song. Joplin and ragtime conformed in this respect.

The harmonies of ragtime are mainly the basic harmonies and harmonic contrivances ('banjo' chords) of the popular music of the day – the drawing-room songs and ballroom dances. Joplin's first publications were a couple of innocuous songs in the conventional vein and the harmonies were much the same as he used in his first ragtime compositions. Later rags, as we would expect, became more ambitious, but basically there is nothing that we can pinpoint as being exclusively ragtime harmony.

The rhythms of ragtime are a mixture of conventional European-based march or dance rhythms, generally in 2/4 time, the left hand keeping very much to the regular beat, only varying a vamped accompaniment by an occasional shifting of the bass notes from the first and third beats of the bar to the first and fourth (a device common in all kinds of music of the period) and by regular whole tone or semitone ascents and descents to give momentum. The bass figures are an essential characteristic of Joplin's music and other ragtime and give it much of its flavour : for instance, a great deal of the character of *Maple Leaf Rag* comes from its very mobile left-hand movements. It might be noted here that much of the basic left-hand or bass beat of jazz is also a straightforward 2/4 or 4/4 and a lot of nonsense is talked about 'jazz rhythms'. In jazz, as in ragtime, what makes for a distinctive 'rhythm' is the way that the top, melody line is set against the bass line. The syncopation, which has always been a basic element of ragtime, is almost always achieved by a *melodic* note being delayed or advanced for half a beat or an eighth-note. While this happens regularly throughout most ragtime pieces there are also whole sections of ragtime compositions that are not syncopated at all – for example, the second strain, oddly enough, of a Joplin piece called *Elite Syncopations*. Syncopation is simply a placing of the emphasis in the melodic line, where it would not be expected to fall in a 'straight' rendering of a piece; generally over an unstressed beat or between beats. In ragtime it is usually a simple shift of a quaver by means of a tied note or a dotted note, using a syncopation that can be accurately written out in normal notation; whereas, in jazz it is a much subtler business and cannot be accurately notated, hence the essentially improvised nature of jazz and jazz phrasing.

These melodic shifts are essentially those that you find in earlier minstrel songs and in the banjo rhythms that accompanied them. Ragtime, melodically, is clearly based on what had become the traditional folk music of the slave plantation, at least its dances (jigs, struts, hops, cakewalks, etc.) which had been printed as the popular and minstrel songs of Negro composers (and certain white imitators like Stephen Foster) in the decades of the nineteenth century before the rise of ragtime. So there is no great mystery as to where ragtime's melodic and rhythmic characteristics came from. Probably long before Joplin and others got down to composing and publishing ragtime, there were itinerant Negro pianists and other instrumentalists playing a similar music in the saloons and dives of the South. How much Joplin borrowed from unwritten sources we will never be able to ascertain. His originality can only be measured against the published works of his contemporaries and there is little doubt of his superiority in this context.

In spite of having seen Joshua Rifkin performing in 'tails' at London's Royal Festival Hall, we can still affirm that ragtime was originally conceived as a dance. Joplin and his brother pianists would doubtless have been surprised to have found many people standing around and simply listening to their music. Joplin's creative life was directed towards trying to make ragtime a concert music (the whole reason for writing it down and publishing it), but he spent most of his career playing it as background to conviviality and debauchery and was said to perform with a driving rhythm most conducive to dancing. Along with instrumental ragtime came the ragtime song which was to lead the way to Tin Pan Alley's various dilutions – but that is a later chapter.

The form of ragtime is most commonly an AABBACCDD pattern – that is four distinct strains repeated as indicated, or close variants, sometimes returning to A to round off matters or using

21

it as a rondo theme – and is essentially the scheme of most European and American marches (Joplin was very much in the Sousa era) and of many dance-forms such as the quadrille. Indeed many of the early rags are either marked as 'tempo di marcia' or 'march time' or actually called marches or subtitled as such. Other facets obviously borrowed from the march tradition that flourished in Joplin country was modulating to the subdominant in the Trio or C section, with a two or four-bar leading-in modulation. The form of most ragtime pieces and their allied key-changes is very much that of the march tradition.

In summary we might say that ragtime was very much a child of European ancestry, certainly in form and harmony. Only its melodies and syncopated melodic lines show Negro ancestry and affirm its second- or further removed-cousin relationship to jazz, part of which came from the same sources. The inherited ragtime element in jazz is essentially the gayer element, the march-based square-rhythmed, melodic Dixieland-styled music. The freer-formed, essentially improvised and generally darker side of jazz came from the far deeper African part of the Negro's ancestry, from the blues tradition. Ragtime is nearer to West Indian than African origins, where we can find its links with the Creole type of melody exploited by that unusual American composer Louis Moreau Gottschalk.

That is ragtime in abstract terms, later to be clarified in nature by listening to genuine examples which we will list. Where did it get its name? There is not, so it seems, all that much mystery there. Someone simply asked at some time for some more of that 'ragged' music. As ragtime, before about 1897 and its first publications, was generally referred to as jig-time music, the substitution of 'rag' for 'jig' was a fairly simple colloquialism. So it became ragged or ragtime music, the music with the broken, jagged melodic line. Scott Joplin never liked the name 'ragtime' which he described as 'scurrilous'.

That is ragtime! Ragtime in narrow and fairly precisely defined terms as it was written in the 1890s and early 1900s by the classic ragtime composers like Scott Joplin, Tom Turpin, James

Scott, Joseph Lamb, Louis Chauvin, Scott Hayden. But RAGTIME
in its broadest sense is more of an elusive spirit than something
you can define. It is that element of syncopated gaiety that runs
through all kinds of jazz-influenced popular music; while the more
introspective element stems from the blues. There was ragtime in
the music that came before Joplin's time; in the minstrel songs
and the dance music of the Negroes. There was the ragtime that
was played by countless unknown and unrecorded pianists from
whom Joplin drew his inspiration. There were the ragtime songs
that were being created at the same time as piano ragtime which
led to the Tin Pan Alley ragtime of Irving Berlin and the other
songsmiths. It was there in the Charleston and the raggy tunes of
the twenties and thirties. It was an element of early jazz, in the
music of the Original Dixieland Jazz Band, the New Orleans
Rhythm Kings, King Oliver's Creole Jazz Band, the music of Louis
Armstrong. It came back into power with Muggsy Spanier and his
Ragtimers and the revivalist strains of the Yerba Buena Jazzband.
In England Humphrey Lyttelton, George Webb, Chris Barber, Ken
Colyer founded their music on an instinctive understanding of
ragtime. The jazz pianists of the golden era that followed Joplin
– Jelly Roll Morton, James P. Johnson, Fats Waller – may have
smoothed it out and added new chords, but the spirit of ragtime
was still there. It was revived and nurtured by ragtime addicts
like Ralph Sutton, Knocky Parker and Max Morath. It was knocked
about a bit by the funny hat and tin-tack pianists like Joe 'Fingers'
Carr and Winifred Atwell, but it was still ragtime. It was there in
the foot-tapping rhythms of the pioneer dance bands of Paul
Whiteman, and in England in the music of Lew Stone and Roy
Fox, Ambrose, Jack Hylton, Jack Payne, Harry Roy. Through the
influence of a great composer like Gershwin it filtered into Europe
as a new element in musical comedy. It is still there in much of
the pop music we hear today. Generally it was called jazz; but it
was the ragtime strain of jazz that most tickled the ears of the
uninitiated. Serious composers like Debussy, Satie, Hindemith,
Stravinsky, Milhaud, Honegger, Poulenc, Copland, Ravel, Krenek
and Weill had a try at manipulating its elements for their own
uses. Ragtime was in all of these. But to understand how much it

gave to popular music one must first absorb the characteristics and flavour of pure classical ragtime; a rich, formal, delicately hard-hitting music that has survived because it has the strength and individuality of all the great strains of popular music that evolved slowly and naturally by finding the right balance of ingredients from folk music and written music of the past to create a dish of unmistakable and unforgettable flavour.

The English critic Ernest Newman said as long ago as 1927 that jazz could never be the basis of a genuine and lasting new direction for academic music because once you bent it to the mainstream of musical development you lost its 'own peculiar physiognomy' and it ceased to be jazz. The years have more or less borne out his contention. But in returning to the root music of ragtime we may yet be able to start all over again and create music that is based on the written art of ragtime. It may not happen, but it could.

Scott Joplin I

The Entertainer

Maple Leaf Rag

COMPOSED BY

SCOTT JOPLIN.

PRICE 50¢

SEDALIA, Mo.
PUBLISHED BY
JOHN STARK & SON

Musicians are unpredictable animals and have added their own wilful confusion of musical terms to the predictable inaccuracies of those engaged in publicising it. There has thus been much confusion over the use of the word 'rag'. Employed as a verb it loosely means to liven up, to add a general air of syncopated hilarity to a popular or jazz-styled composition. Appended to such jazz titles as *Panama Rag*, *Bugle Call Rag* and *Tiger Rag*, and as performed by popular entertainers such as Mr. Pee Wee Hunt, the word signifies an effervescent Dixieland-styled performance. Carelessly used the word 'rag' is more or less synonymous with words like 'stomp' and 'strut', indicating a fast-tempo piece full of dance spirit with perhaps a grain of true ragtime in its ancestry. Used in the strict (I hesitate to say 'academic') sense, a rag is specifically a ragtime composition in the formal style and shape of such compositions already defined in the previous chapter. Talking of ragtime in an appropriately pure spirit it is safe to say, without fear of challenge, that Scott Joplin was quite clearly the greatest and most consistently inspired of all ragtime composers.

A modest and retiring man and an accomplished though not a virtuoso performer, he achieved only the respectable fame that musical history offers composers, in contrast to the contemporary adulation that is poured upon musical executants. The result, unfortunately, is that not very much has been committed to print that offers detail or insight into his life and character. Now, as also frequently happens, he has achieved posthumous fame and exploitation and his name means something to that unpredictable creature the 'man in the street', there is no doubt that some worthy and assiduous American scholar will do his best to remedy the situation by some difficult research into the misty past to produce a definitive Joplin biography.

At the present time the few facts available are fairly basic and oft-repeated. Scott Joplin was born on a Tuesday on the twenty-fourth day of November 1868 – just coming under the sign of Saggitarius and all that it portends. He was born in the small city of Texarkana, which has the unusual distinction of being a twin city having entities in both Texas and Arkansas. The Joplins resided in the Texan town which was then known as Bowie County.

His father, Giles Joplin, was a railroad labourer who came from North Carolina. He had been born and reared as a slave and had only obtained his legal freedom from this bondage some five years before Scott Joplin was born. He played the violin and had performed in a plantation dance band during his slave days. He did all that he could to promote a family interest in music and must take at least some of the credit for his son's musical genius. Joplin's mother, Florence Givens Joplin, was a freeborn Negro who came from Kentucky. She helped to keep the family alive by working as a laundress and had musical talents as a singer and banjo-player. There was an elder brother, Monroe, and two musically inclined younger brothers: Will, who was a singer, guitarist and violinist; and Robert, who was a singer and composer of forgotten popular songs. There were also two sisters, Myrtle and Ossie.

Taking whatever was at hand (and cheapest) Scott Joplin made his first excursions into music on the family guitar and for a time blew a bugle in a local band. But it was his discovery of a piano in a friendly neighbour's house that revealed his natural gifts. In a poor black community music tended to be allowed as the one affordable luxury and Scott's early talents were so much appreciated that his father, overlooking family poverty and a natural desire for his son to become apprenticed to some solid wage-earning trade, was persuaded to buy him an old piano. In spite of its shortcomings, it was played with unflagging zeal by the young pianist who became a proficient executant and improviser by the time he was eleven. He was heard by a local German music teacher who was so impressed that he offered free lessons both in piano playing and elementary harmony. He also aroused Joplin's interest in music by playing him the compositions of the great composers – amongst which, no doubt, at that stage of American history, would be the piano works of the late great Louis Moreau Gottschalk then commonly seen on the top of America's parlour pianos. The name of the German teacher has not been recorded, but Joplin never forgot his benefactor and sent him various gifts of money when later he was aged, ill and poor.

By now Joplin's only ambition was to make his way in the musical world with the desirable result, he had no doubt, of enhancing his family's fortune beyond its wildest dreams. His father thought differently and still tried to make him take a steady job. The deciding moment came when his mother died in 1882. He finally quarrelled with his father and, just coming up to fourteen years of age, left home to seek fame and fortune. This was not an uncommonly early age for a Negro boy to make such a move in those days of domestic hardship; in fact, many like him would have been pushed out to fend for themselves.

Neither did it matter much what your age was if, as a musician, you had the right sort of ability. No government department was worrying itself about child employment or further education. Joplin simply wandered around Texas and Louisiana, up and down the Mississippi, playing in honky-tonks, gambling and gaming halls, cafés and brothels, joining travelling shows for a period, earning low wages but gathering quite a good living in tips from those who appreciated his youthful talents. We can imagine the rich harvest of experience that he gained in hearing Civil War songs and plantation melodies, the dance music that accompanied the minstrel shows or was played at local hops, as well as the more sophisticated songs of the whites and the earthy blues and work songs of the blacks. Whatever its moral desirability, it was an experience that could never be gained in a musical academy. He also heard the other 'professors' of the piano, the well-known and the up-and-coming, who played in the folky, syncopated, banjo-based style that he was eventually to crystallise in his ragtime compositions.

We are too short of definitive evidence as to what the typical minstrel and plantation music of the period was like to be able to say with certainty that this was the basis of ragtime. Ann Charters in her introduction to *The Ragtime Songbook* is somewhat scathing about the theorists who firmly found ragtime on plantation banjo melodies. Nevertheless we have to assume that it came from some such public folk-music source and no doubt many Joplin melodies could have been based on unpublished songs long forgotten. Even in a very thorough book like Marshall Stearns' *Jazz Dance*, the steps of the dances are given in detail but he carefully avoids describing the music that they were danced to beyond a mention of banjos, tambourines, etc. The word 'ragtime' doesn't even get into the index – so that trail is very quickly lost. We do know that early songs, like *Jim Crow* (*c.* 1828) and the few published songs and cakewalks of the rest of the nineteenth century up to the time of Joplin's emergence as a composer, all bear some relationship to ragtime in their melodic patterns.

By 1885, when he was just in his seventeenth year, Joplin first arrived at the Mecca of all wandering musicians, the Mississippi riverboat centre of St Louis. An early trading post, St Louis had become a typical fast-living levee city. Here there was a continual to-ing and fro-ing of river traffic. The labourers unloading the boats were still treated like slaves. But there was lots of money around from trading, cattle, cotton and other Mississippi industries. It was a focal point for gamblers and the quickly-rich and packed with saloons, gambling joints and brothels. It was an easy place in which to thrive as an entertainer, for in spite of the hard competition the demand was endless. The pianists would gather at what had become a sort of unofficial musician's union headquarters at 'Honest John' Turpin's Silver Dollar Saloon. There they waited for a request to provide entertainment at whatever establishment needed their temporary services. Most of the seedy and bawdy venues used by the Negroes were on either Chestnut Street or Market Street and the air there was alive with the sound of out-of-tune pianos.

On Top of the Parlour Piano

Musical Background

OJOS CRIOLLOS

(Les yeux Créoles.)

DANSE CUBAINE

Caprice brillant

pour deux mains

COMPOSÉ PAR

L.M. GOTTSCHALK.

6

NEW-YORK

WILLIAM HALL & SON 543 BROADWAY.

Chicago.
ROOT & CADY.

New Haven Conn.
SKINNER & SPERAY.

Rochester.
JOS P. SHAW.

Entered according to Act of Congress A. 1864 by Wm. Hall in the Clerks Office of the District Court of the Southern District of N.York.

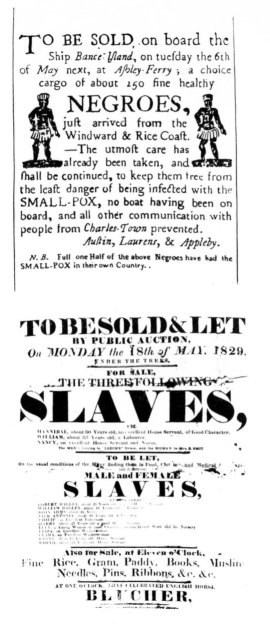

1 and 2 Posters for slave auctions. Joplin's father was born a slave and only obtained his freedom in 1863

3, 4 and 5 Romantic views of plantation life *Above: Old Kentucky Home* by Eastman Johnson 1859 *Left:* Selecting a banjo *Right:* A plantation in the West Indies

6 *Above:* A typical Mississippi port – the Levee and railway station, New Orleans 1866

7 *Below:* A street scene, New Orleans 1870s

8 *Above:* Loading cotton on the Mississippi, 1870

9 *Below:* Bar-room dancing

10 and 11 *Above:*
Negroes dancing, 1880
Left: A 'Nigger' min-
strel, 1884

12 *Above:* James Bland (1854-1911), composer of *Carry Me Back To Old Virginny* (1878), whose many popular songs would have been heard by Joplin as a child

13 *Right:* Louis Moreau Gottschalk (1829-69), the classical composer whose use of Creole melodies and habanera rhythms greatly influenced Joplin

14 John Philip Sousa (1856-1932), bandmaster and composer of marches which were so influential on Joplin's music

Pause for a moment at this formative stage of Joplin's somewhat haphazard career to imagine what he might have heard and assimilated in the years between his tenth birthday, when he would be likely to be absorbing musical ideas for the first time and the days when, as a seventeen-year-old adventurer, he was about to make his mark as a composer – the years between 1878 and 1885.

We shall never know what pieces of music lay on top of the Joplin parlour piano; we can only make the wildest guess at what they might have been. We know that the German teacher led him unsuccessfully towards the standard classics, possibly lending him one of those curiously inconsequential folios of piano music which generally contained an apparently aimless mixture of European popular masterpieces and the works of contemporary virtuoso composers. The editorial policy might well have been based entirely on what was most cheaply available. Such an album might contain *Ojos Criollos* by L. M. Gottschalk; *Pas de Sabots* by Sydney Smith; *Viccolo* – grand galop de concert, by Chas. D. Blake; a suite *Aquarellen* by Niels W. Gade; Brahms' *Hungarian Dances* (very popular fare); a Chopin *Nocturne*; an uncredited arrangement of Bach next to a piano selection from *The Beggar's Opera*; followed by *Un Rêve du Ciel* by Kinkel and a couple of waltzes by Johann Strauss Sr and Gung'l. In all of these we could find elements that Joplin might have absorbed.

The polite songs of those days, which Joplin was to copy in his own ballads, had titles like *My Blue-eyed Nelly* (Charles Blam-

33

phin); *By The Sad Sea Waves* (Benedict); *Blissful Dreams Come Stealing O'er Me* (Abt); *Where Are The Friends Of My Youth* (Barker); *There Are Friends That We Never Forget* (Winner) and *Oh, No! We Never Mention Her!* (Bishop). Joplin's own songs suggest a close acquaintance with the works of America's great popular songwriter Stephen Foster, whose song-writing career ended in 1863. He wrote sentimental ballads in the European vein but is best remembered for his famous pseudo-Afro-American songs whose echoes are as inherent in most American music as the songs of Purcell are in English.

Immensely popular songs of the 1850s and 60s, whose influence would linger on, were items like *The Arkansas Traveller* by Mose Case; songs of unknown authorship like *Billy Boy*; *Over There* (not the Cohan one but a song with unlimited possibilities of adaptation ranging from 'Oh! potatoes they grow small over there' to 'The eagles they fly high over there' – nobody revealing where 'over there' actually was); *Vilikins And His Dinah* which came over from the early London music hall, as did *Captain Jinks Of The Horse Marines* (with a brisk 6/8 melody) and *Up In A Balloon*; together with all the Harrigan and Hart songs that were the latest thing on Broadway and often reflected America's unflagging interest in the problems of alcohol – like *I'll Never Get Drunk Any More* and *I Never Drink Behind The Bar*.

A chronological list of music published between 1878 and 1885 reveals the trends of American popular song as it might have affected a musically aware child like Joplin. 1878 : *Carry Me Back To Old Virginny* (Bland); *A Flower From Mother's Grave* (Kennedy); *Tell Me The Old, Old Story* (Doane). 1879 : *The Babies On Our Block* (Braham and Harrigan); *Oh! Dem Golden Slippers* (Bland). 1880 : *Never Take The Horseshoe From The Door* (Braham and Harrigan); *Why Did They Dig Ma's Grave So Deep* (Skelly). 1881 : *Goodbye* (Tosti); *Wait Till The Clouds Roll By* (Fulmer). 1882 : *I'll Be Ready When The Great Day Comes* (Putman); *When The Clock In The Tower Strikes Twelve* (Braham and Harrigan). 1883 : *Forget-me-not* (Macbeth); the first appearance in print of *There Is A Tavern In The Town* (anon). 1884 : *Always Take Mother's Advice* (Lindsay); *White Wings* (Winter). 1885 :

Poverty's Tears Ebb And Flow (Braham and Harrigan); *Sleep, Baby, Sleep* (Handley); etc., etc.

It seems fairly certain that Joplin was much influenced by the musical shape and spirit of the great march tradition. Foremost the name of John Philip Sousa who, between 1879 and 1885, published some fifty marches, dances and songs – though most of his best-known titles came later in Joplin's career and remained an ever-present influence. The band of Patrick S. Gilmore had been touring the States since the 1850s, following in the steps of the great maestro Jullien.

It might be reasonable to assume that Joplin would be at least as much influenced by black music as white; except that its accessibility would certainly be more limited. It was not until he himself was flourishing that the publication of music by Negro composers was at all commonplace. The main outlet was in the cheap books of banjo music and minstrel songs that accompanied the minstrel shows of the mid-80s. Joplin's father had played his violin in minstrel bands and dance orchestras and may well have retained some of the publications. It is even more likely that he would have passed on his repertoire in true folk style. The professional minstrel tradition began paradoxically with troupes of white performers 'blacked up' and unquestionably playing and singing anglicised versions of true Negro slave music. Ann Charters, in *The Ragtime Songbook*, mentions pieces like *Grape Vine Twist* (*c.* 1843) which had little to distinguish them on paper from the traditional Irish jigs. This might equally well be said of the celebrated song *Jump Jim Crow* (*c.* 1828) by the 'black-face' performer Tom Rice (1808–60). It was his success with this song that initiated the fashionable craze for minstrel shows. The best remembered names are those of the Christy Minstrels, the Virginia Minstrels, the Ethiopian Serenaders, the Buckley Serenaders, the Moore and Burgess Minstrels and the Mohawk Minstrels. Most of these troupes became universally famous and London was equally enraptured by their art. British troupes were formed in imitation. The *one* name that became synonymous with minstrelsy was that of Edwin P. Christy, who specialised in singing Stephen Foster songs and even published many of them under his own name.

Christy did not have a long or exceptionally distinguished career but, by one of those quirks of public acceptance, minstrel shows were widely referred to by a majority of people as 'Christy Minstrel' shows and many troupes that had nothing whatever to do with him used his name.

Reflecting the slave status of the majority of black Americans, Negroes themselves were not allowed a footing on the professional stage until well into the 1870s; but they were making their mark amongst their own people as singers and musicians at plantation dances and entertainments. A West Indian Negro called Picayune Butler achieved fame when he won a banjo competition in New York in 1857 and was immortalised the following year in a song called *Picayune Butler's Come To Town*. The songs by Negro composers were often used without their names being credited. One of the first to achieve national recognition was James A. Bland (1854–1911), who had written *Carry Me Back To Old Virginny* in 1878 and had provided the minstrels with one of their most popular end songs, *Close Dem Windows*, in 1881.

There doesn't really seem to be much question that the melodic nature of ragtime and the preceding minstrel songs and dances had their origins in banjo playing. The pauses and syncopations that distinguish ragtime come naturally to the plucking hand which catches the strings in a rapid to and froing action. The characteristics were picked up and imitated by the pianists and fiddlers whose contribution to the emerging inspiration of Scott Joplin will never be credited. It can be seen in a piece like *Root Hog, Or Die*, published in Septimus Winner's *New Primer for the Banjo* in 1864 and in the banjo tune *Civil Rights Juba* published in 1874. Both of these may well have come Joplin's way. Also Thomas J. Armstrong's *Rag Baby Jig* (a significant title) that appeared in the 1885 *Banjo Companion*.

The dance music prevalent in the 1870s and 80s was that which was written for set dances like the quadrilles and lancers. Each of these is made up of a series of dance movements requiring a distinctive musical section. The music for them is always written with three or four or more distinct sections, similar to the march form and that used in the extended waltzes of Lanner, Strauss and others. The similarity between such dances and the ragtime compositions of Joplin and others is very marked. The nature of the succeeding movements is very much linked with the traditional quadrille, which started by using various popular country dances of the day for its sections before specialised music was written for the purpose. A predecessor of the quadrille was the cotillon which also used a number of folk tunes for a round dance. In *Dandy Jim Of Caroline Cotillion* (1844), which has an American-styled tune, the bare bones of a Joplin rag can be discerned.

Long before ragtime became established, composers had been using banjo imitations and syncopations in their music, notably Louis Moreau Gottschalk (1829–69). His most famous composition is *The Banjo*, which is not a dance but a very elaborate and difficult concert piece with a tune that almost verges on *Camptown Races* and some extremely virtuoso banjo imitations. Gottschalk's use of Creole melodies and habanera rhythms brings the pieces that use these very close to the lilting and sweet strains of Joplin's rags, notably *Bamboula*, *Le Bananier* and *La Savane* – which have been described as his 'Louisiana trilogy'. Similar in atmosphere are his West Indian and South American influenced pieces like the delightful *Ojos Criollos* (described as a 'danse Cubane'), *Danza* and *La Gallina* (The Hen), which all resulted from several visits to Cuba, Puerto Rico, Haiti, Latin America and the West Indies. Joplin rarely used blatant habanera rhythm (*Solace* is a distinguished exception) but there is always a hint of its smooth, gliding movement in most of his creations. The nearest Gottschalk ever came to writing a piece of ragtime was perhaps in his *Pasquinade*, a caprice in polka form.

One can discern strains that Joplin might have picked up in a variety of dance pieces like Septimus Winner's *District Quickstep* and so on; but we actually come nearest to true ragtime in the strains of the cakewalk, whose history is so intertwined with ragtime that it is often difficult to untangle them. Joplin wrote several pieces that he described as cakewalks. Some well-known cakewalks are very close to ragtime, some are nearer to marches. The basic requirement is, of course, a compulsive kind of march rhythm which encourages the high-stepping antics of the cakewalk; and ragtime, as exemplified by pieces like *The Ragtime Dance* (Joplin), is ideal material. The cakewalk is thus described in Dannett and Rachel's *Down Memory Lane*: 'The Cake Walk came into vogue around eighteen-eighty in the South. It originated in Florida where, it is said, the Negroes got the idea from the Seminole Indians. These consisted of wild and hilarious jumping and gyrating steps, alternating with slow processions in which the couples walked solemnly in couples. The idea grew, and style in walking came to be practised among the Negroes as an art. There were classes for the sole purpose of teaching it, and the simple feat of promenading in a dignified manner developed into the cake walk. Prizes were given to the best performers – first, ice cream and chocolates; later on, huge decorated cakes. At the end the winner cut the cake and shared it with the other dancers. This custom, according to a reliable source, gave rise to the expression: "That takes the cake". When Florida became a fashionable winter resort, the Negroes began to dress in a special style for the performances – the men in long-tailed coats with high collars, the women in fluffy white gowns with bouquets of flowers. From Florida the cake walk spread to Georgia, the Carolinas, and Virginia, until it reached New York, where the Negroes organised clubs and gave champion belts to the best walkers, and diamond rings to the women'.

It has been suggested that beneath all the high jinks and rhythmical zest lay a deeper strata of satire, as the Negroes aped the postures and poses of the white society people who ruled their lives. Anyway, the cakewalk probably helped to give the ragtime music that went with it its initial impetus and quick popularity. The white composer David Braham, who was responsible for most of the music in the popular Harrigan and Hart extravaganzas, from which so many of the hit songs of the 1870s came, wrote a novelty number in 1877 called *Walking For Dat Cake*. It was described in the publisher's advertisements as an 'exquisite picture of Negro Life and Customs' and the words were as follows:

'Twas down at Aunty Jackson's dar was a big reception
Of high-toned society people so full of sweet affection;

Such singing and such dancing, we made the ceiling shake.
The cream of all de ev'ning was a-walking for dat cake.
So gently on de toe we dancers step out so,
Easy and so gracefully around de room we go.
De wenches captivate, we all perambulate,
High-toned society people dar a-walking for dat cake'.

Which all bears out the satirical import. There was not, however, a great deal of ragtime in Braham's music.

The cakewalk vogue continued well into the 1900s. It fostered a good deal of cakewalk (ragtime) music. Films were made of it, some still around to be seen. The French composer Debussy wrote his *Golliwog's Cakewalk* in 1908 and *Minstrels* in 1910. The cakewalk had spread abroad by then. It became popular in England, particularly in Lancashire where there was a strong tradition of social dancing and clog-dancing championships had long been a popular sport. The jig (remember that ragtime was originally called jigtime) and the clog-dance were the two staple dances in the minstrel shows. Clog-dancing (basically dancing with wooden-soled shoes) evolved into tap-dancing; the jig evolved into 'soft shoe' dancing. Both developed alongside ragtime.

The point we reach now is where someone had to get the first true bit of ragtime down on paper. It would be pleasant to be able to say, for our purposes, that it was Joplin. But it wasn't. Most textbooks give the credit to Krell's *Mississippi Rag* published in 1897, closely followed by Turpin's *Harlem Rag* the same year. But this is only making an academic distinction. As Ann Charters points out, ragtime of a kind had been around since Gottschalk's time. She is inclined to give the title to Charles Gimble's Paraphrase de Concert on *Old Black Joe* published in 1877, the final variations of the set having every appearance of ragtime and the required syncopations. Joplin's first published piece of ragtime was to be his *Original Rags* in March 1899.

Scott Joplin II
St Louis - School of Ragtime

Respectfully Dedicated to the "PAWNEE CLUB" ST LOUIS, MO.

WEEPING WILLOW

Ragtime Two Step

By

SCOTT JOPLIN

The King of Ragtime Writers

5

Published by
VAL. A. REIS MUSIC Co
1210 OLIVE ST — ST LOUIS, MO.

St Louis in 1885 was a free-and-easy city with that special cosmopolitan sinfulness about it that is common to ports-of-call all over the world from Hong Kong to Liverpool to New Orleans. It was geographically a long way from being a seaport, but had gradually become a commercial frontier town as the blossoming trade and life of America followed a natural course up the Mississippi.

As early as 1803, the Mississippi basin claimed half a million settlers spawning out from the early established city of New Orleans. Very few of them originally were English-speaking. By 1825 the population of the Mississippi basin was around five million and settlements like Memphis and St Louis were beginning to call themselves cities. Long before roads and railways established their hold, the big waterways of the world acted as natural trade routes. Every kind of boat you could imagine from light canoes, sturdy keel boats, great heavy flat-bottomed barges to the luxurious passenger-carrying paddle steamers were soon thronging the broad, muddy and often dangerous waters of the Mississippi, carrying a constant stream of itinerant humanity and the commercial pickings of a rich, though often tragically flooded valley. Cotton and other agricultural and mining products went down to New Orleans; the multifarious trappings of civilisation came up.

As natural accompaniment to an incredibly hard, exhausting

life that was a continuous battle against the treachery of the river and its pirates and rogues, came the two natural solaces: hard liquor and song. As they carried the needs of life – cloth, furnishing and cooking utensils, flour-mills and coal – with ant-like determination up the river against its powerful currents, the boatmen drank, sang and danced to a primitive accompaniment of jug-blowing, paper and comb, banjo and fiddle. The bigger steamers carried their calliopes and bands. And when they got to the principal unloading ports like St Louis, they expected wine, women and song on a grand scale and to highly professional standards.

It would need, and has probably already taken, five hundred scholars and thousands of books to document a quarter of the music-making that went on up and down the Mississippi, let alone the rest of America. Some of the musicological trails are too long and too tenuous to follow. The elements that were to be crystallised in ragtime, which is also a crystallisation of all the racial ingredients that make up the American nation, had already filtered their way through every port in the world. If you seriously wanted to, you could find something of every shade of folk and written music that ever existed in ragtime, from Irish jigs and Spanish fandangoes to African tribal dances.

In St Louis in 1885, Scott Joplin made himself a temporary base, living in the most respectable boarding house he could find or afford, not so much studying music as having it poured through his ears and filtered through his brain at almost every waking hour of the day. Certainly he must have looked at and absorbed the lessons of all the printed music he could find; but most of his education would have been in listening to the countless other itinerant pianists and musicians like himself who translated the unconsidered elements of the world's musical offerings into a foot-tapping, melodic music that pleased the drunken and boisterous clients of the saloons and brothels of St Louis and other American towns and cities. Their approval would at least earn you that immemorial reprieve 'don't shoot the pianist – he is doing his best'; their wholehearted approval would mean a reliable source of income; their disapproval would not bear thinking about.

Where exactly Joplin found the peace and quiet actually to sit down and write his considered pieces of music would be anybody's guess. Perhaps in some lodging-house that had a parlour-piano; perhaps in the comparative lull of the afternoon before the customers had sobered up ready for another night-long session of drunkenness and debauchery. As they waited for a messenger from some establishment who needed a pianist to entertain the customers, or the better-known players went to their regular posts, most of the pianists would gather at 'Honest John' Turpin's Silver Dollar Saloon, which became a sort of unofficial union headquarters. It was here that ragtime grew out of talk and comparisons, competitive solos or friendly duets, each pianist having to make his mark in the most critical and uncompromising company in the world – that of his fellow professionals. Musicians are as humane and friendly as the next man in most respects but they have no mercy on bad or pretentious performers. Those who can are allowed to; those who can't either go into commerce, become critics or jump into the river.

Joplin began to spend much of his time in St Louis and, no doubt, a considerable part of it at John Turpin's place. Between times he would fulfil engagements in surrounding towns like Hannibal, Columbia, Carthage and Sedalia, occasionally going as far as Cincinnati or Louisville. This life continued for many years, and we have few details of the particulars. There was a rewarding visit to Chicago for the Chicago World's Fair in 1893, which attracted pianists and entertainers from all over America. Joplin led a small orchestra there in which he played both piano and cornet; and then held various steady jobs in the Chicago Tenderloin District.

When the Fair ended he returned to St Louis for a short time and then found himself settling for almost a year in Sedalia. Memories of Joplin all suggest that he was a quiet, friendly and ever polite person, with an intelligent face. In spite of the tumultuous background of his early 'schooling', he seemed to have had positive and determined leanings towards social and musical respectability. We can imagine him torn between his desire to be a respected and published composer and the need to be where the

45

righteous but bawdy sources of his inspiration lay. In Sedalia he modestly played second cornet in the Queen City Concert Band, sang in choirs and quartets, and took genteel employment as a piano accompanist. His unpublished compositions, which became an increasing part of his musical interests, were cosy Victorian songs in the whitest of veins, piano pieces, marches and waltzes for local performers.

His nature suggests that he was very happy moving in decent and sober society. Nevertheless he was soon back in St Louis. Around 1895, the headquarters of ragtime had become the Rosebud Café on St Louis's Market Street run by Thomas Million Turpin. The son of 'Honest John', Tom Turpin was born around 1873, an immense and rugged man with a heart of gold. He was a pale-skinned Negro who could easily mix with whites. He and his brother Charlie acquired shares in a gold-mine near Searchlight, Nevada; and Tom, passing for a full-grown man, spent a few unsuccessful years as a gold prospector. Tom returned to St Louis in his early twenties and, following in his father's footsteps, opened his own saloon at 2220 Market Street, very much in the sporting district. Being an accomplished musician, ragtimist and composer, the Rosebud Café became the new HQ of the ragtime cult. Turpin was to be credited with the first published black American rag, *Harlem Rag*, and was, no doubt, a strong source of inspiration as well as a good friend to Joplin.

In Chicago Joplin had become firm friends with one Otis Saunders, who had accompanied him to Sedalia and now to St Louis again. Saunders was an early believer in Joplin's genius and, as well as making his own living as a pianist, became an unofficial manager to Joplin and did his best to push the talents of his modest and retiring friend. They became inseparable; wherever one was seen, the other would be somewhere around. With Saunders' help, Joplin drew the threads of his first ragtime writings from the inspiration of not only Turpin's very large and thunderous hands but also from musicians he had heard in Chicago : banjoist 'Plunk' Henry, whose banjo rhythms probably put ragtime notions into his head; and a celebrated pianist called Johnny Seymour, who eventually opened a saloon in Chicago that became a similar pianists' HQ to Turpin's – and those gathered in the Rose-bud: Louis Chauvin, Charles Warfield, Sam Petterson, Artie Matthews, Joe Jordan, Charlie Thompson and Rob Hampton. In a wine bar at the back of the Rosebud, mammoth cutting compe-titions went on. The cream, spiced by visiting virtuosi from St Louis and elsewhere, would be invited to further all-night sessions at Mother Johnson's house across the way. Many of the names mentioned above would be mere teenagers. Joplin was now in his mid-twenties and, by general standards, was a late starter, but becoming very much a figurehead in ragtime circles by virtue of his long experience.

Ragtime Strains

What did the music sound like that Joplin and his friends were formulating? Ragtime is essentially a bright music. But it has a light-hearted and delicate sort of gaiety, rather than the forceful, brash kind that you get in Dixieland jazz. All music, classical and otherwise, that has an underlying nimble, foot-tapping rhythm tends to sound bright and friendly. Yet, at the same time, because there is this delicacy, almost fragility at times, about it (as in the music of Mozart or Chopin, all of which is essentially rhythmical) it has a melancholic streak too. It is this intriguing mixture of moods that makes music, poetry and people fascinating; as Walter J. Trelby said, the 'sweet and sour sauce that adds flavour to the human rice'.

On the whole, we just take it for granted that the musical language of popular music today (and for the last fifty years or so) has been jazz-based. How often do we stop to think how curious it is that such a comparatively simple device as 'jazzing' turns out to be should not have occurred to anyone in the whole previous history of European music. Now it is the natural way to play a popular song or tune and it is even a curious experience to listen to a well-known song from the fringe days of jazz acceptance sung, by theatrical artists not yet acquainted with the jazz idiom, in a 'straight' style. Once accepted by the white world, the black idiom of jazz became natural to all races; we only wonder why it took so long for it to be discovered.

It is now so natural to white musicians as well, that there are critics and historians who have tried to make out a case for the white invention of jazz – but it is hardly a convincing philosophy in view of the accumulation of evidence to the contrary.

Jazz and ragtime came from the same background of private black entertainment music which was quite naturally flavoured by the heritage of African music brought to the USA by the slaves, who were mainly concen'rated in the Southern parts of America where their services were most needed in agricultural pursuits. The whole basis of jazz, and to a lesser extent of ragtime, is the desire to make the rhythmic characteristics as exciting and as propulsive as possible. This rhythmic excitement, achieved by moving other rhythmic parts (in the case of African drum music) or the emphasis of the melodic line away from the main beats of the bar, usually anticipating the beat, gives the whole music a runaway feel, a sense of drive and urgency. This we can clearly hear in African music of all kinds. The most accessible and clearly illustrative example of this rhythmic heightening is to be found in records of Negro church services, where the music often starts in plain 4/4 and then, urged on by the preacher's exhortations, the whole congregation responds to an intoxicated sense of rhythm, excitement grows, until, in modern parlance, the whole thing is really 'swinging'. This is something that inevitably happens spontaneously and infectiously. The ingredient of 'swing' (or whatever we may call it) is essential to jazz. The curious and interesting thing is, however, that most white people and many black can equally appreciate the propulsive African rhythms of jazz and the straight four-square rhythms of most 'classical' and 'light' music, and are able to switch from one to another with ease.

Because the world's knowledge of jazz came with the growth of recorded music in the late 1910s and early 1920s, its background history was once considered to be mainly a twentieth-century phenomena. In fact, the jazz element was always there in black music-making, simply moving from one continent to another. What the Negroes originally did for their own musical entertainment on the plantations, was probably always very much in the ragtime-cum-jazz idiom. We can only rely on verbal reports and ancient memories for these conjectures. Gradually, what was a private music became a public idiom, as Negroes became emancipated and slavery was abolished. They became trained musicians in their own right, composers and writers, professional entertainers. By then they had access to the sophisticated instruments of Western music.

In fact, nobody has ever written down jazz successfully; but there is no questioning that songs published as early as the 1830s – such as *Turkey In The Straw* (originally known as *Old Zip Coon*) – were phrased and accented in a manner that clearly shows them to be ancestors of ragtime and of modern popular song; and these, of course, were only approximations to their improvised performances. The early success of Negro minstrel shows fostered a curious black-faced imitation by white performers, the first intimation that the generally despised black music was about to become the universal language of the world's popular song.

We needn't go too far into discussing the nature of jazz at this stage. Jazz rhythm is something approximating to what you get mathematically when you impose a group of three notes on the space of time taken up by a group of two underlying notes, then more finely of six over four, of twelve over eight – and so on. Only the first notes or beats of these patterns coincide exactly. The melodic notes, phrased in triplets, are missing the beats by fractions that cannot be properly notated by our usual system.

All this is a little academic for our purposes, because such considerations do not actually concern ragtime whose 'classical' syncopations, involving quarter, eighth or sixteenth notes, can be written down and played, with effect, exactly as written. Perhaps there was more of a jazz element in pre-ragtime playing than we know of. Probably Joplin and his contemporaries played far more freely than the printed music suggests. All that we do know for certain is that ragtime became known to the world via the carefully notated printed copies as a strictly syncopated music. Even on this basis it had enough excitement about it to become a universal craze, and it was naturally its printed form that had most influence on composers and musicians whose sphere of activity did not lie within Negro saloons and other places of entertainment.

Scott Joplin III

Original Rags

Having absorbed every available 'cultural' influence and having otherwise survived the good-time sordidness of St Louis night-life, Joplin once more returned to the comparatively peaceful life of Sedalia.

Towns like Sedalia grew in the mid-nineteenth century with a rapidity and absence of planning that is hard to conceive of in our planned and budgeted age. In 1859 General George R. Smith simply looked for a good site to start a town. He found it about 189 miles west of St Louis and 96 miles east of Kansas City. It was set in the middle of the vast and fertile agricultural area of Missouri, most of it then rolling prairie with highly productive development following the railroad as it spread its tentacles throughout America. A railroad was planned to go through the very spot that General Smith chose, the main reason, of course, for his choice. He bought a thousand acres of land and started his town by developing a farm and its attached community, which he called Sedville. The name was given after his daughter Sarah who was known to the family by the nickname of Sed. He then decided that Sedville should be the centre of his wider community and intimated his plans to develop a town of some two and a half square miles ready to meet the railroad when it should arrive. The first settlers responded to the call in 1860 and the railroad got there in 1861. During the Civil War Sedalia, as it was now called, became a Union military post and remained so until 1864.

With the war ended, Sedalia continued to grow and flourish and by the 1890s had a population of around 15,000 people. It was even considered to be important enough to be the site of the annual Missouri State Fair. At one time it was considered as a potential state capital, but had to be content with becoming the county seat of Pettis County. The country around was wonderfully fertile and Sedalia became mainly a centre for the distribution of agricultural produce. Eventually it benefited from its railroad connections by becoming the junction of no less than seven different lines; the terminal of four branches of the Missouri Pacific Railroad and of three branches and main lines of the Missouri, Kansas and Texas Railroad Company, who established their main rolling-stock repair works in the town. The surrounding country produced corn, wheat, oats, vegetables, and a variety of fruits as well as livestock, all of which flowed into Sedalia for packing and distribution. The abundance of work naturally encouraged a great influx of Negro labour, mainly to be employed in the processing, packing and shipping firms. By 1895, when Joplin drifted back there, it had its prosperous and well-kept streets with large red-brick houses, while trees of the elm and maple variety provided shade and distinction. Parks were planned : Forest Park on the southern side and Sicher Park where the Pettis County Fair and later the State Fair were held. The Negro community, of course, settled in rather poorer areas, but even so Sedalia was less of a ghetto town than either St Louis or New York turned out to be. The fact that Sedalia had been a Union post had drawn a Negro population there right from the start so that they were already founder members of the community. The railroad brought more of them, and the plentiful demand for labour brought a further influx so that eventually they made up almost half the population. Naturally they created their own entertainment, their own hotel and service industry; and wherever black Americans settled in large numbers it was inevitable that, with their rich musical heritage and love of song and dance, their saloons and dives must flourish. Sedalia, for the Negro, was a pleasant environment with much less racial prejudice than was found in many Southern towns. There were adequate Negro schools and several Negro newspapers. And in the east end of its

Main Street, there grew a black quarter where clubs, honky-tonks and brothels abounded.

And of course, the money rolled in. Pay was good as a result of the town's general prosperity and the workers, both white and black, asked for nothing better than a carefree evening of entertainment when the hot toil of the day was over. The liquor flowed freely and pianists and other entertainers were in great demand. In the 1890s Sedalia boasted some eight hotels, twenty-odd restaurants and thirty-plus saloons of all kinds and classes. You could get a ten cent meal in the lowest 'transport' café kind of establishment; or you could lash out twenty dollars in one of the lush joints like Pehl's Fulton Market which specialised in seafood.

And music flourished. There were two first-class bands of a respectable nature: The Sedalia Military Band, around eighteen woodwind and brass players with an associated string orchestra of twelve, and the twelve-strong Independent Band. These were both white organisations but similar black groups existed. Pianists were in great demand. King among them was a Negro called Blind Boone who toured the Missouri area and often appeared in Sedalia. He had a reputation locally such as a pianist like Art Tatum achieved nationally at a later period. He could play anything that was asked for, whether it was folk, popular, classical or grand opera. A large Negro, totally blind, he was even accompanied by a manager, a sure symbol of status, and his technique was the admiration of all the other players. The local boys, who included Arthur Marshall and Scott Hayden, were frequently joined by the itinerant players like Joplin, Otis Saunders, Tom Turpin and Louis Chauvin.

Joplin himself has been described by Brun Campbell and Roy Carew as 'a very black Negro, solidly built, about five feet seven inches tall [others have suggested that he was much taller]; a good dresser, usually neat, but sometimes a little careless with his clothes; gentlemanly and pleasant, with a liking for companionship. He liked a little beer, and gambled some, but he never let such things interfere with his music. Judging from a picture taken about that time, it can be seen that he had poise, and a sort of calm determination in the expression, with confidence in his ability to look out for himself'.

Once settled in Sedalia Joplin found himself regular employment in one of the taverns which had a gambling room upstairs. Here he played nightly. 'Even in those early days,' write Campbell and Carew, 'Joplin had developed a piano style that was unusual, and his chords and harmonies sounded different from those of the ordinary pianist; he had the gift of perfect pitch and could recognise and identify any chord he heard, even though he couldn't see the player.' His friends gave him good advice in suggesting that he should study music further and get sound tuition. In Sedalia there was even a music school, the Smith School of Music, a department of the George R. Smith College for Colored People, located in the suburbs, built on a twenty-four acre site that had been donated to the town by the daughters of its now honoured founder, General George R. Smith. Joplin enrolled as a student and learned how to dot his crotchets.

So, by the end of 1895, Joplin was back on the musical course that he must have had in mind in the German professor's front-room in Texarkana. Composers generally have to make their start by having somebody or something to write for. Joplin now found his mouthpiece in a male vocal octet (really a double quartet) which called itself the Texas Medley Quartette and which included his two younger brothers, Will and Robert. Joplin was the leader, conductor and soloist. They started their career in and around Sedalia and, quickly gaining a local reputation, were able to embark on a tour under the auspices of Oscar Dame of St Louis and the Majestic Booking Agency. Their repertoire was made up of plantation medleys and popular songs of the day and, most important, of new songs written by Scott Joplin Esq. In 1895 they got as far as Syracuse, New York, and it was there that Joplin sold his first two works to music-publishers. The music store of Leiter Brothers printed *A Picture Of Her Face* and M. L. Mantell *Please Say You Will*. The most that can be said of Joplin's two first publications is that they are well constructed and harmonised, otherwise they might have been written by any sentimental lady composer of Victorian days and, as Rudi Blesh has said, show 'no intimations of genius'.

The following year the Quartette toured Louisiana and Texas, and in the town of Temple in Texas Joplin had his first pieces of piano music published. These were *Combination March* and *Harmony Waltz* printed by Robert Smith and, of somewhat greater importance, *The Crush Collision March* which was published by John Ř. Fuller, an influential publisher with an international market and an outlet in London through Chas. Sheard & Co., an important firm making their mark in the music-hall market and with their famous 'Musical Bouquet' series of publications.

The Quartette (Octet) embarked on a second and final tour in 1897 which ended, appropriately enough, in the town of Joplin, Missouri; after which it disbanded. Scott Joplin had a few weeks as a soloist in the town's red-light district, then returned to his organised life in Sedalia. It was in this year that he wrote what was to be his most important rag, *Maple Leaf*. Joplin had no doubts about its qualities or anything but a clear vision of the kind of music that he wanted to write; classic ragtime, a synthesis of all the primitive American musics that he heard around him, was already a steady image in his mind. His own words, when he later (in 1899) referred to it to Brun Campbell as 'my first rag', make *Maple Leaf* an even more remarkable composition. He told his friend Arthur Marshall, another young Sedalia composer, after he had finished it: 'one day the *Maple Leaf* will make me King of Ragtime Composers'. He lodged in the family home of the then fifteen-year-old Marshall while he continued to work in the honky-tonks and saloons of the Sedalia Tenderloin district. Eventually when he did become well-known he took great trouble to help Arthur Marshall on his way, collaborating with him on several rags and urging publishers to accept his other works. One of Joplin's best remembered traits was that he was always ready to help a fellow composer and never uttered a word of jealousy or condemnation.

Joplin became very much the centre of Sedalian black musical activities. His friends and colleagues included Otis Saunders, Jim

Hastings and another young student at high school, Scott Hayden. Joplin's own quiet respectability helped to make ragtime acceptable. He continued to play in the brothels and clubs for he knew that this was the only place where he could get the earthy inspiration that he needed. Tom Turpin was doing his share of pioneering at the Rosebud Café, while Joplin became resident professor at the Maple Leaf Club to which he gratefully dedicated his masterpiece. The owners of the Club were justly proud of Joplin's composition long before it was published.

It would be fair justice to be able to point to Joplin as the first man to publish a ragtime composition but, as so often happens when a new music is formulating itself, the same seeds spread to many fertile grounds and commercial exploitation is the result of opportunism and luck. Joplin must have sensed that the time was coming. In New York, early in 1896, a pianist from Kentucky called Benjamin Robertson Harney had introduced ragtime (then referred to as 'jig' piano) to the variety stage at Tony Pastor's popular music-hall. It was a resounding hit amongst white and black folk alike. Coupled with a spreading vogue for the cakewalk, ragtime was to become a national craze within the year. Nine months after Harney's pioneering efforts, the first piece to bear the name 'rag' was published. It was written ironically enough by a white Chicago band leader called William H. Krell. It was called *Mississippi Rag* and was copyrighted on 27 January 1897. Its claim to be 'the first ragtime two-step ever written' was far from the truth, but at least it opened the doors for ragtime to be called for and later demanded by every music-publisher in the country. The same paradoxical situation was to be repeated twenty years later when it was a white band, the Original Dixieland Jazz Band, that was given the opportunity to be the first genuine jazz group to make a recording.

Joplin offered his *Maple Leaf Rag* to the Sedalia publishing firm of A. W. Perry & Son, but they turned down the offer. For the moment he didn't try Sedalia's other music store run by John Stark (who mainly published sentimental ballads) but concentrated on getting more ragtime on to paper. The first Negro ragtime composer to get a rag published was, in fact, Joplin's old friend and rival Tom Turpin, who got his *Harlem Rag* put out by a St Louis publisher in December 1897.

At the end of 1898 Joplin went to Kansas City with several manuscripts. The publisher Carl Hoffmann proved equally un-discerning and turned down *Maple Leaf*. He did, however, accept a composition called *Original Rags*, a compilation of traditional airs which Joplin put together with the help of Chas. N. Daniels – according to the cover. It has enough Joplin flavour about it to disguise its origins and its modest success proved a most important step in Joplin's career. He could now call himself a ragtime com-poser. But this didn't release him from the bond of teaching and playing in clubs. Perhaps it was just as well otherwise that histori-cal occasion, when the respectable and bearded publisher John Stark dropped into the Maple Leaf Club on Sedalia's Main Street, may not have materialised. Although Stark mainly published po-lite songs and piano arrangements of the classics, he certainly had an appreciation of the world's folk music as his various homely blurbs and sayings were to testify. Hearing the sounds of ragtime from a piano in the back room he went over and listened to Joplin playing his *Maple Leaf Rag*. He enjoyed its vigorous strains and tapped his foot to the music before asking Joplin if it was his own composition. Assured that it was he asked Joplin to bring it over to the music store the following day. An account by Mrs Will Stark, John's daughter-in-law, elaborates the next day's happen-ings. Joplin came in, *Maple Leaf* in one hand, a small boy held by the other, whether deliberately conscripted we are not told. He sat down and played ragtime and the small boy danced. John Stark was somewhat perturbed by the obvious difficulties of the piece which he thought might deter customers. But he liked it so much and was so impressed by its terpsichorean effect on the boy that he decided to take the plunge. He gave Joplin a fifty dollar ad-vance and the promise of a royalty on all sales. The presses set to work and *Maple Leaf* was scheduled to appear in September 1899.

Joplin, no doubt feeling assured of a great future now that his masterpiece was sold, started work on an ambitious creation called *The Ragtime Dance* which he conceived as a ragtime ballet, based on folk dances of the period with a narration written by the composer. The dance steps included were *Ragtime, Clean Up, Jennie Cooler, Slow Drag, World's Fair, Back Step Prance, Dude Walk, Sedidus Walk, Town Talk* and *Stoptime* (with its foot-stamping accompaniment). At the end of 1899 he rented the Woods Opera House and put on a performance with four dancers, Will Joplin singing and himself at the piano with a small orchestra. The orchestrations had taken a lot of labour with Arthur Marshall helping out with the copying of parts. The Stark family were invited with a view to being urged to publish the work, but the time was not yet ripe to embark on anything so ambitious. Later it was to become something of a bone of contention.

But now *Maple Leaf* appeared in the shop. It was an immediate sell-out in Sedalia and its fame soon spread abroad. Stark was able to arrange outlets in the surrounding towns and eventually all over America. In six months they had sold 75,000 copies and Stark thought it advisable to move his business to the larger centre of St Louis. They tried nobly to cope with the flood of orders on a hand-operated press in a hotel room while a proper printing plant was set up in Laclede Avenue. The sales continued unabated. The Starks bought themselves a fine house on Washington Boulevard. The whole family spent their days in shirt sleeves helping their small labour force to pack and despatch copies of *Maple Leaf Rag* to towns and cities all over the country.

It was a wild success story of fairy-tale proportions. Stark was already fifty-nine when this bolt from the blue entered his life; Joplin was coming up to thirty-one. Success had come slowly and reluctantly. It wasn't many years before *Maple Leaf Rag* had sold its million copies and it continued to sell when most other ragtime compositions had been long forgotten. For years before the ragtime boom came upon us, it was the only Joplin work that one could buy in London and it kept the name of Joplin alive through all ragtime's lean years. It has been played and recorded more than any other ragtime piece, in every possible style.

It changed Joplin's own fortunes. On the strength of it Joplin married Scott Hayden's widowed sister-in-law, Belle Hayden, and they followed the Starks to St Louis and bought a house at 2658A Morgan Street. Joplin gave up his nightclub activities, no doubt with a thankful heart, and became a much respected teacher. They lived for three years at their first house, Mrs Joplin adding to the family exchequer by running it as a boarding house. Joplin didn't desert his old friends and acquaintances. He still dropped in to the Rosebud to see Turpin, Chauvin, Patterson and the rest of his old cronies, but now he went as a celebrated visitor who might be persuaded (without too much pressure) to sit down and play the celebrated *Maple Leaf Rag* for the delight of the paying customers.

The Stark presses were now hungry for more Joplin compositions. He obliged in 1900 with *Swipesey* – a cakewalk which he wrote with Arthur Marshall to help his friend on the road to fame – and in 1901 with *Peacherine Rag, Sunflower Slow Drag* (with Scott Hayden) and *The Augustan Club Waltzes*. Apparently Joplin did not, as has sometime been supposed, sign an exclusive contract with Stark, for at the end of 1901 he published *The Easy Winners* under his own name. A song *I'm Thinking Of My Pickaninny Days* and a march *Cleopha* appeared with other St Louis publishers in 1902, but he gave Stark some first-rate rags in *A Breeze From Alabama, Elite Syncopations, The Entertainer* and *The Strenuous Life* – all published by him in 1902.

It had been clear from the start that Joplin was ambitious and saw ragtime's future in many forms and as something beyond the simple folky dances of untutored Negroes. He arranged another private performance of *The Ragtime Dance* song. Abetted by Stark's daughter Nell, he at last managed to persuade Stark to publish the work. It was nine pages long, expensive to produce and was a comparative failure. Disagreement over this was said to have soured the Stark and Joplin family relationships somewhat and after the next work *March Majestic*, Joplin spread the favour of publication amongst a number of St Louis firms, not returning to the Stark imprint until 1904.

In 1903 Joplin bought a large house in one of St Louis' better neighbourhoods on Lucas Avenue and continued to teach and compose. John Stark continued to maintain that ragtime should remain a popular musical form without ideas beyond its station, but Joplin had other things in mind. How else should one now acknowledged on many covers as 'The King of Ragtime Composers, justify his title? A journalist and composer in New York called Monroe H. Rosenfeld made this clear to the world in an interview with Joplin published in the St Louis *Globe Democrat*. 'Joplin's ambition,' he wrote, 'is to shine in other spheres. To this end he is assiduously toiling upon an opera, nearly a score of the numbers of which he has already composed and which he hopes to give an early production in this city.'

Leaving Joplin assiduously toiling, let's look for a moment at what the other ragtime composers were up to . . . .

Grace and Beauty
The Classical Ragtime Composers

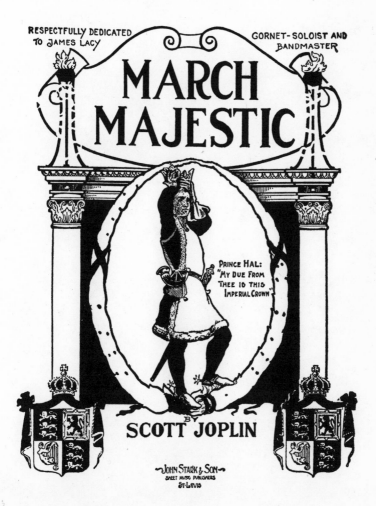

RESPECTFULLY DEDICATED
TO JAMES LACY

CORNET-SOLOIST AND
BANDMASTER

MARCH MAJESTIC

PRINCE HAL:
"MY DUE FROM
THEE IS THIS
IMPERIAL CROWN"

BY
SCOTT JOPLIN

JOHN STARK & SON
SHEET MUSIC PUBLISHERS
ST. LOUIS

We have already encountered Tom Turpin (1873–1922) whose influence and friendship interweave themselves as a natural background to Joplin's formative and successful years. As the owner of the Rosebud Café in St Louis, which became the unofficial HQ of the pianist entertainers from around 1895, he may have had more influence on ragtime than we can possibly ascertain or guess at this time. He finds a firm niche in ragtime history by being the first Negro to publish a piece of ragtime – that is a distinct piano composition with the name 'rag' attached – his *Harlem Rag* of 1897. One gathers that Turpin was a forceful big-handed pianist compared to Joplin, a sort of early Fats Waller, and he has been described as a purveyor of folk-ragtime. This contradictory label can be deciphered to mean that his performances and compositions were near to the unwritten kind of jig piano that was being played by the unschooled majority of entertainers around at that time. *Harlem Rag* bears this out. Although it has the melodic nature of a typical minstrel tune, it is almost devoid of ragtime's deliberate syncopations and is really a primitive dancing march which translates easily into the Dixieland jazz style with a modicum of ragtime flavour. Performances by Ken Colyer and Wally Rose with the Yerba Buena Jazz Band (both with a pleasant opening strain added probably by Rose) are a good illustration of this. It has a solid four-square nature and its second strain, in the piano version, is one of those root-tooting bass melodies for trombone or tuba.

His later rags: *The Bowery Buck* (1899); *A Ragtime Nightmare*

(1900); *St Louis Rag* (1903) and *The Buffalo Rag* (1904) (which makes up the sum total of his published works) were possibly increasingly influenced in their turn by the activities of clever men like Joplin and begin to show more intricacy. *St Louis Rag*, for example, could almost be taken for a moderately successful Joplin piece; it found considerable favour as a band piece being first recorded by Arthur Pryor's band in 1904.

The two composers who are generally bracketed with Joplin as being leaders in the classic ragtime field are James Scott and Joseph Lamb. James Scott, also a Negro musician, was born in Neosho, Missouri in 1886 and mainly taught himself the necessary elements of music. He was a small man, weighing about 140 pounds, very shy and studious, and generally known as the Little Professor. In 1900 he made his centre of activities the town of Carthage in Kansas. His early compositions like *A Summer Breeze* and *The Fascinator*, both published in 1903, and *On The Pike* (1904) are very much in the cakewalk style. In 1906 Scott became associated with Joplin and the other ragtime pianists in St Louis and Sedalia and, influenced by Joplin to some extent, began to cast his works in true ragtime style. John Stark & Sons added him to their publishing stable and Scott was a steady producer of tuneful and well-constructed rags that sold well and established for him a reputation second only to Joplin's in the true ragtime world. He wrote and published steadily from 1906 to 1920 with inventive and exciting pieces like *Frog Legs Rag* (1906); *Sunburst Rag* (1909); *Grace And Beauty* (1910); *The Ragtime Oriole* (1911) and *Climax Rag* (1914); all of which also became popular band pieces. Untroubled by Joplin's hankerings after ragtime grandeur, he experimented within the natural expanding framework of ragtime and was still producing some of his best rags at the end of his writing career; for example, the high-spirited *New Era Rag* with its indebtedness to Joplin's *The Cascades*; the wonderfully delicate *Troubadour Rag* (both 1919) which uses a dotted note melody in a way that looks forward to much of the ragtime-based salon music of the 1920s and 30s written by composers like Felix Arndt (*Nola*) and Billy Mayerl (*Marigold*); and the equally delicate and almost Chopinesque *Modesty Rag* of 1920 – all written when the ragtime boom was merging into the Charleston era. By that time they appeared old-fashioned and were not greatly appreciated by the general public, and yet they looked forward to music far ahead and had qualities that make them come up now as fresh as a daisy. William Bolcom has referred to our future discovery of what may be 'the American classical musical style' in compositions like these. For the moment they hold 'a feeling of splendid isolation – the pride of being the latest and most luxuriant flowering of a style'. Long after he stopped composing, he worked in Kansas City as an arranger, conductor and theatre organist, and died there on 30 August 1938. The ragtime revival quickly rediscovered quintessential works like *Frog Legs* and *Grace And Beauty* which had found their way on to various piano rolls, and there is no doubt that Scott deserves to be publicly recognised again just as Joplin has been.

Essentially a lyrical and melodic composer, his rags have less delicacy than Joplin's but comparable strength and a good dramatic sense in the comparative nature of their various sections. In some he shows an obvious reaction to the influence of white salon music of the rippling kind and in works like *The Ragtime Oriole* is ambitious in his attempts to write descriptive music. Some writers even rate him above Joplin in several respects. Schafer and Riedel say : 'there are things in Scott's music apparently beyond Joplin's talents. The sense of integrity in a piece like *The Ragtime Oriole* is very strong; there seems to be a kind of melodic treatment which is absent from Joplin's rags. Scott displays a sense of the *organic* possibilities of simple themes, using them elastically; while Joplin's themes are carefully finished, each one built, polished and set aside as the composer moves on to another. The four themes of *Grace And Beauty* seem to originate from a sustained mood or idea, while the themes of many Joplin rags seem less consistent and, in fact, are often deliberately contrasted.'

Joseph Lamb, who was born in Montclair, New Jersey on 6 December 1887, is often used as an 'astonishing' illustration of the fact that a white composer could even begin to write rags comparable to the Negro output. At a time when ragtime was in the doldrums, many writers were led to assume that he was, in fact, a black mid-western contemporary of Joplin and Scott. Until he was rediscovered and recorded in his last years, his quiet and unassuming nature had led to his almost complete neglect. The interesting and important link with Joplin was re-established in the recording he made for Folkways at his home in Brooklyn on 12 and 22 August 1959. Lamb had met Joplin, purely by accident in 1907 when he happened to drop into the Stark Music Store in New York. He recalls:

'There was a colored fellow sitting there with his foot bandaged up as if he had the gout, and a crutch beside him. I told Mrs Stark that I liked the Joplin rags best and wanted to get any I didn't have. The colored fellow spoke up and asked whether I had certain pieces which he named. I thanked him and bought several and was leaving when I said to Mrs Stark that Joplin was one fellow I would certainly like to meet. "Really," said Mrs Stark, "Well, here's your man." I shook hands with him, needless to say. It was a thrill I've never forgotten. I had met Scott Joplin and was going home to tell the folks.'

Learning that Lamb had already submitted a couple of rags to Stark, Joplin became interested. They walked up Twenty-third Street and into Madison Square and there sat and talked on a bench. The upshot was that Joplin asked Lamb to bring some of his music over to his house which he did a few evenings later. Joplin asked Lamb to play his pieces to him and several black musicians who were there at the time. When he played his *Sensation* they took interest. Joplin said: 'That's a good rag – a regular Negro rag', which pleased Lamb more than anything else that could have been said. Joplin offered to present *Sensation* to Stark saying: 'We will put along with your name "arranged by Scott Joplin". People do not know you and my name might help to sell the rag.' Joplin kept his word and a week later Lamb got a letter from Stark offering him twenty-five dollars and the same sum after a thousand copies had been sold. 'He could have had it for nothing,' said Lamb. All he wanted was to see it published. The other twenty-five dollars came within a month and Stark also bought and published his *Ethiopia Rag* and *Excelsior Rag*. Others that made their mark later were *American Beauty Rag* (1913); *The Ragtime Nightingale* (1915) and *Top Liner Rag* (1916).

Here was a parallel case to what was happening in jazz: a white musician, loving and understanding the music, able to absorb it sufficiently to be taken for a black musician. And why not. There is nothing in ragtime, as we have said over and over again, that a gifted white musician could not put into equal terms. In jazz, perhaps, one has to absorb more racial characteristics and few white musicians have reached to the emotive soul of the blues. But later musicians, hampered by a pale skin, have absorbed the music and played it with as much success and flair as its originators. Indeed, the whole world has absorbed the jazz idiom by now and uses it, to some degree, as the natural language of popular music.

'Lamb,' write Schafer and Riedel, 'wrote very lively and completely organised rags; their thrust was not toward technical or emotional complexity but toward lyrical flow, transparent vitality, and constant motion.' Whitney Balliet reprints an interview with Joseph Lamb in his *Dinosaurs in the Morning* which resulted from the issue of the Folkways record. Lamb, then seventy-two, told him that since the publication of Blesh's *They All Played Ragtime* he had started writing rags again. Between 1908 and 1919 he had published twelve. Now he had many more that he had written. Lamb died in Brooklyn on 3 September 1960 and thirteen rags under the title 'Ragtime Treasures' were published by the Belwin Mills Publishing Corp. in 1964, with a foreword by Rudi Blesh: 'They are simply beautiful music, waiting to sing their beguiling melodies . . . they confirm their creator's place with the immortals of American music.' But in 1917, when Lamb had submitted some of his latest works to publisher Irving Mills, Mills had asked him: 'Can't you write some novelettes like *Nola*? That's what they want!'

Scott Joplin IV
The Missing Guest of Honor

STOPTIME RAG

BY
SCOTT·JOPLIN
COMPOSER OF
"GLADIOLUS RAG"
"SEARCHLIGHT RAG"

The year 1903 was a disturbed one for Joplin. There was an increasing coldness in his relationship with John Stark. It was simply that they both realised how much they owed to each other – and yet they could not reconcile their opposing views on ragtime's future. Joplin completed several rags during the year but none of them were published by Stark. *Weeping Willow* went to the Val. A. Reis Music Company in St Louis; as did a new collaboration with Scott Hayden, *Something Doing. Palm Leaf Rag* was published by Victor Kremer in Chicago; while a rather forgettable song called *Little Black Baby*, with milk-curdling words by Louise Armstrong Bristol, also came out in Chicago under the imprint of the Success Music Company.

But it was chiefly Joplin's obsession with writing a ragtime opera that made the Stark Publishing Company's blood run cold. For many years Joplin had been nagging at Stark to take it on. Sometimes the publisher would nearly relent, at one point going so far as to say that if Joplin could find a better libretto it might be considered. Or was this because he knew that the obstinate Joplin would never envisage this? Publication was diplomatically postponed. Hopes rose that Joplin might have forgotten the whole thing; but he was not to be thwarted that easily. It was not to be the last time that the composer would almost bankrupt himself by faithfulness to an ideal. Joplin desperately cast the work and to test out the public reaction put on a public dress-rehearsal in a large dance hall in St Louis. Arthur Marshall has recorded that it 'was taken quite well' and there were rumours that Joplin almost persuaded a theatre circuit manager to undertake its production. But this must have failed for the opera *A Guest Of Honor* was never heard of again apart from another amateur run-through in Sedalia. What did Joplin, who was no doubt deeply depressed by this wasteful failure, do with the score?

A file card in the Washington Copyright Office was found by the Joplin expert Roy Carew in 1946. '*A Guest Of Honor*, a ragtime opera, written and composed by Scott Joplin' was entered on 18 February 1903. 'Copies never received' was added to the entry. While many people claim to have remembered some beautiful and effective music, the original manuscript has never been seen again. His second wife suggested that it might well have been in a trunk of clothes, books, letters and photos that Joplin had left for security against an unpaid bill in a Pittsburgh boarding-house between 1907 and 1909, just before their marriage, when he was undertaking vaudeville tours. The trunk was never reclaimed and even the address of the house concerned is not remembered. Did Joplin perhaps use the material for later compositions? Were the delightful strains of *The Cascades* perhaps a part of it? Probably we will never know. Ragtime researchers have long puzzled their heads over this one and reports of the music's rediscovery have materialised from time to time, without any concrete evidence to support them.

The conjecture that arises is how, if *A Guest of Honor* had been produced and successful, it would have affected Joplin's career. It might even have made *Treemonisha* a better work. Perhaps Joplin's judgment might have been proved right, for in those days of ragtime fever a ragtime opera might have been well received. In any case the first true black opera, by a black composer on a black theme and an all-black cast, to get to Broadway was Harry Lawrence Freeman's *Voodoo* produced there in 1928. Freeman and Joplin were acquainted and who knows what ideas passed between them. Freeman himself had an opera produced in Denver as far back as 1893 called *The Martyr*.

With *A Guest Of Honor* a closed page, there would appear to have been a healing of the Stark/Joplin relationship. *The Cascades* and *The Chrysanthemum* were both published by Stark in 1904. *The Favorite* made a tardy appearance under the imprint of A. W. Perry of Sedalia, the publisher who originally turned down *Maple Leaf Rag* in 1898 and who, according to Trebor Jay Tichnor, a St Louis pianist, had bought *The Favorite* in 1900. *The Sycamore* was published by Will Rossiter of Chicago and New York. 1904 was the year of the St Louis World Fair and it was the tableau Cascade Gardens at the Fair which inspired one of Joplin's finest rags. Stark also published, with presumably less need of persuasion, a song version of *Maple Leaf Rag*. With adroit professional lyrics by Sydney Brown that lived up to the excellence of the music, *Maple Leaf* got a further boost to its continuing sales and kept Joplin in the style to which he was becoming accustomed.

1905 was not, however, to prove a happy year. Joplin's first marriage was beginning to break up, the process hastened by the birth of a baby girl who died after a few months. The first Mrs Joplin had little real interest in music. She was miserable, although she did her best to be pleasant to Joplin's musical friends and pupils who continually drew on her hospitality. Composing and teaching was not easy in this atmosphere and it was not a particularly fruitful year. There was only one piano ragtime piece published – *Leola* (which by some quirk had its first registration at Stationer's Hall in London). It was not successful and was very much a forgotten Joplin opus until the 1950s. Other publications were *The Rose-bud March*; *Binks' Waltz*; a song *Sarah Dear* with words by Harry Jackson and based on a folk melody; and the charming *Bethena* waltz in which, with hindsight, we might sense Joplin's melancholy disposition at this time.

Eugenia, one of the first pieces to get simultaneous orchestral publication, led into an unsettled 1906. Early in the year Joplin and his wife finally parted. Joplin went to Chicago to stay for a while with his friend and collaborator Arthur Marshall, who records that Joplin had his sights set on New York. When he left the Marshall house it was the last that they ever saw of one another. It was not surprising that very little music came to life at this time. Stark published a march *Antoinette* and a piano version of *The Ragtime Dance*, condensing it to normal ragtime proportions with hopes of making up for the considerable loss made on the original song-cum-ballet version, which had caused so much early contention.

Throughout his career Joplin was always ready and willing to help other composers and often lent his name and reputation to collaborative efforts with those not so fortunate as himself. It was while he was in Chicago in 1906 that he went to see the unfortunate Louis Chauvin, a handsome Keats-like figure rapidly dying of opium-smoking and syphilis. A talented pianist and composer, Chauvin had sketches for future compositions lying around in his poverty-stricken lodgings. Joplin took two beautiful themes and, adding one of his own, published the joint work as *Heliotrope Bouquet* the following year; unfortunately too late to be able to help his friend. Stark was very much taken up with the piece, advertising it in his usual flowery style as 'the audible poetry of motion'. Probably during his last stay with Arthur Marshall they wrote another collaborative piece *Lily Queen* which was also published in 1907.

During the year he moved to New York and seemed to find a new impulse in works like *Searchlight Rag* and *Gladiolus Rag* which were published there by Joseph W. Stern. *Rose Leaf Rag* was published in Boston; *Nonpareil* by Stark in St Louis; and an undistinguished song *When Your Hair Is Like The Snow* by its lyric writer Owen Spendthrift also in St Louis. There was also a song called *Snoring Sampson* with words by Harry La Mertha which seems to have disappeared without trace. The number of his 1907 compositions is surprisingly large in view of his unsettled state and the fairly busy life that he was leading at the time. It was during this period that he undertook a series of vaudeville appearances, living for months on end in hotels and boarding houses (in one of which he lost his belongings as we have already noted), feeling that some public appearances were needed to keep his name known. Thus Joplin, billed as 'King of Ragtime Composers – Author of *Maple Leaf Rag*' appeared before his public. This was to be a prelude to a more settled period in his life, until yet another operatic venture brought the final earthquake.

Ragtime Days
1896-1907

EUGENIA

by

Scott Joplin

Composer of
"MAPLE LEAF RAG"
"CASCADES" &c.

Published for
BAND and ORCHESTRA

(References in square brackets throughout these sections refer to either music, e.g. [PTR] – see Appendix 2; or records, e.g. [AL3563] which are listed in Appendix 3.)

Looked at in isolation (as we have tended to do in previous chapters) Joplin's ragtime writings may seem like a pure river of music flowing through a featureless plain. But this is an entirely wrong impression, leading us to the conclusion that Joplin might well have invented, developed and ended the ragtime era all on his own. This is very far from the truth. Joplin grew up and wrote his first rags when ragtime was being formed of many elements – a feverish activity to be compared to the growth and joining of living cells under a microscope. Hundreds of composers, musicians and entertainers contributed to its beginnings. Joplin was isolated only by his superior genius – even perhaps hampered by it. As Samuel B. Charters wrote in *Jazz: A History of the New York Scene* : 'The tragedy for Joplin was that the Negro musicians with whom he associated in New York rejected him even more completely than the white audience did . . . They felt that ragtime music was low-class, and as members of an insecure middle class (i.e. successful musicians like J. Rosamond Johnson, Chris Smith and James Reese Europe) they seemed to be afraid to associate with the music in any more than a very superficial manner'. While he continued to write pure ragtime along with a handful of other black composers, the rest and the white imitators simply jumped on the band-wagon of the rag craze and exploited it in every possible way. But then such commercial exploitation is never all bad : it keeps the music and a lot of people alive; moreover it is a natural course for any musical fashion to take. How else can it get to the people – the proverbial man in the street? The privileged historian can sort out the muddle later and dig back to the pure sources.

In the year 1896 there was no actual printed exploitation of the word 'ragtime' nor, apparently, much call for piano solo music in this vein. But already the Tin Pan Alley songs of the day were beginning to latch on to the cakewalk craze and more than a nip of ragtime flavouring could be found in Ben Harney's *You've Been A Good Ole Wagon* [RS] and *Mr Johnson, Turn Me Loose* [RS; GTR]; Barney Fagan's *My Gal Is A Highborn Lady* [RS]; Ernest Hogan's *All Coons Look Alike To Me*; the dancer Bert Williams' *Miss Brown's Cakewalk*; Kerry Mills' *Happy Days In Dixie* and *Rastus On Parade*; and that national anthem of good times coming *There'll Be A Hot Time In The Old Town Tonight* [ST499; RS] by Theodore M. Metz and Joe Hayden. The world, as a whole, was still basking in the pleasant Palm Court strains of shows like 'The Geisha' and was unaware of the full import of the musical revolution about to take place – tasted without fear of addiction in the 'black-face' minstrel shows.

By 1897 we witness that strange social phenomenon where a word, hitherto a private colloquialism, a very 'in' word, suddenly begins to have a meaning on a nation-wide basis; within a year perhaps world-wide. Suddenly the word 'rag' and 'ragtime' is all over the music covers. William H. Krell, a white bandleader, is generally given credit for publishing the first piece to carry the banner with his *Mississippi Rag* [GTR], but it would take careful work with old and unreliable publishers' lists to be absolutely sure of that. The same year saw such publications as *Rag-ma-la* by Shaw and Anderson; a *Rag Medley* (obviously of folk material) collected and arranged by Max Hoffman – one of many that he was eventually to publish; *Ragtime March* by Warren Beebe; *Bundle Of Rags* by Robert S. Roberts; *Missus Johnson's Rent Rag Ball* by Fred Hammel and D. A. Lewis; and *Coontown Capers* by Theodore Morse (1873–1924). Countless names about whom we know nothing come and go in the tragic cavalcade of popular music's lottery. Of more lasting fame were Theo. H. Northup's *Louisiana Rag* [AL3563] and the 'first' true Negro rag (though it was much more of a dancing march), Tom Turpin's *Harlem Rag* [LAG12030]. While in New York, the pioneering Ben Harney had already published a *Ragtime Instructor*. This year and for several more, the name 'ragtime' was to be inextricably interwoven, mixed, muddled and substituted for or by the word 'cakewalk'. As far as most folk were concerned they were both two-steps for convivial dancing, so some of the pieces like *Who'll Win De Cake Tonight* by Walter Hawley (described as an Ethiopian Schottische – what a mongrel); *Alabama Cakewalk* by O. J. de Moll and *Cakewalk To The Sky* by Cad L. Mays were probably just as much deserving of the title of rag. The one acknowledged masterpiece in that vein was Kerry Mills' *At A Georgia Camp Meeting* whose infectious strains have been translated into every possible musical guise [AL3563]. One of the big songs of that year with its minstrel-cum-barbershop tones was Paul Dresser's *On The Banks Of The Wabash*. How many of these items impinged on Joplin's ready ear we shall never know.

By 1898, while Joplin brooded over the negligible sales of his published marches, waltzes and songs, the flood tide was visibly mounting. In the year of Kerker's 'The Belle of New York', the cakewalk provided much localised entertainment to such items as *Prize Cakewalk Of The Blackville Swells* by Walter V. Ullner; *Eli Green's Cakewalk* [SDL210] by Sadie Koninsky; *Belle Of The Cakewalk* by F. C. Lowder and W. M. Lind; *Carolina Cakewalk* by Max Dreyfus; and it even showed its age in a song called *De Ole Time Cake Walk* by W. Moody and Lee B. Grabbe. That ragtime already had a very specific meaning was shown by the words of a song *Play Dat Rag Time, Play It Right* by Fred Meyer; and by the sub-titles that many publications carried such as *Darktown Belles* – 'rag time march and dance' by Alfred Paulsen; and the song *She's A Thoroughbred* – 'coon song à la ragtime' by Ned Wayburn. The mixing of terms was still confusing : *Queen Of The Raggers* by A. Bafunno was called 'march rag time or cake walk'; *Dat Blackville Wedding* by Robert Cone was rather vaguely called a 'characteristic march and two-step'. This vagueness was to be perpetuated even by Joplin in many of his later works. There were a number of unspecified works like *Mandy's Broadway Stroll* by Thomas E. Broady; *Alabama Jubilee* by C. C. Moffett; a popular song *Who Dat Say Chicken In Dis Crowd?* by Will Marion Cook and Paul Laurence Dunbar that was to have many imitators; a march *Cotton Blossoms* by Milton H. Hall described as a 'march comique' which suggests ragtime associations. Already ragtime was beginning to get its quota of snide comments from the Press, the fate of any new-fangled craze: 'Rag time,' wrote one critic, 'is a term applied to the peculiar, broken, rhythmic features of the popular "coon song". It has a powerfully stimulating effect, setting the nerves and muscles tingling with excitement. Its esthetic element is the same as that in the monotonous, recurring rhythmic chant of barbarous races. Unfortunately, the words to which it is allied are usually decidedly vulgar, so that its present great favour is somewhat to be deplored.' Another writer suggested that 'the faculty for it must be acquired, much like a taste for caviar' – with the rider 'another of its peculiarities is that its best exponents are generally execrable musicians'. While the music still waited for its Joplins and Scotts to arise, it was already interpreting its message under a wide variety of fanciful titles beginning with Tom Turpin's *Bowery Buck*; followed by *Watermelon Rag* by E. F. Dillebar (there was to be a strong horticultural flavour to numerous ragtime titles); *My Rag Time Lady* by Charles N. Daniels and Albert Brown; *De Ragtime Dance* (anticipating Joplin) which was an arrangement by Max Dreyfus from Harry Von Tilzer's song *When You Do De Rag Time Dance*; similarly *That Rag Time Dancing* by H. J. Breen and T. Mayo Geary; *Alabama Rag Time* by J. E. Hennings; *Boom-e-rag* by Warner Crosby; *Bunch Of Rags* – an arranged medley by Ben M. Jerome; *Ma Rag Time Baby* by Fred S. Stone; a song *Ragtime Liz* by Alfred E. Aarons and Richard Carle; and the very forward-looking *Dar's Rag Time In De Moon* by Seymour Furth and Maurice Shapiro. Max Hoffman supplied his yearly quota of pickings in a medley called *Ragtime Rags* – a very positive title.

So by the time Joplin got around to getting his first ragtime piece *Original Rags* published in 1899, he was simply ragtime's Mozart appearing out of the confused ragtime baroque period. A ranking he richly confirmed by the publication of *Maple Leaf Rag* later in the year, a piece with a success story that was to unleash an even greater flood of rivals and imitators. It was a vintage year apart from Joplin's efforts, bringing forth several other classics in associated vein: Abe Holzmann (1874–1939), a New York born, academically trained musician who worked in Tin Pan Alley as composer and arranger, added a classic cakewalk to the lists with his *Smokey Mokes* [SDL132] [SDL210]; which Frederick Allen Mills (1869–1948), a Philadelphia born, New York publisher better known as Kerry Mills (and already well established with his classic *At A Georgia Camp Meeting*) rivalled with the popular *Whistling Rufus* [SDL210; GTR]. Ben Harney (1871–1938) penned a success with his *Cakewalk In The Sky*; Arthur Pryor (1870–1942) with his *African Beauty* and *A Coon Band Contest*; and the immortal Eubie Blake (still alive and playing) started off his composing career with *Charleston Rag* [SH8463] at the tender age of sixteen. Cakewalks and dances continued to be published: *Cake-Walk Of The Day* (with ragtime chorus) by Tony Stanford; *The Katy Flyer* – an early cakewalk by the up-and-coming ragtime composer George Botsford; *A Tennessee Jubilee* by Thomas F. Broady; *Scandalous Thompson* and *Doc Brown's Cake Walk* by Charles L. Johnson, who we shall also be mentioning later as a well-known ragtime composer; *Clorindy, The Origin Of The Cake Walk* by Will Marion Cook; *Alabama Cake Walk* by George D. Barnard (described as a 'ragtime cakewalk'); *Alabama Coon's Jubilee* – a ragtime two-step by Chauncey Haines; *Alabama Tickle* by George Southwell – a march and cakewalk [AL3563]; *Aunt Dinah's Cake Walk* by William Weidenhammer – a ragtime march; *Belle Of The Creoles* by Harry P. Guy – a cakewalk and two-step; *Black Venus* – a cakewalk by G. N. Blandford; *Dixie Doodle* – a rag and cakewalk by C. N. Buchanan; *Shuffling Jasper* – a ragtime two-step by W. H. Scouton; *Jasper Johnson's Jubilee* – a cakewalk and two-step by Paul Rubens (well-known writer of musical comedies); *Mississippi Side Step* – a cakewalk by Leo E. Berliner; *Mobile Buck Wing Dance* by Dan J. Sullivan; and one that became very popular, the *Dusky Dudes* cakewalk written by Tin Pan Alley composer Jean Schwartz who was to add some distinguished items to the ragtime lists. In all these we find the old-fashioned terminological confusions still existing. One of the more lasting ragtime pieces was *Tickled To Death* [SDL132] [VLF2] by Charles H. Hunter (1878–1907). Born in Columbia, Tennessee, he was almost completely blind, self-taught as a musician, and made his living as a piano-tuner. His rags had a clear affinity with folk music and *Tickled To Death* remained one of his greatest successes. 1899 was a bumper year for ragtime titles. We cannot list them all but the movement was getting into full swing (still without contributions from what were to be most of its best writers) with: *St Louis Rag* by Leo Grabbe; *Ragtime Patrol* by Charles Jerome Wilson; *Ragtime Skedaddle* [SDL132] by George Rosey (George W. Rosenberg 1864–1936); *Ragtime Lancers* by Samuel Hosfeld; *You're Talking Ragtime* by the Beaumont Sisters; *It Takes A Coon To Do The Ragtime Dance* by Charles L. Johnson with words by Robert Penick; *Bos'n Rag* by Fred S. Stone; *Banjo Rag Time* by Arling Shaeffer; and *His Rag-Time Walk Won The Prize* by Nathans Bivins. With all these variations about it was perhaps not surprising that a song appeared called *I Don't Understand Rag Time*, written by one Irving Jones. Comment from the American *Musical Courier* in 1899: 'A wave of vulgar, filthy and suggestive music has inundated the land. The pabulum of theatre and summer hotel orchestras is coon music. Nothing but ragtime prevails and the cakewalk with its obscene posturing, its lewd gestures. It is artistically and morally depressing and should be suppressed by press and pulpit.'

Joplin's only contribution to the epochal year **1900** was *Swipesey Cake Walk* which he wrote in collaboration with Arthur Marshall. Tom Turpin contributed *A Ragtime Nightmare* [H-71257]; and a good cakewalk and future band and jazz number *Creole Belles* [SDL117; LAG12030; GTR] was written by the Danish composer J. Bodewalt Lampe. Born in Ribe, he later concocted the pen-name of Ribé Danmark. He emigrated to America in 1873, studied music at an academy, then worked as a composer, arranger and conductor. He wrote many orchestral arrangements of rags for all kinds of instrumental ensembles and ended his musical career as musical supervisor of the Trianon Ballroom in Chicago and as director of the Dell Lampe Dance Orchestra. *Creole Belles* provided a classic cakewalk right at the end of the cakewalk heyday. Other items in like vein were *Whistling Remus* by Thomas E. Broady, cashing in on an earlier success; *After The Cakewalk* by Nathaniel Dett; *The Bowery Spielers* by William H. Krell; *Bunch O' Blackberries* by Abe Holzmann; and two highly successful songs of the year were *In Dahomey* by James Weldon Johnson and *A Bird In A Gilded Cage* by Harry Von Tilzer and Arthur J. Lamb. Ragtime titles included *A Tennessee Tantalizer* by Charles H. Hunter; *Ragtime Intermezzo* by Maxwell Silver which described itself as a syncopated symphony; *A Hot Rag* by S. R. Lewis (an early use of the adjective); *Ragged Rastus* by O. H. Anderson; *Ragtime Insanity* by Chris Praetorius; and a song called *I'm Living A Rag-Time Life* [GTR] by Robert S. Roberts and Gene Jefferson. The subject of their song is the poor fellow who found ragtime taking over his whole existence: 'I got a ragtime dog and a ragtime cat, a ragtime piano in my ragtime flat; wear ragtime clothes, from hat to shoes; I read a paper called the "Ragtime News". Got ragtime habits and I talk that way, I sleep in ragtime and I rag all day; got ragtime troubles with my ragtime wife . . . I'm certainly living a ragtime life.' One leading journal took it upon itself to explain ragtime to its readers: 'This music got its name from the rough appearance of the bands which are called rag-bands, and the music rag-music or "rag-time" music. The popularity of "rag-time" music is certainly not diminishing, and it remains to be seen what effect it will have on the American music of the future.'

1901 (the year of Joplin's *The Easy Winners*; *Peacherine Rag*; and the *Sunflower Slow Drag* collaboration with Scott Hayden) saw the publication of Abe Holzmann's finest march *Blaze Away*. But the great success of the year was undoubtedly Charles N. Daniels' *Hiawatha* which was described as an Indian intermezzo. Daniels (1878–1943) came from Leavenworth in Kansas. He was a busy song-writer and arranger who was called in to put Joplin's *Original Rags* into shape, and was also a music publisher in a small way. His *Hiawatha* [OU2035] [LTZ-U15072] [33SX1158] eventually earned him some $10,000 and started quite a craze for Indian pieces. Sousa's playings and recordings of it helped to spread it all over the world; the previous year they had embarked on the first of five European tours. Daniels published it under his usual pseudonym of Neil Moret and the next year brought out a song version with words by James O'Dea. There is no denying its catchy qualities, and there were many imitators. Daniels himself tried to repeat his success with *Silver Heels* in 1905. Charles L. Hunter had two good rags – *'Possum And 'Taters* [AL3523] and *Cotton Boles* that year; others were *Jagtime Johnson's Ragtime March* by R. Ryder; *Rag Pickers Rag* by Robert T. O'Brien and *Ragtime Jubilee* by James W. Seeley, Holzmann also published *Hunky-dory* – a characteristic cakewalk march; and two songs worth mentioning were the long lasting *Ain't Dat A Shame* by Walter Wilson and John Queen; and the short-lived *Coon! Coon! Coon!* by Leo Friedman.

In **1902** (Joplin: *Elite Syncopations; The Entertainer; The Ragtime Dance* song; *A Breeze From Alabama; The Strenuous Life*) found its best-seller in near ragtime vein in a song with a true background – *Bill Bailey, Won't You Please Come Home* by Hughie Cannon. It broke up his marriage. Several now well-established names come up again : Joe Jordan with *Double Fudge*; Charles L. Johnson with *Black Smoke*; Abe Holzmann with *Alagazam Cake Walk* (it is noticeable that this particular strain is dying out); and Tony Jackson wrote his *Naked Dance* later to be effectively revived by Jelly Roll Morton. Otherwise a rather mixed bag : *Trombone Johnson* by E. J. Stark; *Cotton Picker Rag* by C. Tyler; *Easy Pickins'* by Tin Pan Alley stalwart Egbert Van Alstyne; *Levee Rag* by Charles Mullen; *Ragged Raglets* by James M. Fulton; *Ma Ragtime Queen* by John F. Barth; *A Ragtime Reception* – a cakewalk by Irwin L. Sperry; *When The Band Played Ragtime* by John Cole; and *Kitchy Koo Cake Walk* by Gus Edwards (1879–1945). Arthur Pryor took a somewhat gloomy view of the situation when he wrote *The Passing Of Ragtime*. The real craze was still a few years ahead. A top selling ragtime song was Bob Cole's *Under The Bamboo Tree.*

1903 (Joplin: *Weeping Willow; Palm Leaf Rag; Something Doing* [with Scott Hayden]; and the ill-fated *A Guest of Honor*) saw the first publication by James Scott – *A Summer Breeze*, and Turpin's *St Louis Rag* [AL3515; GTR]. Works by a second generation of ragtime composers begin to appear. Joe Jordan, who was born in Cincinnati in 1882 and brought up in St Louis, was very much in the creative ragtime circles of the time. He moved to Chicago eventually to become a well-known figure in popular music circles, working as a bandleader and arranger, teaming up with Ernest Hogan to produce a number of popular songs of the day, forming a singing group called the Memphis Students, and finally working with Will Marion Cook and enjoying a long career as leader of his own band. He died in 1971. The most worthy of his rags are listed in 1904, 1905 and 1909. *Nappy Lee* of 1903 was one of his pioneering efforts. Percy Wenrich, who was born in Joplin, Missouri in 1880, was another ragtimer who veered towards Tin Pan Alley and was to write some enormously successful songs like *Put On Your Old Grey Bonnet, Moonlight Bay* and *When You Wore A Tulip* at the height of the commercial ragtime boom. His *Ashy Africa* came in 1903 to be followed by many more good quality rags that are noted later. Other rags of 1903 were *Alabama Shuffle* by Joseph Ott; *Carpet Rags* by Raymond W. Connor; and *Rag-Time Drummer* by J. Leubrie Hill. It was also the year of the first of Axel W. Christensen's *Ragtime Instruction Books* which were to be the foundation of his nation-wide piano schools and correspondence courses and went through nine or ten volumes and numerous editions between 1903 and 1937.

1904 (Joplin's *The Favorite; The Cascades; The Sycamore; The Chrysanthemum*; and the song version of *Maple Leaf Rag*) saw Tom Turpin's *The Buffalo Rag*; Joe Jordan's fine *Pekin Rag*; and the popular *St Louis Tickle* [AL3523; RS] by Barney and Seymour. Charles Seymour also had a success with *Panama Rag* [SDL132] [JGN1001] (not to be confused with the later *Panama*), while Kerry Mills collaborated with Andrew B. Sterling on the immortal song *Meet Me In St Louis, Louis*. It is interesting to note how the syncopated ragtime strains creep into successful theatrical songs like *Give My Regards To Broadway* which George M. Cohan was singing in 'Little Johnny Jones' that year. Other rags of the year were: *Crazy Chord Rag* by Albert Carroll (which Jelly Roll Morton revived in 1949); *Havana Rag* by Maurice Kirwin; and *Buff Rag* by Robert Bircher.

During **1905** and up to 1907 ragtime appears to be simmering ready to come to the boil in 1908 and 1909. Joplin's only notable contribution to 1905 is the waltz *Bethena*; Joe Jordan published *J. J. J. Rag* and Percy Wenrich his *Peaches And Cream*. Joseph Northup, a name that frequently appears from now on, has a success with *The Cannonball* [AL3542] (it was also published in London), and the name of the highly successful Negro orchestra leader James Reese Europe is seen on a piece called *Coon Band Parade*. Two successful ragtime songs of the year were *Rufus Rastus Johnson Brown (What You Goin' To Do When The Rent Comes 'round)* [RS] and *Wait Till The Sun Shines, Nellie* by Harry von Tilzer and Andrew B. Sterling. Tilzer, one of a family of Tin Pan Alley songwriters was to dabble frequently in the ragtime idiom with many songs in the vein and occasional popularised rags. From Indianapolis, Harry (1872–1946) and his brother Albert (1878–1956) founded a highly lucrative publishing empire in New York and produced many of the top pops of the times between them. Other ragtime compositions of 1905 were: *Baltimore Buck Rag-Time* by Harry Brown; *Black Cat Rag* by Wooster and Smith; *Calico Rag* by Lee B. Grabbe; *The Coon Band Played Rag-Time* by E. Denville; *Peek-a-boo Rag* by Warren Edwards; *Jungle Time* [AL3523] by E. Phillip Severin; and *Sassafrass Rag* by J. Levy. Another Tin Pan Alley stalwart who penned many rags in between his popular songs was Egbert Van Alstyne (1882–1951) who was born in Chicago and had a thorough musical training. He worked for many years as a travelling ragtime pianist in vaudeville and road shows, then began to write his songs in partnership with people like Harry Williams and Gus Kahn. Barber-shop favourite *In The Shade Of The Old Apple Tree* was his 1905 hit.

1906 was a quietish year before the storm but it has some notable publications like Joplin's *The Ragtime Dance*; James Scott's delightful *Frog Legs Rag* [AL3542] [33CX10061]; Arthur Marshall's *Kinklets*; and Charles L. Johnson's forthright *Dill Pickles Rag*

[PTR] [AL3563] [OU2035] – all of which have remained great favourites. Charles L. Johnson, who also wrote as Raymond Birch, was born in Kansas City in 1876 and spent his whole life there, dying in 1950, in the music-publishing business. *Dill Pickles* keeps his name alive, but he also wrote in 1906 one of those popular Indian pieces called *Iola*. Percy Wenrich wrote *Noodles* and *Chestnut Rag Medley*; and there was also *Bric-a-brac Rag* by Maurice Porcelain; *Holy Moses Rag* by Charles Seymour; *The Grand Old Rag* and *Popularity* by George M. Cohan (1878–1942) and the song *Dat Lovin' Rag* [ORS-2] by Bernard Adler and Victor H. Smalley. It was also the year of a very popular march called *National Emblem* by E. E. Bagley.

1907, the last year we deal with here before the ragtime explosion, had three good rags by Joplin – *Nonpareil;Gladiolus Rag* and *Rose Leaf Rag*; as well as *Heliotrope Bouquet*, his memorable collaboration with the ailing Louis Chauvin (1881–1908). James Scott had a classic in *Kansas City Rag*; Charles L. Johnson contributed *Fine And Dandy*; and Percy Wenrich gratefully sub-titled his *The Smiler* [AL3542] as 'a Joplin rag', a timely tribute. He also published *Dixie Darlings*; and there was *Powder Rag* by Raymond Birch (Charles L. Johnson); *Down South* – a ragtime march, by C. A. Grimm; *Fluffy Ruffles* – a slow drag, by C. Duane Crabbe; and *Sumthin' Doin'* [RP] by F. H. Losey. The big commercial success of the year owed a great deal of its catchiness to Robert Schumann and his *Merry Peasant* – Kerry Mills' 'Indian' song *Redwing* – but owed very little to ragtime.

Scott Joplin V
The Final Gesture

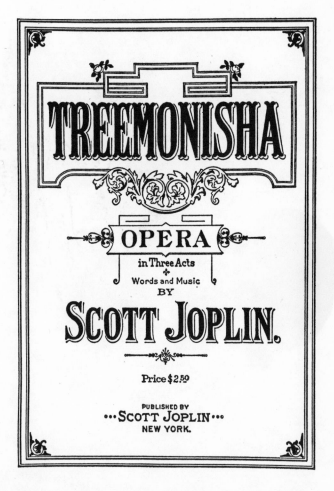

TREEMONISHA

OPERA

in Three Acts

Words and Music

BY

SCOTT JOPLIN.

Price $2.50

PUBLISHED BY
···SCOTT JOPLIN···
NEW YORK.

15 *Walking For Dat Cake* – a song sheet showing a cakewalk competition

16 and 17 The contrast between the cakewalk as practised in its native form and as adopted by high society in the drawing-rooms of Paris, 1903

18, 19 and 20 Different versions of the cakewalk

21 and 22 *Above left:* William H. Krell, whose *Mississippi Rag* (1897) was one of the first pieces of ragtime to be published *Above right:* Joseph Lamb, one of the few white men to write rags that were as good as the very best black compositions

23 and 24 *Above:* Ben Harney, who had the first New York hit with piano ragtime in 1896 *Right:* Blind Tom, who was able to repeat the most complex piano compositions after one hearing, including the mistakes often planted to trap him

25 *Right:* Williams and Walker, a vaudeville team that spread the gospel of ragtime

26 The Queen City Negro Band 1896 – the first band to play ragtime in America

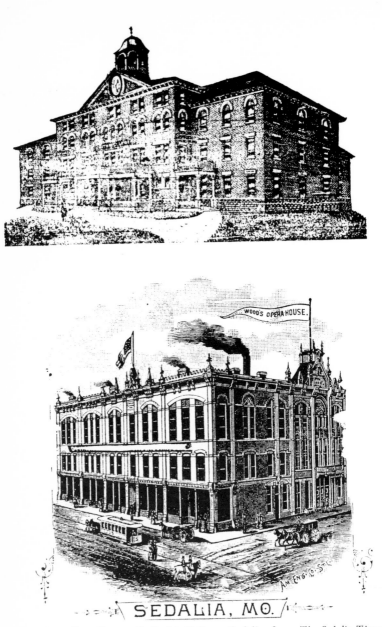

WOOD'S OPERA HOUSE.

SEDALIA, MO.

27 and 28 *Top:* George R. Smith College, Sedalia, from *The Sedalia Times,*
31 August 1901 *Above:* Wood's Opera House, from *Sedalia Today* 1904

29 and 30 *Above:*
Building at 119 East
Main Street, Sedalia,
that housed the Maple
Leaf Club *Right:* View
of the Ferris Wheel
and the Moorish
Palace, World's Col-
umbian Exposition
1893 (*By courtesy of the
Chicago Historical
Society*)

31 The Great Hall of Festivals and Central Cascade, St Louis Exposition 1904

By the time he reached New York, Scott Joplin was beginning to tire of the wandering life and decided that this must be the place for him to settle. Here the ragtime craze was making big money for all kinds of entertainers and songwriters, though not necessarily for a purveyor of pure classical Negro ragtime from the Mississippi. Here too he met a girl called Lottie Stokes, this time someone who would take an interest in his music and do her best to help him achieve his ambitions. They first met while he was still touring and she began to accompany him round the. vaudeville circuit.

During 1908 Joplin put some of his teaching experience into a small book of six exercises which he called *The School of Ragtime*. It sold for fifty cents and took a serious view of the music – or at least of the 'high-class' kind that Joplin purveyed. It came a long time after Ben Harney's *Rag Time Instructor* which had been published in 1897, and just too early to cash in on the coming public interest in pseudo-ragtime when amateur pianists would be flocking to schools like those run by Axel Christensen with branches in twenty-five American cities. The vogue for teach-yourself piano courses and tutors was to continue right through to the 1930s both in America and England, at each period slanted towards the music that was in fashion, in the 1900s to ragtime, naturally.

1908 also saw the publication of *Fig Leaf Rag* by John Stark; and of *Sugar Cane* and *Pine-apple Rag* by the Seminary Music Co.

of New York. The pre-occupation of ragtime with the vegetable world is something that has not been fully explained.

In 1909 Joplin and Lottie Stokes were married and bought a house at 252 West Forty-Seventh Street which Lottie ran as a theatrical boarding-house and Joplin as a ragtime conservatory. It was a happy period of regular meals, a steady income and paid bills, and conducive to work. Joplin wrote many rags but he could have written more had he not already become pre-occupied with his second venture into the operatic world. *Treemonisha* was unprofitably taking up much of his composing time.

In 1909 and in his early forties Joplin could probably have looked forward to a prosperous old age had he tried to repeat his *Maple Leaf Rag* success and perhaps if he had set his sights more firmly on the Broadway theatre and written a musical comedy. But, now in a good enough, though barely good enough, financial position to compose, it was the old nagging ambition to write an opera that led him astray. There were still good rags and other pieces to come. 1909 saw the publication of the dramatically sub-titled *Wall Street Rag*; *Country Club*; *Euphonic Sounds* and *Paragon Rag*; as well as the fine *Solace* – defined as a Mexican serenade – and another ragtime waltz called *Pleasant Moments*. All these were published by the Seminary Music Co. By 1907 Stark had set up a branch in New York but found it an unprofitable venture. Classic Negro ragtime did not sell particularly well in New York and most of its sales were still to be found in the more Southerly states. The Tin Pan Alley watering-down was more to the public taste; simple songs rather than intricate piano pieces. The price wars had started in Tin Pan Alley through the five-and-ten-cent stores. Stark's wife was also seriously ill. When she died in 1910 Stark closed down his New York branch and went back to St Louis and to the more modest business that he had maintained there before *Maple Leaf* came along with a promise of the big-time. So another old friend went from Joplin's side.

In 1910 the work on *Treemonisha* meant that there were only two other publications, *Stoptime Rag* and a song version of *Pineapple Rag* with words by Tin Pan Alley writer Joe Snyder. 1911 saw another collaboration with Scott Hayden on *Felicity Rag*. In fact, we may note now, that there were to be only three more new rags published in his lifetime: another collaboration with Hayden called *Kismet Rag* published in 1913; and two solo efforts, both excellent – *Scott Joplin's New Rag* in 1912 and *Magnetic Rag* in 1914.

But 1911 saw the beginnings of the *Treemonisha* disaster. Firstly Joplin was unable to get a publisher for it and had to bring it out at his own expense which, of course, was considerable. (See page 144 for further comment on the opera.) Even today its full worth is still to be properly assessed through good professional performances; but no doubt, with the interest in Joplin, this will now come. Enough has been heard through the enterprise of ragtime enthusiasts to know that it is potentially a stageable work.

It was first published for eleven voices and chorus with piano accompaniment. Next Joplin realised that it must be orchestrated if there was to be any chance of a full production. The writing of rags was abandoned and money had to be raised by taking on more pupils. They moved to a smaller house at 163 West 131st Street. He employed a young ragtime musician from St Louis, Sam Patterson, to help him copy the parts of the orchestral score that now took up most of his non-teaching hours. They slaved at it long into the night. The money dwindled. Determined to get the opera some publicity he further strained the budget by publishing parts of the opera separately – revised versions of *A Real Slow Drag* and the *Prelude to Act 3* in 1913; and *Frolic Of The Bears* in 1915. His pre-occupation with *Treemonisha* was now nothing less than a mania and even his teaching began to suffer. Many pupils left and others were neglected. His wife believed in his work to such an extent that she descended to running the house as a brothel, in which sordid atmosphere Joplin still laboured.

The orchestration was now finished, but Joplin had no success at all in getting any of the New York managers to put on the opera. He put on a performance, with himself playing the piano, in a dismal hall in Harlem in 1915 with a largely invited audience. Sam Patterson remembers that: 'without scenery, costumes, lighting or orchestral backing, the drama seemed thin and unconvincing, little better than a rehearsal, and its special quality, in any event, would surely have been lost on the typical Harlem audience that attended'. Joplin had driven his cast at rehearsals with high hopes. Now he was heart-broken.

He tried to get back to other writing but his spirit had gone. Unfinished manuscripts littered his desk. A helpful publisher commissioned him to orchestrate some of his earlier rags. Unfinished orchestrations of *Stoptime Rag* and *Searchlight* were among the things he left behind him, along with half-written songs and piano pieces. Deep depressions alternated with periods of sporadic work. An attempt to make some new piano rolls, which he once did with fluent ease, was a disaster. As his mind went so did his physical co-ordination and finally he was taken to the Manhattan State Hospital on Ward's Island. Occasionally he would come to life for brief moments and start jotting down music, but his mind slowly lost its grasp and lapsed into a state of incomprehending dullness. He died on 1 April 1917.

His greatest wish had been to have *Maple Leaf Rag* played at his funeral but even that was denied him. His wife thought it was hardly suitable music. The death certificate said that he had died of 'dementia paralytica-cerebral' which had partly been brought on by syphilis; but it didn't add that it had been hastened by a violent addiction to *Treemonisha*.

The thread that kept Joplin's name alive in the world was a tenuous one. As the ragtime craze built up on a basis of works generally inferior to his own, it swamped his reputation. Only *Maple Leaf* and a handful of other rags continued to be played. David A. Jasen in his *Recorded Ragtime 1897–1958* lists sixty-eight recordings made of *Maple Leaf Rag* ranging from versions by the US Marines Band and Fred Van Eps Orchestra, through many of the great names in jazz, to the revival performances by such as Ralph Sutton and Knocky Parker. Many more have been added since then; and, fortunately, all his other fine pieces are now recognised as masterpieces of popular music-making. *Treemonisha* has been staged in New York and that fact alone has probably made poor old Joplin settle more comfortably in his grave.

The Ragtime Explosion
1908-30

It was an explosion in two ways: an explosion in sales potential and the popular interest in ragtime which took it to the heights of a real craze; and an explosion in which ragtime blew itself sky-high and scattered bits and pieces all over the musical world. From 1896 to 1907 the movement gathered strength and momentum. In the next few years things really began to snowball, though the directions that ragtime took were, as seems inevitable in the popularisation of a folk art, away from its purest and, as we can see in retrospect, strongest form; towards those varied dilutions that appear necessary to make any art-form saleable to a vast non-specialist public.

There were several practical reasons for ragtime's real boom coming so late. In the days before the turn of the century everything took longer. You didn't see your favourite music-hall star at the turn of a knob on a TV set; you had to wait for them to visit your local palace of variety. The other way that music got around was via the sheet-music bought for the family piano. In the 1890s it was surprisingly expensive and it was quite common to find a copy of a popular song selling for anything up to two dollars – which was then quite a lot of money. But after 1900 they found cheaper ways to print music and gradually booming sales brought along the 25c songsheet. Then there was the pianola and piano player, two variations of a mechanical system that brought piano playing within reach of those who couldn't. Blesh lists well over four hundred ragtime titles available in piano-rolls in *They*

All Played Ragtime, calling it a selective list; we know there were many more. To cap it all came the phonograph and the gramophone, with Mr Edison's cylinders and Mr Berliner's discs vying for popularity and between them spreading the ragtime gospel. The machines had become standardised and comparatively cheap by 1896 but it obviously took some years for the new-fangled contraptions to catch on. In 1903, for example, a well-known London dealer had a stock of 100,000 records and offered sixty different makes of machine to play them on. The turnover was forty machines and 3,000 records a day. The cost of a cylinder in 1907 was around 50c to 75c, and records were much the same. The silent cinema contributed its mite by supplying jerky pictures of people cakewalking, slow-dragging and two-stepping to the accompaniment of the cinema pianist. In other words ragtime grew up exactly at the time when the means of promoting it were also growing up. It was the first music to make itself widely popular outside the confines of theatre and dancehall; its message coming right into people's homes.

One can see the momentum gathering around **1908** ready for the bang that was to come a year or two later, in about 1911. In 1908 the classical composers were even beginning to take note. We don't know what it was that Debussy listened to in 1907 or 8; he may even have been contaminated on his visits to London, but he certainly heard some cakewalks somewhere and contributed his own *Golliwog's Cakewalk* as part of the *Children's Suite*. It added an air of respectability to the whole thing. Having said 'I find these times particularly ungracious in that a lot of noise is made about things of no importance', he is reported to have thought highly of Joplin's music. In 1908 Joplin wrote his very seriously intended *School of Ragtime* exercises, as well as *Fig Leaf Rag*, *Sugar Cane* and *Pine-apple Rag*; and he helped the up-and-coming Charles Lamb to get his *Sensation Rag* [FG3562] [HSU5010] into print by lending his name to its publication. Percy Wenrich wrote *Crab Apples* and *Memphis Rag*. There were several intimations of new ragtime directions, firstly in the smoothed-out lines of one of those works that have a lasting appeal for the tinny piano exponents – George Botsford's *Black*

And White Rag [AR1; PTR], which is not to be sneered at as it has joyful and athletic memories of its own and has much caught the public fancy. But it has already, in 1908, made a clean break with the Joplinesque mode, though the nearer to that idiom you play it, the better it sounds. 'George Botsford (1874–1949) came from Sioux Falls, South Dakota and, making his start in the cakewalk style, became a commercial songwriter and music-publisher. Later he was to collaborate with Irving Berlin. In 1908 he also published *Klondike Rag*. Jean Schwartz (1876–1956), another Tin Pan Alley man who had successes with *Bedelia* (1903) and *Chinatown, My Chinatown* (1906), penned a likeable rag in Botsford vein called *The Whitewash Man*. We begin to see the commercial use of the ragtime idiom in songs like *Shine On, Harvest Moon* by Jack Norworth and Norah Bayes (though Norworth and Albert von Tilzer also published *Take Me Out To The Ball Game* in the older waltz style); and *Down In Jungle Town* by Theodore Morse and Edward Madden. George M. Cohan exploited what he called the 'new kind of step' in *Cohan's Rag Babe*, showing that the theatre was cottoning on; while the warning message that anything in the world could be ragged if need be came with *Coontown's Merry Widow* – 'a rag time arrangement of the famous opera' by Edward Laska and Charles Eliott. Other rags of the year were Arthur Marshall's *Ham And – Rag* and *The Peach* [OU2035]; Blinde Boone's *Rag Medley No. 1*; *Bolo Rag* by Albert Gumble (1883-1946); *Daisy Rag* by Fred Heltman; *The Devilish Rag* by Lew Roberts; *Dusty Rag* by the popular feminine exponent May Aufderheide; *Powder Rag* [AR1] by Raymond Birch; *Wild Cherries Rag* by Ted Snyder [Herwin 402]; *Old Time Rag* – a song by Madden and Morse.

1909 has notable Joplin works in *Wall Street Rag; Solace; Euphonic Sounds* and *Paragon Rag*. James Scott published *Great Scott Rag* [H-71299], *Sunburst Rag* [LAG 12030] and *The Ragtime Betty*; Joseph Lamb *Excelsior Rag* [FG3562] and *Ethiopia Rag* [H-71257]; and other familiar names were represented by *Piano-phiends Rag* [AL3563] and *Texas Steer Rag* by George Botsford; *Temptation Rag* [SDL132] [PTR] and *Ole South* by Henry Lodge; *Boone's Rag Medley No. 2* by Blind Boone; and *Porcupine Rag* by Charles L. Johnson. A new and significant name that year was J.

Russell Robinson whose career most decidedly spanned the transition from ragtime to early-jazz. Robinson became the pianist of the Original Dixieland Jazz Band when Henry Ragas left and, touring with them in England in 1919, was probably as much responsible as anyone for introducing ragtime and jazz piano to British audiences. He was born in the ragtime town of Indianapolis (birthplace also of May Aufderheide and Paul Pratt) in 1892 and in 1909 published his *Sapho Rag*. He died in 1963 having written a good many famous jazz standards. The songs that promoted the ragtime idiom with commercial success in 1909 were *By The Light Of The Silvery Moon* by Gus Edwards and Edward Madden; and *Put On Your Old Grey Bonnet* by Percy Wenrich and Stanley Murphy. There was also a song called *That Mesmerising Mendelssohn Tune* by Irving Berlin and *I'm Alabama Bound* [VLP2] – a ragtime two-step by Robert Hoffman. Other tantalising titles were *Vanity Rag* by Paul Pratt; *The Thriller Rag* [SDL118] and *Buzzer Rag* [SDL132] by May Aufderheide; *Calico Rag* by R. G. Behan; *Candy Rag* by Robert Bircher; *Poverty Rag* by Harry J. Lincoln; *Cauldron Rag* by Axel W. Christensen; *Cincinnati Rag* by W. C. Powell; *Clover Leaf Rag* by Charles Seymour; *Oh! You Devil Rag* by Ford Dabney; *Rag-bag* [RP] by Harry Lincoln and *Rag Baby* [RP] by F. H. Losey. Neil Moret tried a follow-up to *Hiawatha* with a piece called *Silver Heels*.

As Joplin gradually faded from the competition (*Stoptime Rag* and the *Pine-apple Rag* song were his only contributions to 1910), others came to the fore, notably James Scott, who may be worthy of being regarded as Joplin's equal, with his distinctive *Grace And Beauty* [DNO-3] [OU2035] [AL3515] [SDL118], the lively *Hilarity Rag* [SDL118] [DNO-3] and *Ophelia Rag*. George Botsford had another commercial success with *Grizzly Bear Rag* [RP] [AL3523] [SDL132] [SDL210] which was also available with words added by Irving Berlin and sometimes referred to, as in the Victor Dance Orchestra's *Two-step Medley No. 10*, as *The Dance Of The Grizzly Bear*. This was the beginning of that ragtime song catch-phrase 'it's a bear, it's a bear' which caught on with great rapidity. Then there was *Red Pepper* [VLP2] by Henry Lodge; *Glad Rag* [AL3542] by Ribé Danmark; *Walhalla* [SDL132] – a 'two-step craze' by Paul

Pratt; *Dynamite Rag* [AR-2] by J. Russell Robinson; *Aggravatin'
Rag* by George L. Cobb; *Champagne Rag* by Charles Lamb; *Franco-
American Rag* and *Black Beauty Rag* [AL3563] by Jean Schwartz;
Blue Ribbon Rag by May Aufderheide; and an intriguing novelty
that mustn't be confused with Joplin's beautiful *Entertainer* – Jay
Roberts' *The Entertainer's Rag* [AL3542] [LTZ-UI5072], which
ingeniously combined the tune of *Dixie* in one hand and *Yankee
Doodle* in the other, then reversed, which is difficult and effective,
while the rest of the rag is a respectable one in the 'modern'
streamline style. It was a popular item in ragtime contests for
many years and a clever executant could usually depend on win-
ning the audience, and often the contest, with a dexterous performance. The popularised ragtime song now begins to come
strongly on to the market. Irving Berlin, who was born in Temum,
Siberia in 1888, the son of a Jewish Cantor and with the real name
of Israel Baline, seems an unlikely candidate as one of the principal figures in Tin Pan Alley's history. But as Constant Lambert
has written in *Music Ho!*, it was the cosmopolitan Jew who took
over popular music from the Negro so that Tin Pan Alley became
a 'commercialised Wailing Wall'. Berlin came to America when
he was four and wrote his first published song in 1907, supplying
the words in this case. His incredible facility, leading to a vast and
often inspired output, remains unequalled. By 1910 he had firmly
cottoned on to the ragtime urge and the word 'rag' became very
much a money spinner for him. *Grizzly Bear*, which became best-
known now as *Doing The Grizzly Bear* (to George Botsford's
melody) was introduced with tremendous success by Fannie Brice
in the 'Ziegfeld Follies of 1910'. Now he began to write many ragtime songs, mainly with lyrics by Ted Snyder, which in 1910 included : *Dat Draggy Rag*; *Piano Man*; *That Opera Rag* which was
introduced by May Irwin in 'Getting a Polish'; *Stop That Rag
(Keep On Playing, Honey)* and *Sweet Marie, Make a Rag-a-time
Dance With Me* from the Bayes and Norworth show 'The Jolly
Bachelors'; and *That Beautiful Rag* which Berlin and Snyder performed themselves in 'Up and Down Broadway'. It was the
theatre's exploitation of ragtime that started the real boom. There
were other good and lasting songs in the idiom like *Put Your Arms*

Around Me Honey [ORS-1] by Tilzer and McCree; *Some Of These Days* by Shelton Brooks; *That Fussy Rag* [ORS-2; AR-2] by Victor H. Smalley; and the jazz orientated *Washington And Lee Swing* by Thornton Allen. Other piano rags of the year were: *Chanticleer Rag* by Albert Gumble; *Chile Sauce Rag* [PTR] and *Pepper Sauce* [PTR] by H. A. Fischler; *College Rag* by William Hunter; *Dogzigity Rag* [RP] by Billy Taylor; *Redhead Rag* by Irene Franklin and Burt Green [LTZ-UI5072]; and *Tangle Foot Rag* [PTR] by F. H. Losey. Abroad Monsieur Debussy continued his tributes towards the cakewalk spirit by writing *Minstrels* as one of his first book of *Préludes*. John Stark, now fighting a rearguard action for the classic rags he believed in, was drawn out into a desperate attack on the Tin Pan Alley perpetrations in a 1910 advertisement for his wares: 'We mean just what we say when we call these instrumental rags classic: They are perfection of type . . . they are used in the drawing rooms of culture. Of course the name "Rag" is a scurrilous misnomer, and filthy songs have done much to drag the name in the dirt, but no name could hold down our classy instrumental numbers. That person who flouts them at this date is exposing a verdancy and ignorance that is pitiful.' And, of course, from a purist point of view, he was quite right.

The song that really caught the public's imagination and made everyone ragtime 'mad' was, of course, *Alexander's Ragtime Band* in **1911**. It was introduced by Irving Berlin at the Friar's Frolic of 1911, a private affair. It was first performed publicly in Chicago by the deep-voiced Emma Carus and it was much popularised by Lew Dockstader's Minstrels, by Al Jolson and, in vaudeville, by Eddie Miller. There is no doubt that it had some magical quality for it spread like a prairie fire. The ragtime historians, like Stark, have taken every opportunity to decry the song and its impurities. The truth is that we so rarely hear *Alexander's Ragtime Band* [SDL210] and other pre-war ragtime songs played in a ragtime fashion. If one applies to them the same technique that one applies to a Joplin rag, it can quickly be discovered that they have a considerable genuine ragtime element in them. The verse of Berlin's song makes an excellent ragtime theme; *Darktown Strutters' Ball* makes a good ragtime number if played in the right idiom. It was the performers who tended to take the music away from the true ragtime idiom more than the music itself. Irving Berlin thrived by supplying the public with what they wanted; Joplin failed by insisting on writing his ragtime opera *Tree-monisha*. With these two events counterbalanced in 1911 it looks like the pivotal point of ragtime history. Interestingly Berlin once said: 'Syncopation is the soul of every true American. Ragtime is the best heart-raiser and worry banisher that I know.... Someday I'm going to write a syncopated grand opera.' Joplin also wrote *Felicity Rag* with Hayden, but otherwise continued to fade from the scene. Berlin prospered additionally with *That Mysterious Rag*; *The Ragtime Violin*; *Dying Rag*; *Whistling Rag* and, another great success, *Everybody's Doing It Now* – which was certainly an apt motto for ragtime. Classic rags were still being written by those who kept to the straight and narrow path. James Scott wrote *Quality Rag* and a charmer in *The Ragtime Oriole* [AL3515] [SDL132]; George Botsford wrote *Honeysuckle Rag*; Charles L. Johnson *Tar Babies Rag*; and Percy Wenrich *Sunflower Rag*. Two other items of note were bandleader Wilbur Sweatman's *Down Home Rag* [33CX10061] [ST499], which is really even less of a rag than *Alexander's Ragtime Band* and a clear straightening out of the notes ready for subsequent jazz use; and a popular song that brought ragtime into the music-halls – *Oh, You Beautiful Doll* which was written by Nat. D. Ayer who came over to England with the Ragtime Octette and stayed to spread the new gospel. Other publications of 1911 were: Kerry Mills' *Ragtime Dance*; *April Fool Rag* by Jean Schwartz; *That Flying Rag* and *Canhani-balmo Rag* by Arthur Pryor; *Barnyard Rag* by Chris Smith; *Bees-wax Rag* [PTR] by Harry J. Lincoln; *Ramshackle Rag* [VLP2] by Ted Snyder (1881–1965); and Harry Tierney's *Checker Board Rag*; *Black Canary Rag*; *Fanatic Rag*; *Fleur-de-Lys Rag* and *Innocent Rag*. The obvious tendency is to treat ragtime as something comical rather than the poetic and lyrical music that it was in the hands of Scott Joplin. There was the song *Where You Goin'* by Albert von Tilzer and Lew Brown; *That Fascinating Rag* by Walter Rolfe; *Corrugated Rag* by Ed. J. Mellinger; *Foolishness Rag* – a buck dance by Mort Weinstein; *Harmony Rag* by Hal. G. Nichols;

Hot Chestnuts – a rag medley by G. J. Trinkhaus; *Hurricane Rag* by F. G. Johnson; *Jay Roberts Rag* and *Jolly Rag* by Jay Roberts; *Nonsense Rag* [LTZ-UI5072] by R. G. Brady; and *Weeping Willow* [RP] [AL3542], *Black Wasp Rag* and *Hot Scotch Rag* [RP] by H. A. Fischler. The titles suggest the necessity for offering scope to sheet music illustrators rather than actual sources of inspiration.

1912 brought a prosperous spate of ragtime songs: *Ragtime Cowboy Joe* [ORS-1] with words by Grant Clarke and music by Lewis F. Muir and Maurice Abrahams; *Ragging The Baby To Sleep* [ORS-1] by Lewis F. Muir and L. Wolfe Gilbert; *Hitchy-koo* [ORS-1] by Lewis F. Muir, Maurice Abrahams and L. Wolfe Gilbert which was so popular that it lent its name to a successful series of revues; *Pucker Up Your Lips, Miss Lindy* [ORS-1] by Albert von Tilzer and Eli Dawson; *Ragtime Goblin Man* by Harry von Tilzer and Andrew B. Sterling; *Row, Row, Row* by James V. Monaco and William Jerome; *My Little Lovin' Sugar Babe* [ORS-2] by Henry I. Marshall and Stanley Murphy. Berlin contributed *At The Devil's Ball*; *Ragtime Mocking Bird*; *Ragtime Soldier Man*; *That Mysterious Rag* (music by Ted Snyder) [SDL210]; *Ragtime Jockey Man* used in 'The Passing Show of 1912'; *That Society Bear* used in 'The Whirl of Society' and confirming the use of the word 'bear' as a dance name; *Ragtime Sextette* (a parody of 'Lucia di Lammermoor' in the same show); and, his biggest success of the year, *When The Midnight Choo-choo Leaves For Alabam*. It was very much the year of ragtime everything. It was also the year of a new stream of music that started to popularise the blues – notably with W. C. Handy's *Memphis Blues* – ready for the eventual mixture with ragtime in the jazz days to come. Joplin had a last fling with *Scott Joplin's New Rag*; George Botsford wrote *Eskimo Rag*; Charles L. Johnson *Swanee Rag*; Henry Lodge his *Black Diamond Rag* [SDL210] and J. Russell Robinson *That Eccentric Rag*. Christensen issued his *Instruction Books for Vaudeville Piano Playing*, Vols. 1–5, wherein he put due emphasis on the need to know your ragtime style to be in the vogue. Both Neil Moret and A. J. Weidt published pieces called *That Banjo Rag* (which at least showed a historical sense). For the rest there was: *That Daffydill Rag* by Bill and Frank Mueller; *Slippery Elm Rag* by C. Woods; *Mandy's Rag-*

time Waltz by J. S. Zamecnik; *Popular Rag* by Webb Long; *The Turkey Trot* [AR-3] by Ribé Danmark; *Red Onion Rag* and *Winter Garden Rag* by Abe Olman (b. 1887); *That Chopstick Rag* by Grant Clarke, William Jerome and Jean Schwartz; *Fiddlesticks Rag* [AR-1] by Al. B. Coney; *Fashion Rag* [RP] by Chas. Cohen; and *Rig-a-jig Rag* [AR-3] by Nat D. Ayer. Probably the public had no idea of the ancestry of the music they were humming when they bought such songs as *Way Down South* [ORS-2] by Geo. Fairman and *Waiting For The Robert E. Lee* by Muir and Gilbert, but they enjoyed the flavour.

Through all the furore of ragtime making and breaking, earnest opinion was beginning to sense the music's impact. The American *Current Opinion* wrote: 'It would seem that the cultivation of Negro music is an important step – one of the most important steps – in the development of American music' – and that was quite a bold thing to say in 1913. In London *The Times* wasn't quite so sure and warned that 'there are sincere and sensitive musicians who hold that "ragtime" is decadent and deplore its popularity as an evil sign of the times'. Of course, this wasn't entirely true for many classical musicians of sincerity and sensitivity were finding Afro-American music a fascinating source of inspiration. Dvořák had confirmed his interest in the early 1890s with his 'From the New World' symphony and his 'American' quartet, saying: 'In the Negro melodies of America I find all that is needed for a great and noble school of music'. Delius had explored the Negro spiritual even before that. Debussy again contributed in 1913 with a movement in his second book of Préludes called *General Lavine – Eccentric* – a cakewalk that portrayed the celebrated American comic juggler Edward la Vine whom he saw at the Théâtre Marigny. It is, at the same time, sheer snobbishness to talk as if popular music was dependent for its acceptance and survival on the good will of the academics. Its own vitality is its propagator and the support of the common man provides its sustenance.

By 1913 Joplin's contribution to the world was practically over. But other classic ragtime composers were still able to publish and sell their fine works perhaps even aided by the fact that publishers were making a lot of money out of the commercialised brand. There was *American Beauty Rag* [AL3515] [FG3562] [HSU5010] by Charles Lamb; *Incandescent Rag* by George Botsford; *Moonlight Rag* and *Pastime Rag* by Henry Lodge; and *Ragtime Turkey Trot* by Percy Wenrich, with words by Julian Eltinge and Jack Mahoney. Two important names appear on the scene: firstly Artie Matthews, who was born in Minonk, Illinois in 1888, was brought up in Springfield and had a straight musical background. Arriving in St Louis in 1904 he found himself totally unable to compete with the accomplished ragtime pianists there and retreated to Springfield to polish up his technique. By 1907 he was back in St Louis and became acquainted with Joplin and Turpin. In 1913 Charlie Turpin, Tom's brother, founded the Booker T. Washington Theater which presented vaudeville and variety with Matthews and Tom Turpin writing most of the music. Matthews also worked as an arranger for Stark, knocking rags into shape for pianists who had the ideas but not the technical know-how. We can't be sure how much many published rags may owe to his abilities. He published the first of his own series of *Pastime Rags* [CPR] [H-71299] in 1913, a series which drew inspiration from every kind of dance from tap to tango, songs and blues. No. 2 [CPR] [H-71299] has a new kind of ragtime quality using the triplets which were to become part of jazz and foreshadowing the popular kind of salon 'ragtime-based' music that would be heard in works like Felix Arndt's *Nola* and Billy Mayerl's *Marigold*. Matthews also made musical history by being the first to publish a work with 'blues' in the title – *Baby Seals Blues* which came out in 1912 a few weeks before Handy's *Memphis Blues* [SH8474] and Garrett and Wand's *Dallas Blues*. But that is another story. Matthews died in 1959. The other name to take note of is that of Charles 'Luckey' Roberts, who was born in Philadelphia in 1893 and died in New York in 1968. His first rags *Junk Man Rag* [GOR] [AL3563] [SH8463] and *Pork And Beans* [GOR] [HB-U1057] [H-71257] [SH8463] have a forward-looking, sturdy, honest quality that is very much a link between the old ragtime and the new Harlem style piano of James P. Johnson and Fats Waller. 1913 also saw the publication of Jim Burris's *Ballin' The Jack*, material for a new dance vogue. Other rags were: *Alabama Jigger* by Edward B. Claypole (1883–1952); *Checker Rag* by Harry J. Lincoln; *Contagious Rag* by Ed. J. Mellinger; *Movie Rag* by J. S. Zamecnik; *1915 Rag* [SDL132] and *The Tierney Rag* [AR-3] by Harry Tierney (1890–1965); *Tickle The Ivories* [AR-3] by Wallie Herzer; and *That Lovin' Rag* [AR-2] by Bernard Adler. There were a fair crop of ragtime songs: *That International Rag* by Irving Berlin (written while crossing the Atlantic and used on a successful variety tour of England); *Wagner Couldn't Write A Ragtime Song* by Jean Schwartz and William Jerome; *That Ragtime Minstrel Band* [ORS-2] by Pearl and Roth; *Mammy Jinny's Jubilee* [ORS-2] by Lewis F. Muir and L. Wolfe Gilbert; *'Cross The Mason-Dixon Line* [ORS-1] by Henry I. Marshall and Stanley Murphy; *Sailing Down The Chesapeake Bay* by George Botsford and Jean C. Havez; and *He'd Have To Get Under* [ORS-1] by Maurice Abrahams, Grant Clarke and Edgar Leslie. An interesting new approach was penned by Elsie Janis – *Anti-rag-time-girl*; and the vogue was catching on in London where Fred W. Leigh wrote *The Ragtime Yokel (Go To Jericho With Yer Rag-a-time Mary Ann)* – sung by George Bastow.

The early war years found no marked abatement of ragtime fervour. 1914 established another important new name, that of Eubie Blake, who was born in Baltimore and was musically trained in New York. *Chevy Chase* [GOR]; *Fizz Water* [GOR] [SH8474] and *Troublesome Ivories* [GOR] [OU2035] are all ambitious pieces. Max Morath has commented: 'The first two themes of *Troublesome Ivories* strike me as being so naturally founded in the fingering of the A-flat and D-flat chords that it's amazing that nobody ever thought of these patterns before, and a tribute to Eubie's genius that *he did*, expanding them into a fully shaped composition in ragtime'. The other two he found brimming with originality but less ambitious. At present Blake is still playing, the only genuine survivor of the ragtime age. In 1915 he teamed up with bandleader Noble Sissle to produce in future years some standard songs for the theatre, and in 1917 he worked for a time with James Reese Europe. 1914 had classic rags still: *The Lily* [OU2035] [LTZ-UI5072] by Charles Thompson; *Magnetic Rag* by

Scott Joplin; *Climax Rag* [LAG12030] [DNO-3] by James Scott; and it saw the first rag by James P. Johnson (1891–1955) *Caprice Rag* [RP] [AL3540] which is almost outside the true ragtime idiom; as well as his *Carolina Shout*; alongside a piece that was to achieve immense and lasting popularity in the jangly piano world – *Twelfth Street Rag* by Euday Bowman (1887–1949). Other rags were: *Cataract Rag* [33CX10061] [LTZ-UI5072] by Robert Hampton (1891-1944); *Hot House Rag* [33SX1158] by Paul Pratt; *Music Box Rag* [GOR] [VLP2] by 'Luckey' Roberts; *Calico Rag* [AR-1] [SDL210] by Nat Johnson; *Hysterics Rag* [LTZ-UI5072] by Paul Biese and F. Henri Klickman; *Steamboat Rag* by Ernie Burnett (1884–1959); *Castle House Rag* [GOR] by James Reese Europe; *Colonial Rag* by Ernest R. Ball and Julius Lenzberg; and *Smash-up Rag* [AR-2] by Gwendoline Stevenson. Irving Berlin's output included *He's A Rag Picker*; *Syncopated Walk* and his very successful song *Play A Simple Melody*; while Percy Wenrich published his great hit *When You Wore A Tulip*. Outstanding items of future importance were Lew Pollack's *That's A Plenty* [LAG12030] and the immortal *St Louis Blues* by W. C. Handy (1873–1958).

Hiram K. Moderwell fully recognised ragtime's significance and value when he wrote in 1915: 'You can't tell an American composer's "art-song" from any mediocre art-song the world over (with a few notable exceptions). You can distinguish American ragtime from the popular music of any nation and any age.' To back up his contention there was: *Evergreen Rag* [AL3523] by James Scott; *Cleopatra Rag* [FG3562] [HSU5010]; *The Ragtime Nightingale* [FG3562] [HSU5010]; *Reindeer Rag* [OU2035] [HSU5010] and *Contentment Rag* [FG3562] by Joseph Lamb; *Agitation Rag* by Robert Hampton; *Alabama Slide* by Charles L. Johnson; and *Ragging The Scale* by Edward B. Claypoole (1883–1952). But production of good rags was tending to fall off as other crazes took their place in the queue. The songs of the year in ragtime vein were *Oh! Mr Rubinstein* [ORS-2] by Philip Braham, Fred Thompson and Douglas Furber; *Loading Up The Mandy Lee* [ORS-2] by Henry I. Marshall and Stanley Murphy; and *Alabama Jubilee* [ORS-1] by George L. Cobb and Jack Yellen. An up-and-coming composer called Jerome Kern dabbled with the idiom in his own particular way in *How'd You Like To Spoon With Me*; but would be following other courses. Henry Marshall published his *Weary Blues*. Dr Karl Muck said: 'Ragtime is *poison*. It poisons the source of musical growth, for it poisons the taste of the young!'

1916 still had enough rags to show us that the vein was by no means extinct (ragtime was to linger on well into the 1920s) and had some quite notable titles: *Daintiness Rag* [RP] [AL3540] [SDL118] by James P. Johnson; *Honeymoon Rag* and *Prosperity Rag* by James Scott; *Top Liner Rag* [FG3562] [HSU5010] and *Patricia Rag* [FG3562] by Joseph Lamb; *Miss Samantha Johnson's Wedding Day* by Tony Jackson; Artie Matthews published *Pastime Rag No. 3* [CPR] [H-71299] which this time exploited a *Tea For Two/I Want To Be Happy* sort of show-type tune; both Will Held and Pete Wendling published works called *Chromatic Rag* [33CX10061-Held]; Maceo Pinkard and Irving Berlin both pleaded *Just Give Me Ragtime Please*; Joe Hollander *Two Key Rag* [SDL210]; Edward B. Claypoole *Spooky Spooks*; and Shelton Brooks went *Walkin' The Dog*. There was still a place for ragtime songs like *They Called It Dixieland* [ORS-2] by Richard A. Whiting and Raymond Egan; and *When Paderewski Plays* [ORS-2] by R. P. Weston, Bert Lee and the Two Bobs.

1917 was the year that jazz music offered its first real challenge and the first time that a newspaper, the *New York Times* of 2 February 1917, spelt it 'jazz'. And in March, the Original Dixieland Jazz Band made their first recording – repeating the old story – a white band being given the first opportunity to profit by a black music. In items of their repertoire like *Original Dixieland One-step*, credited to the ODJB and Joe Jordan, much of the ragtime element still remained. But it was significant that that fertile barometer of musical taste, Mr Irving Berlin, published no 'rag' title this year but neatly shifted his allegiance with a song called *Mr Jazz Himself*, while the following year he found the solution to the War with the title *Send A Lot Of Jazz Bands Over There*. James Scott still published his *Efficiency Rag* [H-71299] and *Paramount Rag*; but there was more of the future in James P. Johnson's striding *Harlem Strut* [AL3511]. Guy Hall and Henry Kleinkauf published *Johnson Rag* [AR-1]; Paul Pratt borrowed his *Springtime Rag* from Mendelssohn. There was at least one good raggy song in Shelton Brooks' *The Darktown Strutters' Ball* [ORS-1] (which could be played as an excellent bit of ragtime); but new names were beginning to dominate the scene, although one of them, George Gershwin, still hankered after the old days in his *Rialto Ripples* – and called it a piano rag solo. Erik Satie (1866-1925) had a success in France with his modern ballet 'Parade' which had a movement in it called *Ragtime de Paquebot*.

By **1918** the few examples began to look very much like survivors from another age, although Artie Matthews made his tango-style *Pastime Rag No. 5* [LAG12025] [H-71299] quite forward-looking; and James Scott wrote *Rag Sentimental* which was a new angle for a classic rag. The name that struck a new and formidable note (see jazz chapter) was that of Jelly Roll Morton who entered the battle with his *Frog-i-more Rag*. George L. Cobb (1886-1942) found unusual inspiration in Rachmaninov's C# minor prelude for his *Russian Rag* [AR-1]. Max Darewski wrote a piece called *Monkey Blues* [AR-3] which might not be significant; and the ODJB retained the flavour in that excellent composition by Larry Shields and Henry Ragas called *Clarinet Marmalade* and in *Reisenweber Rag* by Nick la Rocca (1889–1961). Almost too late the celebrated composer Igor Stravinsky (1882–1971) noticed what had been going on and wrote his *Ragtime For Eleven Instruments* and added the flavour to *L'Histoire du Soldat* – but so missed the feeling of ragtime that it made no significant contribution either to the dying idiom or modern music.

In **1919** James Scott made an almost defiant tribute to Joplin's *The Cascades* in his boldly titled *New Era Rag* [H-71299] which really did go back to the old style; while his *Troubadour Rag* [H-71299] went into the future by being delicate and stylish with a dotted note melody that brought a new feeling to ragtime without losing touch with the past. As did *Dixie Dimples*. *Sister Kate* by A. J. Piron, which was to become a great jazz standard, staunchly described itself as a cakewalk; while *Fidgety Feet* by Nick La Rocca and Larry Shields had something of the old feel about it. Songs like *Dardanella* by Fred Fisher and Clarence

Williams' *Baby, Won't You Please Come Home* were now as much influenced by the Handy flavour as the Joplin. Stravinsky had another stab at it in his pastiche *Piano Rag Music* which was uncomfortably self-conscious about the whole thing. Joseph Lamb's last published work for the moment was *Bohemia Rag*.

1920 finds us looking hard for survivors. We find them in Artie Matthews' *Pastime Rag No. 4* [CPR] [H-71299] (published after 5); and James Scott's *Pegasus* [H-71257] and *Modesty Rag* [H-71299]. 1921 was less favoured with *Keystone Rag* by Willy Anderson; *Pianola Concert Rag* by Otto Welcome; and a new novelty piece that started a craze for light-fingered frivolities called *Kitten On The Keys* by Zez Confrey (1895-1971). The Eubie Blake–Noble Sissle hit *I'm Just Wild About Harry* showed their upbringing in the ragtime school. 1922 had a relic called *Nitric Acid Rag* by Ed Hudson; J. Russell Robinson wrote his *Aggravatin' Papa*; Edward B. Claypoole *Dusting The Keys*; Felix Arndt had a tremendous success with *Nola* (which had a vague ragtime ancestry); and you could just catch the flavour in songs like Gershwin's *I'll Build A Stairway to Paradise*.

1923 was an important year, not for the perpetuation of classic ragtime but for its complete digestion into the stomach of jazz. Even the word 'rag' had now lost its clear meaning and was used simply as a gay piece of music that was patently not a blues. It was the year of emerging jazz : the New Orleans Rhythm Kings, King Oliver and the young Louis Armstrong, the domination of the new striding Harlem style in the piano world. The titles that we end with, taking us up to 1930, are a random selection of those which, with the dour determination of musical historians, we feel we can still link in spirit and style to Joplin and his contemporaries, that still have an ancestral link with ragtime. 1923 : *Old-fashioned Love* [LA8548] and the trend-setting *The Charleston* [AL3511] by James P. Johnson; *The Pearls* [JRM-1], *Grandpa's Spells* [JRM-2] [AL3534, AL3519] and *Kansas City Stomps* [JRM-1] [AL3534] by Jelly Roll Morton; *Wildcat Blues* by Fats Waller; *Bugle Call Rag* [PTR] by Pettis, Meyers and Schoebel; *High Society Rag* by Joe Oliver (arr. Lil Hardin); *Snake Rag* [AL3504] by Joe Oliver and Alphonse Picou; *Dusting The Keys* by Walker O'Neill

[AL Siegel on Herwin 402]; *That Futuristic Rag* by Rube Bloom (1902–); and *Weather Bird Rag* [AL3504] by Louis Armstrong. **1924**: *King Porter Stomp* [JRM-1] [AL3529, AL3559] and *Perfect Rag* [AL3534] by Jelly Roll Morton; *Bouncing On The Keys* by Edward J. Claypoole; *Nighty Night* by Axel W. Christensen; and it was the year of Gershwin's *Rhapsody in Blue* and that classic jazz song *Cake Walking Babies From Home* [ST499] by Clarence Williams which revived the cakewalk style in recordings by Alberta Hunter and Bessie Smith. **1925**: *Carolina Shout* [LA8548, AL3540] by James P. Johnson; and *Milneberg Joys* [JRM-2], *Shreveport Stomp* [JRM-1] [AL3534] and *Midnight Mama* [AL3519] by Jelly Roll Morton. 'What is ragtime? Ragtime is no longer mentioned,' wrote W. J. Henderson around this time. **1926**: *Keep Off The Grass* and *Jingles* [LRA10022] by James P. Johnson; *Black Bottom Stomp* [JRM-1] by Jelly Roll Morton; *Heebie Jeebies* by Boyd Atkins. **1927**: *St Louis Shuffle* by Fats Waller; and *West Coast Rag* [AL3539] by Will Ezell. **1928**: *Marigold* by Billy Mayerl [SH189]; *Yamecraw* by James P. Johnson; *Mixed Up Rag* by Will Ezell [AL3539];*Wildflower Rag* [AL3561] by Clarence Williams; and *South Bound Rag* [AL3560] by Blind Blake. **1929**: *Valentine Stomp* and *Ain't Misbehavin'* by Fats Waller; and *Atlanta Rag* [AL3537] by Cow Cow Davenport (1894-1955). **1930**: *You've Got To Be Modernistic* [LRA10022] and *Riffs* [LA8548] by James P. Johnson; and *Handful Of Keys* [RD-7915] by Fats Waller. Just a handful of titles; there were many more of course. And in Germany a show called 'Viktoria und ihr Husar' by Paul Abraham was still perpetuating the 'it's a bear' style to a growing continental audience.

Scott Joplin VI
Joplin's Music

Peacherine Rag

BY THE KING OF RAGTIME WRITERS

SCOTT JOPLIN

COMPOSER OF

MAPLE LEAF RAG SWIPSEY CAKE WALK

SUNFLOWER SLOW DRAG AUGUSTAN CLUB WALTZES

1 *Please Say You Will* – a song (w. Scott Joplin) (1895). Simple ballad in 3/4 time. The verse has more melodic and harmonic interest than the chorus which also suffers from somewhat trite and ill-constructed lyrics:

> 'Must I plead   must I kneel   and you not forgive
> Has your heart   love been sealed   do you love me still
> You have al-ways been true   now why not forgive
> I don't love none but you   please say you will –'
> (there is no punctuation)

Scott Joplin is credited as 'of the Texas Medley Quartette' and the song is obviously written with barber-shop type singing in mind. (p. M. L. Mantell) (CW:2; KR)

2 *A Picture Of Her Face* – a song (w. Scott Joplin) (1895). In similar vein to the above song, better constructed in some ways but over-long and rambling. In the same 'music-hall' style with harmonies later to appear in several rags, the chorus has echoes of the verse. The name Grace is brought in to rhyme with face. (p. Leiter Bros) (CW:2; KR)

3 *The Crush Collision March* (on cover – *Great Crush Collision* – march) (1896). Described by Blesh as a 'period piece of a special sort'. A brisk march with a good first section and adventurous harmonies. It was dedicated to M. K. and T. Ry. (Missouri, Kansas and Texas Railway) which runs through the town of Temple (where the piece was published) and crosses

another railway line at that point. It might be assumed that it portrays a train crash of recent occurrence. Blesh suggests that Joplin could have added the effects to an already written piece. The first three sections are march movements of not especially descriptive character. The fourth section represents an early attempt to put train sounds into music (chords over a quaver bass) 'train running at 60 m.p.h.'; (crushed notes) 'whistling for the crossing'; more train noise; 'whistle before crossing'; 'the collision' – ff chord of F 7th; return to normal march section. Although a typical march of the period it has intimations of ragtime in the opening octaves and in the melodic nature of the second and third themes which are not written in syncopated form but easily lend themselves to ragtime styling. (p. John R. Fuller, Temple, Tex.) (CW:1; KR; EPR)

4 *Combination March* (1896). Straightforward march with a modicum of distinction. Might be a lesser known Sousa and could well be put into brass or military band guise with a catchy enough tune to be remembered. The potential ragtime quality is there in the last strain. (p. Robert Smith, Temple, Tex.) (CW:1; KR; EPR)

5 *Harmony Club Waltz* (1896). Ingenious waltz of considerable charm, with chord changes from section to section which give it a sort of 'perpetuum mobile' effect, the rippling section in F leading neatly back to the initial Bb. Grant Hossack's pleasant orchestration of the middle sections in 'Prodigal Son' shows that it could become a useful addition to the light orchestral repertoire at any time. The chromatically descending arpeggios of the fourth to eighth bars of the second section, cleverly developed in the thirteenth to sixteenth bars, foreshadow a device that Joplin was often to use generally at the end of many ragtime sections, and appear as one of his first distinctive hallmarks. (p. Robert Smith, Temple, Tex.) (CW:1; KR)

6 *Original Rags* (picked by Scott Joplin; arranged by Chas. N. Daniels) (1899). The first Joplin rag to appear in print, accepted by the Kansas City publisher who turned down *Maple Leaf*, it is the first of several of what we might call Joplin's 'happy' or

'dance' rags, obviously written with cakewalking possibilities in mind. It has much of American hoedown fiddle music in its makeup. As in all the Joplin rags the original 2/4 time tempo should be maintained throughout. We can either say that it is unusual in having five themes or that Joplin evolved to a four-theme form in most of his later rags, probably finding it more to his liking. Its first theme is similar to later pieces like *The Ragtime Dance, Sunflower Slow Drag* and others that must be considered samples of Joplin exploiting the typical march tempo ragtime pieces that were probably most commonly used for dancing and general public entertainment. The initial section has a distinctive enough melody but is foremost an essay in ragtime syncopation with the fourth and fifth quavers of the bar characteristically tied. The second theme with its consecutive thirds, the first bar unaccompanied, is unique in Joplin compositions. The third is one of those simple melodic sections of considerable charm that were to appear in many future compositions. The fourth and fifth sections are ingenious and tricky to play but don't live up to the earlier parts of the work. It has been suggested that this is not an entirely original piece, that, in fact, Joplin may well have taken some of the traditional dance rag themes currently in use, merely selecting them and leaving the final arrangement to Chas. N. Daniels, a composer later to become better known under his pseudonym of Neil Moret and as the composer of *Hiawatha*, which became a great hit in 1901. The music is so typically Joplin, however, that one could doubt this; but we might follow the interesting hypothesis that in these themes Joplin discovered the strains that attracted him and modelled his own future style on them. Daniels may simply have helped or merely been the person who got the work published. The title in itself is interesting in having a sort of deprecatory or humorous allusion to the rag as a genre rather than stating it uncommittedly. The cover shows an old Negro literally picking up rags outside a tumbledown shack. It is a fascinating debut for a ragtime composer and it stands among Joplin's best works, a fact implied by Jelly Roll Morton's adaptation of it in his own distinctive style where it comes to life again, utterly changed but with comparable attraction. Morton's version is transcribed by Richard Thompson and printed in *The Art of Ragtime* side by side with the original Joplin/Daniels version. A metronome marking of around ♪176 is suggested as being about the right tempo for its performance and it is effective played lightly and crisply. (p. Carl Hoffman, Kansas City, Mo.) (CW:1; KR)

7 *Maple Leaf Rag* (1899). The history of *Maple Leaf Rag* is outlined elsewhere in this book. From the musical point of view it is a remarkable composition. We must assume that Joplin had written many unpublished rags and experimented with the form in the blank period between his early marches and waltzes and the appearance of *Original Rags* and this superb work in 1899. In general it exhibits a firm grasp of form, boasts an imperishable main melody, but paradoxically it is by no means a typical Joplin rag. In fact there is no other work of his really like it in character apart from the device of the ascending arpeggios which we find in *The Cascades* and one or two other rags and the fact that the second strain is in the 'dance' style that we have already encountered in *Original Rags*. Without questioning the fact that it has deservedly become Joplin's best-known and most performed work, it is still worth remarking that it is not necessarily among the best in his truly personal and lyrical vein. While unquestionably ragtime it nevertheless retains the true nature of a march and thus has characteristics that make it eminently suitable for jazz-styled performance (which is indeed how we have most often heard it e.g. New Orleans Rhythm Kings [AL3536]) and for straight performance by military band or orchestra. Unlike most of Joplin's pieces it is unharmed by a brisk, even fast performance which has the effect of giving the very mobile and melodic left-hand figure a cohesive life of its own which greatly enhances the contrapuntal nature of the piece. Joplin's own piano-roll performance is very fast and most performers come near to ♪208 rate of knots which still leaves it open-textured and clean-limbed. Taken slower it tends to fall to pieces and

most tardy performances seem cumbersome. The first strain is a miracle of perfection, an inspirational phenomenon, harmonically sophisticated yet completely uncontrived. The third strain has a pounding, unsubtle excitement that Joplin rarely equalled and one can understand how it delighted all who came across it for the first time. Perhaps the total measure of *Maple Leaf Rag*'s power is that it became so popular in spite of being, like most Joplin rags (a fact which has even limited their appeal), extremely difficult to play. Blesh neatly sums it up as being 'alive with announcement and expectation'. (p. John Stark & Son, St Louis) (CW:1; KR; BSJ; PR:1; EPR)

8 *Swipesey* – a cakewalk (with Arthur Marshall) (1900). If the *Swipesey* collaboration with Arthur Marshall seems pale after the glories of *Maple Leaf* it still has an endearing character with four strains of simple, folky tunefulness; an unambitious work as one might expect of a collaboration, but eminently danceable and jazzable. The third section is particularly attractive with a Sousa-like quality about it, a classical descending, imitative melody of mathematical structure. This is the first true *slow* rag; specifically named as a 'cakewalk' it confirms the variations of speed in this dance, obviously being intended for some kind of slow strut in contrast to the flashier quick tempo dances. It needs to go no faster than ♩132 and is still effective as slowly as ♩120. (p. John Stark & Son, St Louis) (CW:1; KR; BSJ; GTR)

9 *Peacherine Rag* (1901). That *Maple Leaf* had the effect of truly establishing Joplin was held without reservation by his friend and publisher John Stark who hailed him on the cover of *Peacherine Rag* as 'The King of Ragtime Writers'. *Peacherine*, apart from its very pleasant and memorable first strain, is not a particularly notable rag. Its opening (those four bars that seemed to be a particular challenge to the ragtime composers' ingenuity) is not inspired and the second strain indicates one of Joplin's repeated failings in trying to make something memorable of three or four on-the-beat block chords – although he did pull it off once or twice elsewhere. The third strain is an unsuccessful echo of *Maple Leaf*. Marked 'not too fast' it seems

to settle nicely at a tempo of about ♪144. (p. John Stark & Son, St Louis) (CW:1; KR; BSJ)

10 *Sunflower Slow Drag* – a ragtime two-step (with Scott Hayden) (1901). If there is some excuse for confusing *Sunflower Slow Drag* with *Swipesey* as both exploit the same initial kind of melody, a slow version of the cakewalk style of ragtime, *Sunflower* turns out to be the more inspired collaboration. Stark has told us that Joplin worked on it 'during the high temperature of courtship . . . while he was touching the ground only in the highest places, his geese were all swans, and the Mississippi water tasted like honey-dew . . . a song without words' – a highly poetical and evocative appraisal. But well justified. As Blesh has said : it is 'among the early gems of ragtime'. It builds from a memorable introductory four bars, through a conventional but memorable ragtime dance measure to a delightful second section which manages, as Stark suggests, to call for words, to introduce the exciting stomp element of *Maple Leaf*'s third strain and to handle a block chord successfully by simply repeating the same three inversions of F7. After a four bar modulation, the third strain turns out to be one of the most ingenious and delightful that Joplin ever wrote, with quietly controlled octave crochet left hand and the inspired use of a natural A in the B♭7 harmonies. Even the fourth strain, often the weak one in a Joplin composition, has a nice floating, cheerful air about it. We don't know how much credit Scott Hayden should be given but it is an unusually distinctive case of collaborative rapport. Speed about ♪ 144. (p. John Stark & Son, St Louis) (CW:1; KR; BSJ)

11 *The Augustan Club Waltzes* (1901). A truly delightful little piece in 3/4 time that has all the grace and lightness of a thoroughly efficient piece of Palm Courtery and, although it makes no claim to being a ragtime waltz, it has a certain degree of typical Joplinesque ragtime charm, particularly in the second strain which has a hint of *The Entertainer* delicacy about it. While ragtime stands as a completely successful piano music, it is no way to judge a waltz and this piece calls for orchestral clothing of the right period flavour to bring it life.

Grant Hossack, in his arrangement for 'Prodigal Son' has done just this and should have set it firmly in the light repertoire. (p. John Stark & Son, St Louis) (CW : 1; KR)

12 *The Easy Winners* – a ragtime two-step (1901). For reasons unknown, Stark did not publish this piece and Joplin had to be his own publisher. Perhaps his puritanical nature could not support a piece that was written in vindication of sport, including horse-racing. This is all in the cover; the music is simply an easy on the ear, melodious rag in Joplin's most flowing vein. It introduces a favourite and most effective flattening of the B♭ and the E♭ in the second and third bars of the first strain and a forward-looking (for its time) bit of 'naturalisation' at the end of the second. It floats along ideally at an easy-paced tempo of about ♪ 144. (p. Scott Joplin, St Louis) (CW:1; KR; BSJ; EPR; GTR)

13 *I Am Thinking Of My Pickaninny Days* – a song (w. Henry Jackson) (1902). A song such as might be found in the repertoire of any 'black-face' minstrel show in America or England, soulfully harmonised by a barber-shop type quartet. Obviously there was still a demand for such material to make the 'King of Ragtime Composers' feel it was worth while deserting his true metier for a time. Very much Uncle Tom sort of material in Stephen Foster vein, now somewhat objectionable. (p. Thiebes-Stierlin Music Co., St Louis) (CW:2; KR)

14 *Cleopha* – a march and two-step (1902). A fairly ordinary march with just enough spirit in it to allow it to survive. It might seem that Joplin was suppressing his natural instincts to write in white vein or was using up unwanted ragtime material in straight style. It almost seems that, in spite of himself, the last strain very nearly became a bit of ragtime. It became part of the Sousa band repertoire so it at least had the merit of carrying Joplin's name around the country and into white America. (p. S. Simon, St Louis) (CW:1; KR; EPR)

15 *A Breeze From Alabama* – a ragtime two-step (1902). It might be that Joplin, having got into the Sousa repertoire with *Cleopha*, thought that he might as well have another try with something that bore the official stamp of ragtime. Essentially

another march two-step with definite march characteristics, and dedicated to 'P. G. Lowery, World's Challenging Colored Cornetist and Band Master', it is also an attempted piece of ragtime in *Original Rags* strutting vein. But, alas, the compromise did not quite work and, although the first strain has possibilities, the rest turns out to be fairly weak with legitimate musical ideas that don't quite catch fire. It seems to trot along best at about ♪ 152. (p. John Stark & Son, St Louis) (CW: 1; KR; BSJ; EPR)

16 *Elite Syncopations* (1902). After several half-hearted works *Elite Syncopations* comes as a sturdy, honest-to-goodness kind of rag that holds a promise of good things to come. After a no-nonsense introduction it has a new kind of first strain that is faintly related to *Maple Leaf* but also looks forward to a good many ragtime songs that were to populate Tin Pan Alley. The second strain is one of Joplin's delightful simple piccolo tunes that lends itself nicely to baroque-style ornamentation and an infinite variety of approaches. It is only modestly syncopated but entirely memorable. The two final strains are pleasant and competent without being inspired the last also having a hint of *Maple Leaf*'s second strain about it. This particular rag might be pointed out as an ideal starting point for aspiring pianists in the ragtime idiom; much less finger stretching than *The Entertainer*; a sort of ragtime primer and probably the easiest to play. Like most, it is marked 'not fast' and falls easily into the ♪ 144 tempo that many mid-period Joplin rags hover around, but it can be much faster. (p. John Stark & Son, St Louis) (CW:1; KR; BSJ; PR:2; GTR)

17 *The Entertainer* – a ragtime two-step (1902). This alluring composition has been one of the reasons for the upsurge of interest in Joplin and this came about partly because we heard it played at a slow and balanced tempo by Joshua Rifkin, and partly because it has responded so well to period orchestral treatment. It is in a completely happy vein, restful, honest, folky but also beautifully constructed and entirely melodious. The simple variant of the typical ragtime opening augers well and leaves us on tiptoe. The first strain is leisurely and the

32 Scott Joplin about 1911

Classical composers influenced by ragtime and jazz

33 and 34 *Above:* Darius Milhaud (1892-1974) *Left:* Erik Satie (1866-1925)

35 and 36 *Above right:* Claude Debussy
(1862-1918) *Below right:* Igor Stravinsky
(1882-1971)

37 Scott Joplin's piano

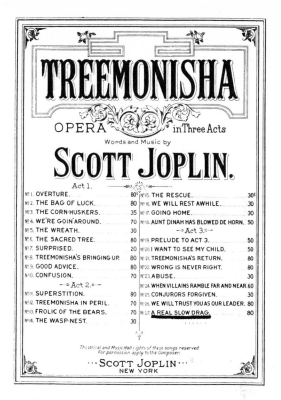

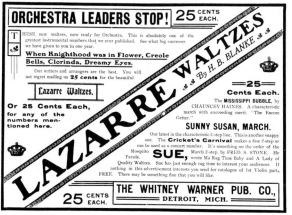

38 and 39 *Top:* The contents list of the sheet music to *Treemonisha*
Above: An advert for sheet music, from *Metronome* 1902

40 *Above:* An advert explaining how to use the new pianola, from *The Graphic* 1903

41 and 42 The new inventions which brought music into the home *Above left:* The piano-roll c. 1910 *Right:* The phonograph

VISITORS TO THE PARIS EXHIBITION LISTENING TO THE PHONOGRAPH.

This grasping, hurrying, money-getting, money-spending, money-boasting, mechanically inventive, successfully scientific, semi-philosophical, sham-religious, sensationally curious, and in- locomotion on land and water; it outdoes the steam-engine, works for us, writes for us, turns night into day, and tells us all manner of secret terrestrial processes, as well as the news of all the civilised world. It is as ready as ever to play with us; and so is that other modern scientific invention, the telephone the combined result of advanced acoustics and

43 and 44 *Top:* Visitors to the Paris Exhibition listening to the phonograph, 1889 *Above:* Listening to the gramophone at home, 1908

WHAT WILL YOU DO

IN THE

LONG, COLD, DARK, SHIVERY EVENINGS,

WHEN YOUR HEALTH AND CONVENIENCE COMPEL YOU TO STAY

INDOORS ?

WHY !!! HAVE A PHONOGRAPH, OF COURSE.

It is the FINEST ENTERTAINER in the WORLD.

There is nothing equal to it in the whole Realm
of Art.
It imitates any and every Musical Instrument,
any and every natural sound, faithfully:

the **HUMAN VOICE**, the **NOISE OF THE
CATARACT** the **BOOM OF THE GUN**,
the **VOICES OF BIRDS OR ANIMALS.**

From

£2 2s.

THE GREATEST MIMIC.

A Valuable Teacher of Acoustics. Most Interesting to Old or Young A Pleasure
and Charm to the Suffering, bringing to them the Brightness and Amusements of
the outside World by its faithful reproductions of Operas, New Songs, Speeches, &c.

EVERY HOME WILL sooner or later have its **PHONOGRAPH** as a **NECESSITY.**

HAVE YOURS NOW ; you will enjoy it longer.

famous French actor, writes:

TRANSLATION OF THE LETTER

" Your wonderful Gramophone has at last given me what I have so much desired : the surprise and
(shall I confess it?) the pleasure of hearing myself! I have heard the recitation ' Des Limaçons, which
I recite in the rôle of M. de la Motte, in the ' Mercure Galant ' of Boursault, and my word . . . . I did
what I have seen the public do for a long time, I laughed. Thank you for having made me amuse
myself—that does not often happen to me—and I congratulate you on your Gramophone, which must
render great services to everybody.

GENTLEMEN,—

" I have much pleasure in stating that I have heard your Monarch Gramophone, and that I consider
it a very remarkable instrument of its kind, and quite the most perfect that I have ever heard. It reproduces
the human voice to such a fine point, that in listening to the records of Caruso, Plançon, &c., it seemed to me
as if those artists were actually singing in my saloons. I have never heard anything to equal it.

45 An advert for an early phonograph

octave chords with an added interior third, although not easy to play, probably have the intended effect of imitating mandolin chording – the piece was dedicated to James Brown and his Mandolin Club. The second strain is one of the most delightful things that Joplin ever wrote, the two bars of syncopated chords beautifully balanced against two bars of flowing melody in his most inspired way. The third more sturdy vein halves the timing of the juxtaposition, moving into forthright F. The last strain has a quiet melancholy about it, hovering in the minor though ending in the major and makes a fine interlude before a return to the early strains – which is not indicated but surely makes good performing sense. A wholly successful composition that is a classic by any standards and might be compared, not too fancifully, to something by Mozart with its superficial gaiety effectively underlined by a hint of melancholy. It responds well to a slow tempo of around ♪ 108 but can be taken, in some moods, up to ♪ 120 and still be effective. (p. John Stark & Son, St Louis) (CW:1; KR; BSJ; PR:1; EPR; S)

18 *The Strenuous Life* – a ragtime two-step (1902). An unpretentious and not particularly significant or effective rag. Joplin's inspiration seems to have flagged a little in this one. There are nice touches in the third strain but it never manages to really get off the ground. (p. John Stark & Son, St Louis) (CW:1; KR; EPR)

19 *The Ragtime Dance* – a song (w. Scott Joplin) (1902). With experience in not only ragtime, but marches, waltzes and a fair amount of vocal music, Joplin was beginning to have ambitions to write something on a larger scale, certainly an opera was hovering very insistently in his mind. His ambition for ragtime was boundless. In this he and John Stark did not see eye to eye. Much as Stark admired Joplin and ragtime he wanted it to stay an unpretentious popular music of solid worth, particularly if it sold in the manner of *Maple Leaf Rag*. Joplin's first venture into an extended song and dance form was *The Ragtime Dance*. He conceived it as a kind of folk ballet with a singer providing the narrative and various popu-

lar dances of the day the choreographic part. The words by Joplin himself showed his old addiction to Uncle Tom corn with lines that nowadays might be taken as rather offensive like 'So many colored folk there without a razor fight twas a great surprise to me' – but it was mainly an exhortation to dance to some marvellous strains in Joplin's best vein. His own faith in the idea was demonstrated when he himself financed a performance at Wood's Opera House in Sedalia, just after he had lined his pockets reasonably well with *Maple Leaf* money. John Stark had not the same faith and the piece was something of a bone of contention between them. It was an expensive piece to print, covering nine pages of music, and Stark long resisted. Eventually he gave in, persuaded by his daughter Nell, and published it and, as he had predicted, sold very few copies. This was the beginning of a rift between composer and publisher, Joplin still convinced that ragtime must be developed and expanded. The more "coonish" elements were abandoned when the piece was republished as a straightforward rag (see below) (p. John Stark & Son, St Louis) (CW:2; KR)

20 *March Majestic* – a march and two-step (1902). With this work Joplin comes to maturity as a march composer. It ought to be part of the standard repertoire of all military bands. The final strain in A minor (before an obvious return to the beginning) is one of those things where the bass department have a good time, here done with considerable ingenuity. Again we are indebted to 'Prodigal Son' for showing us how it can sound. (p. John Stark & Son, St Louis) (CW:1; KR)

21 *A Guest Of Honor* – a ragtime opera (1903) (see history, chapter 'Scott Joplin IV'). Score lost so we cannot comment. Reports suggest that it had some 'beautiful raggy music' in it and it is highly likely that Joplin may have utilised some of it for later rag material.

22 *Something Doing* – a cakewalk march (1903). A pleasant but quite restrained rag that might be said to contain nothing that Joplin had not attempted before. A flowing melodic line with a memorable first strain, matched by an equally flowing and attractive second, after that fairly conventional. But it has an

undemanding charm about it and tickled the ears of Peter Clayton in '14 Miles on a Clear Night' leading him to a highly fanciful account of ragtime's origins. Texturally suited to a steady ♪ 144. (p. A. Reis Music Co., St Louis) (CW:1; KR; PTR; BSJ)

23 *Weeping Willow* – a ragtime two-step (1903). This has the same restrained folky atmosphere about it as *The Entertainer* and its first strain is amongst Joplin's most endearing efforts. Like *The Entertainer* it benefits from a slow, delicate approach and need not be played faster than ♪ 132. (p. A. Reis Music Co., St Louis) (CW:1; KR; BSJ)

24 *Little Black Baby* – a song (w. Louise Armstrong Bristol) (1903). A song totally without distinction except for its general awfulness. Joplin seems to have acknowledged complete lack of inspiration in the trite melody he wrote to accompany such sick-making lyrics as 'What says dis little black baby to little black mammy by its side? Goo-goo-goo-e, goo-garee-goo; Tra-ta-la-ra-ba-ma-oo, Tra-ta-la-raess scaree-ee; Gree goo ta-ma-la-ra-mee.' It would be difficult to imagine anyone, except perhaps G. H. Clutsam, who would be inspired by that. Stephen Foster, at his most awful, rarely managed worse. Even the cover designer ended up with a picture of a little white baby in an effort to forget the title. (p. Success Music Company, Chicago) (CW:2; KR)

25 *Palm Leaf Rag* – a slow drag (1903). With its melancholy first subject alternating tantalisingly between B♭ and G minor, its categorisation as a 'slow drag' and Joplin's instructions to 'play a little slow', this one would seem to call for about ♪ 124, allowing for subtle emphasis in the melodic line. An element of poetry is gradually creeping into the Joplin rags at this stage and we might even hazard a guess that this could have had vocal origins possibly intended for or taken from *A Guest Of Honor*. It has a splendidly contrasted and individual melody in E♭ for its third strain and it is good to find the highpoint coming at this juncture. (p. Victor Kremer Co., Chicago; outlet Chas. Sheard & Co., London – but not traced whether

any of these works did actually get put out in England) (CW: 1; KR)

26 *The Favorite* – a ragtime two-step (1904). A growing refinement in Joplin's rags is absent from this item which dates back to earlier Sedalia days, having been bought by the publisher in 1900 but not published for four years. The same publisher turned down *Maple Leaf Rag*. It is not particularly distinguished and with its triplets in the first measure (which don't really suit ragtime) has more of a march character. It is marked 'slow march tempo' and seems right at about ♪ 126. (p. A. W. Perry & Sons, Sedalia) (CW:1; KR; BSJ)

27 *The Sycamore* – a concert rag (1904). The sub-title 'a concert rag' suggests Joplin's increasingly ambitious view of ragtime and its potential acceptance in polite circles. *The Sycamore* is notable for its interesting harmonies in the second section and apt choice of bass notes. It is a short piece that has something of the air of a ragtime étude about it. A brisk march tempo of about ♪ 160. (p. Will Rossiter, New York & Chicago) (CW: 1; KR; BSJ; EPR; GTR)

28 *The Cascades* – a rag (1904). With supreme confidence this rag is described on the cover as 'The Masterpiece of Scott Joplin'. Its publication was back in the hands of John Stark who had great acumen in these matters. Certainly it has the right to be considered *one* of his greatest masterpieces – if not *the*. It stands halfway in Joplin's really active career and while having some of the characteristics of *Maple Leaf*, e.g. the ascending arpeggio phrase near the beginning and a fourth theme that has some harmonic affinities, it breaks new ground in the third strain which has a demanding bass part in octaves that calls for some good brassy orchestration. The fourth section has a very happy theme but it is the second that is the real peak and which inevitably sets this piece swinging along. Its 'cascades' of notes on the G7 chord and the inner movement of the following C chords are not particularly complex but certainly one of Joplin's happiest inspirations. The rag has a programmatic connection with the Cascade Gardens that were a notable feature of the St Louis State Fair in 1904, a scenic

layout of waterfalls, fountains and lakes. It is altogether a scintillating piece that engenders a considerable swing that we have not connected with ragtime so far. It can be played, and often is, as a very fast piece, but the third strain then often proves a stumbling block, especially when orchestrated. It is most effective in a romping quick march tempo of around ♪ 168 (as played in the 'Prodigal Son' recording) and with considerable bounce. Blesh suggests that the piece asks for a gradual acceleration and, though this is contrary to classic ragtime practice, it does tend to happen without damaging effect. This work is one of the peaks of classic ragtime, a point from which its later developers could take off and it has remained a firm favourite with most ragtime pianists. Without to some extent adulterating the flavour of pure ragtime, the music could not go to greater heights than this. (p. John Stark & Son, St Louis) (CW:1; KR; BSJ)

29 *The Chrysanthemum* – an Afro-intermezzo (1904). 'Afro' simply meant Negro as used here; in fact, there is something of the Gottschalk-exploited Creole element in this charming work. Taken at an easy ♪ 120 the flowing opening section is light and gay. The intermezzo connotation becomes justified in the third section marked *dolce* which is yet another of Joplin's happy and completely individual inventions. A C minor interlude which seems to be leading somewhere, leads, unusually, to a repeat of the *dolce* third section after which the piece is firmly marked END with a firm final chord. One is not expected or allowed to return to the earlier strains. This firm rounding off of the piece is, oddly enough, something we have hardly met before in Joplin, at least in the rags, and shows his increasing awareness of form and sequential rightness. (p. John Stark & Son, St Louis) (CW:1; KR; BSJ; EPR)

30 *Maple Leaf Rag* – a song (w. Sydney Brown) (1904). It was possibly Stark's idea to cash in on the success of *Maple Leaf* by turning it into a song. The catchy melody, missing so far in Joplin's vocal efforts, was there ready made. Instead of sentimental Victorianism, good ragtime melodies inspired a professional lyric-writer to such Ogden Nashisms as 'I dropped into

the swellest ball, the great exclusive IT, but my face was dead agin me and my trousers didn't fit.' Words and music are well suited and the final chorus (which is based on the first strain of the rag) is dashingly exultant. Of course we are entitled to prefer *Maple Leaf* as a rag (a dance is appended to the song) but it also makes a good ragtime song; one which probably inspired Tin Pan Alley to some of its imitative efforts. (p. John Stark & Son, St Louis) (CW:2; KR; DNO3)

31 *Bethena* – a concert waltz (1905). The interest here is not only in music that has melodic character and charm but in what was perhaps the first true waltz written in the ragtime idiom. The syncopations of ragtime used in 3/4 time give a fascinating hesitant effect to the music. The first strain is repeated twice and used in brief for the finale, thus giving the work a rondo-like unity. The fourth strain in F has the most marked ragtime qualities. The weak part of the work is in the long and laboured modulations which at times actually seem to wander away from the key they are trying to get to, to make a desperate plunge at the end. It would have been better to make the change in one or two bars, in the Schubert style. The length and indecision of the third transitional passage in particular holds up the natural flow of the piece without adding anything of real interest or pleasure. In spite of this, *Bethena* is an enchanting and haunting work and one of the most unusual waltzes to have been written. (p. T. Bahnsen Piano Manufacturing Company, St Louis) (CW:1; KR; PR:2)

32 *Sarah Dear* – a song (Henry Jackson). Joplin follows the success of the *Maple Leaf Rag* song with another moderate success in the ragtime idiom, *Sarah Dear* having a genuine minstrel character about it. The chorus is by no means a Joplin original. It is the same tune as used in the concurrent Barney/Seymour rag *St Louis Tickle* and both they and Joplin had lifted it from riverboat history where it had seen long use as a rowdy drinking song. It had previously been adapted for Ben Harney's *Cakewalk In The Sky* published by Witmark in 1899. Its old folksong lyrics: 'Thought I heard Judge Pequette say – 45 dollars – take him away' immediately bring to mind the

Jelly Roll Morton version which he called *Buddy Bolden's Blues* – 'I thought I heard Buddy Bolden say – you're nasty, you're dirty – take it away.' It did good service in the jazz world and as the theme song of the pioneer New Orleans trumpeter Buddy Bolden. Joplin provides subtle differences in the chorus and adds an original verse and makes it into a sturdy little song in politer vein. (p. Bahnsen Music Co., St Louis) (CW:2; KR)

33 *Binks' Waltz* (1905). This has none of the ragtime flavour of *Bethena* and attempts to be little more than a waltz in polite Victorian vein, its cover suggesting that it was either intended for or to be about children. Its melodies have a nice Joplinesque flavour with one or two interesting little twists. (p. Bahnsen Music Co., St Louis) (CW:2; KR)

34 *Rosebud* – a two-step (*The Rose-bud March*) (1905). 'Respectfully dedicated to my friend Tom Turpin' it takes its title, of course, from the famous Rosebud saloon, ragtime's St Louis home. Why it should turn out to be a high-spirited march in 6/8 in that case is something of a mystery. Something sturdy in the ragtime idiom might have seemed more appropriate to Turpin. What we have is very much a gay dance in the typical two-step pattern of the period that must have found a welcome in many a dance-hall and ballroom. Once again we must point to the perfect and apt orchestral dressing that such a lesser-known Joplin piece found in 'Prodigal Son' with the frivolous melody finally handed for comic relief to the horn. It might have come from the pen of many dance writers of the period but it has Joplinesque distinction. (p. John Stark & Son, St Louis) (CW:1; KR)

35 *Leola* – a two-step (1905). This has the distinction of being the first Joplin piece to bear the full health warning: 'Notice! Don't play this piece fast. It is never right to play "rag-time" fast. Author'; and it has no introductory bars but plunges straight into its first 'slow march tempo' theme. It also had the distinction of being 'entered at Stationer's Hall, London, England', the old way of establishing British copyright, but no British publication has been recorded. It is a strange piece with

the unsatisfactory quality of suggesting that Joplin, in his quest for ragtime progress, was stifling some of his natural vivacity in favour of the more conventional strains of the parlour and concert hall. It is dedicated to Miss Minnie Wade. It was not a piece that found much popularity and was not rediscovered and restored until the 1950s. It takes an easy tempo of around ♪ 120 which allows its sweet Spanish flavour to come to the fore. (p. American Music Syndicate, St Louis) (CW:1; KR; PR:2)

36 *Eugenia* (1905–6). We will find a tendency from now on for Joplin rags to stiffen up a little, moving closer to academic music, with less of the early joyful freedom about them and a more self-conscious use of 'clever' harmonies. Some critics hail this as a growing-up, but there are always two sides to this question of naturalness versus artifice. Most of the really popular Joplin rags have now been published, which is not to say that there are not still many masterpieces to come and several that manage to recapture the old carefree gaiety. Early in 1906 Joplin and his wife parted and this may well have had some effect on his creative outlook. *Eugenia* bears the legend 'published for band and orchestra' and this new requirement, as ragtime became more readily available in these forms, may also have laid a hand of responsibility on the composer. *Eugenia* is an involved piece of writing that seems to be going through the motions of ragtime without ever discovering real inspiration – it could have been written under considerable strain. It needs to flow at a slow march tempo of about ♪ 120. (p. Will Rossiter, Chicago) (CW:1; KR; BSJ; PR:2; EPR; GTR)

37 *Antoinette* – a march and two-step (1906). A conventional 6/8 march which might have been written some years earlier according to some authorities. It provides a demanding bass part and, in its third strain, goes into quite ambitious harmonic country. There is barely a hint of ragtime in it. (p. Stark Music Printing & Publishing Co., New York & St Louis) (CW:1; KR)

38 *The Ragtime Dance* (*Ragtime Dance* – a stop-time two-step) (1906). We can be glad that John Stark renewed his faith in Joplin and in this contentious song to re-publish it in pure rag-

time form (even if only to recoup his losses) for it, not un-
naturally, harks back to the old Sedalia ragtime dance vein,
using the second dance section of the song now as its first
strain and tidying up the final stop-time section into something
that makes a riotous piano showpiece in any circumstances.
As the instructions say: 'To get the desired effect of "Stop
Time" the pianist will please *Stamp* the heel of one foot heavily upon the floor at the word "Stamp". Do not raise the toe
from the floor while stamping.' Explicit instructions. The
effect as the stop chords and figures move back into a genuine
driving stomp at the end is ever exhilarating. 'Not too fast'
but it will hold the road safely at anything up to ♪ 160. (p.
John Stark & Son, St Louis) (CW:1; KR; BSJ; PR:1; EPR; S)

39 *Searchlight Rag* – a syncopated march and two-step (1907).
Yet again Joplin pays tribute to his old friend Tom Turpin with
a reflected memory of the goldmining days of Turpin and his
brother Charlie in the town of Searchlight, Nevada, way back
in 1881. It is a good striding piece with Turpinesque rolling
bass that anticipates the developing barrel-house style. The
fourth theme brings in a bit of dissonant humour. ♪ 144 (p.
Joseph W. Stern, New York)

40 *When Your Hair Is Like The Snow* – a song (w. Owen Spendthrift) (1907). Maudlin in sentiment – 'Will your children then
desert you when your hair is like the snow' – and utterly undistinguished melodically or harmonically, it represents one
of the depths that Joplin plunged to in his last decade of composing. (p. Owen Spendthrift, St Louis) (CW:2)

41 *Gladiolus Rag* (1907). A welcome return to ragtime inspiration,
Gladiolus has some of the *Maple Leaf* characteristics, the
ascending arpeggios and the second strain notably, but now
translated into poetical 'slow march tempo' terms, with a delicate and unforgettable first strain and subtle harmonies
throughout. Like *Maple Leaf* it also employs the more difficult
keys of A♭ and D♭ with good effect. This represents Joplin's
successful maturity, the whole piece having a logical sequence
of themes, genuine development and a sense of wholeness.
 ♪ 120 (p. Joseph W. Stern, New York) (CW:1; GOR; PR:1; S)

42 *Lily Queen* – a ragtime two-step (w. Arthur Marshall) (1907). As if to confirm a new found faith and touch in ragtime, Joplin moves into several successful collaborations again – notably *Heliotrope Bouquet* below. With, the cover suggests, a Gibson girl inspiration behind it, *Lily Queen* moves gracefully and charmingly throughout its comparatively simple strains; the first (perhaps the responsibility of Marshall but certainly inspired by Joplin) ingratiatingly melodic; the second flowing; the third with some interesting harmonic contrivances and anticipating *Heliotrope Bouquet*. It is intended to end with its final strain. ♪ 136. (p. Willis Woodward Stuart, New York) (CW:1)

43 *Rose Leaf Rag* (1907). A further development of Joplin's classic rag style, delicate and assured without actually achieving his utmost memorability. The second strain has a touch of originality about it. (p. Joseph Daly, Boston) (PR:2)

44 *Heliotrope Bouquet* – a slow drag two-step (w. Louis Chauvin) (1907). This has been described as one of the masterpieces of ragtime and was a meaningful and memorable collaboration. Louis Chauvin was a dissipated young composer and pianist, a Creole, who was to die at twenty-four through the combined effects of syphilis and opium. Joplin visited him and found him toying with two fine potential ragtime themes. These, harmonised by Joplin with his usual skill, are the first two in the work; to which Joplin added two ideally matching third and fourth strains, described by William Bolcom as 'an affectionate postscript'. The sensuous qualities that Chauvin contributed make this a unique work in the Joplin catalogue. A tempo of around ♪ 138 suits it very well. But Bolcom demonstrates its effectiveness at the much slower pace of about ♪ 112 adding considerable rubato. (p. Stark Music Printing & Publishing Co., New York & St Louis) (CW:1; EPR; GTR)

45 *Nonpareil* (None to equal) (*The Nonpareil* – a rag and two-step) (1907). A gentle piece in an earlier simple vein that may well have been written previously and rested in the Stark pigeon-holes. It has no special melodic distinction but a use of a running quaver bass in parts of the second strain is distinc-

tive and effective. A slow march tempo of around ♪ 120 seems to be indicated. (p. Stark Music Printing & Publishing Co., New York & St Louis) (CW : 1)

46 *School of Ragtime* (1908). A ragtime instruction manual of modest dimensions. It had been preceded by Ben Harney's *Rag Time Instructor* in 1897 and many publications of schools that ambitiously tried to initiate amateurs into the intricacies of ragtime. Joplin's comments on ragtime are the most interesting part of the publication. He certainly makes no bones about ragtime's difficulties and refers to its 'high-class' qualities. The manual offers six exercises, including one with a suggestion of habanera rhythm about it, all of which increase the difficulties of playing ragtime, with a non-syncopated line above the syncopated to offer comparison (but not to be played) and figures which offer no distinctive melodic enticement. It would have been better perhaps to offer simple strains from earlier rags – which would have served a dual purpose of familiarising as well as teaching. The purpose of the publication is curiously summed up as being 'to assist players in giving the "Joplin Rags" that weird and intoxicating effect intended by the composer'. Which gives a curious insight into Joplin's thoughts on ragtime as a genre. (p. Scott Joplin, New York) (CW:1)

47 *Fig Leaf Rag* – a high-class rag (1908). Following two themes in early dance vein, the trio is an ambitious heavily chorded passage and the final section has a choral quality that foreshadows *Treemonisha*. This and the ensuing rags all indicate constant experimentation on Joplin's part, sometimes successful but mostly moving him somewhat uneasily from home base. c. ♪ 144. Curious obsession with being high-class already noted in the above primer, continues in the sub-title of this work. (p. John Stark Music Printing & Publishing Co., New York & St Louis) (PR:1)

48 *Sugar Cane* – a ragtime classic two-step (1908). Joplin's liking for vegetable and fruity titles continues with this likewise experimental rag which has a first flowing quaver theme evolving into dance syncopation. You can find echoes of half-

a-dozen earlier rags in this piece – *Maple Leaf* and *Original Rags* immediately come to mind – but it has sufficient melodic originality to stand on its own as a sturdy and likeable composition. It orchestrates well. Also a middle-course tempo piece of around ♪ 144. Actually the first Joplin piece to have tempo marking = ♩ 100 being suggested. (p. Seminary Music Co., New York) (CW:1; PTR)

49 *Pine-apple Rag* (1908). The third theme of this rag has the vocal quality that probably suggested its future use as a song (see below); otherwise a strange choice. It is not particularly distinctive except for a joyful and very ragged second theme but is well enough constructed and substantial. Again the ♩ 100 is indicated but this seems absurdly fast in view of the 'slow march tempo' instruction and ♪ 168 seems fast enough. (p. Seminary Music Co., New York) (CW:1; PTR; PR:2; S)

50 *Wall Street Rag* (1909). By this time Joplin was in New York, and remarried, his head full of plans for *Treemonisha* and other ambitious outlets for ragtime. *Wall Street Rag* is formally a typical rag of four strains with the difference that Joplin has openly declared his programmatic ideas by adding descriptive headings to each of the movements: 1. Panic in Wall Street, Brokers feeling melancholy; 2. Good times coming; 3. Good times have come; 4. Listening to the strains of genuine negro ragtime, Brokers forget their cares. It would be idle to claim that Joplin was in a position to enter the soul of a Wall Street broker (which might be hard to find anyway) or to speculate what the more catastrophic Wall Street crash of the 1930s might have produced musically if he had still been around. What his programmatic pre-occupations do produce however are some strains of quite remarkable individuality that start to wander beyond the bounds of strictly classical ragtime. The initial 'melancholy' strain has a really emotional quality about it and, with its first four bars utilising a habanera bass and delicate harmonies, it sets Joplin on a rich strain that he was to exploit more fully in his next work. The third section 'Good times have come' has a distinctly vaudeville air about it and suggests the theatrical potential of Joplin's future work; while

the final section with its block chords on the second and sixth quavers of the bar, right in between the beats, is a new trick. Marked to be played in 'very slow march time', William Bolcom's fine performance of it on his 'Heliotrope Bouquet' disc at around ♪120 seems just about right. (p. Seminary Music Co., New York) (CW:1)

51 *Solace* – a Mexican serenade (1909). Employing a slow habanera rhythm in three of its four strains and also marked 'very slow march time', this is a difficult piece to give a correct speed to. Evidence tends to show that Joplin's idea of slow may never have been as slow as many of the metronome markings we have given anyway. His slow probably meant slow in contrast to the breakneck speeds favoured by so many flashy pianists. This is not to deny that there is a right sort of tempo for many pieces, dictated by their nature, and which might even go against what the composer originally indicated. *Solace* can be, and has been, played at tempos in the *andante* range around ♪112 and its languorous melodies are extremely effective handled like this. If this takes it outside the strictly ragtime field, no matter; it is a tango- or Mexican-serenade, full of ardour and warmth. Was it perhaps in tribute to the solace that his new marriage had brought? Whatever its motivation *Solace* is a wonderfully effective piece of writing, his only one in tango rhythm. The adjective 'Mexican' may not accurately reflect its true origins which were more probably Cuban, the sort of music that Gottschalk had heard on his travels and which came into America via its trading ports. It can be compared with Gottschalk's *Souvenir de la Havane*. Known in early American musical parlance as the *tangana*, the first known Negro publication in this form was Jess Pickett's *The Dream* which was played at the Chicago World Fair in 1893. Joplin might also have come across Will H. Tyer's *Maori*, published in 1908. If this motivated him into trying his own hand at tango rhythms, the result was predictably a piece in unmistakable Joplin style that bore no clear relationship to anything that had gone before. (p. Seminary Music Co., New York) (CW:1; PR:2; S)

52 *Pleasant Moments* – a ragtime waltz (1909). A further attempt, in the manner of *Bethena*, to write a ragtime waltz. It is by no means as ambitious or as intricate as its predecessor, sticking to four simple sections without linking passages, nor has it the same melodic distinction. It has a gentle nature and considerable delicacy, but one wonders whether the Seminary Music Co. found much sale for this kind of thing. (p. Seminary Music Co., New York) (CW:1)

53 *Country Club* – a ragtime two-step (1909). The cover portrays a gentleman in full hunting gear on his horse accompanied by one exhausted looking hound. Perhaps the two crochet chords in C with their F♯ crushed note are intended to portray the call to the hunt but in themselves they are not distinguished; nor does the entire piece manage to find real inspiration. It accepts the average rag speed of ♪152 and mixes strains that suggest both dance and song. (p. Seminary Music Co., New York) (CW:1; RP)

54 *Euphonic Sounds* – a syncopated novelty (1909). As its subtitle immediately suggests, Joplin may have been consciously trying to escape from the bounds of strict ragtime in this ambitious and interesting piece of writing. It looks different on the printed page. The customary ragtime stride bass is practically absent, replaced by quaver and broken runs and syncopated block chords alternated. Having established a strong first strain, Joplin alternates this between two other sections introducing for the first time a rag in true rondo form A-B-A-C-A. It is an intricate piece and we stand before it torn between wondering if Joplin has deserted his true metier or is rightly looking forward to a new music. The well-schooled pianists who followed him found it a piece very much to their liking, making it very much of a showpiece for the advanced player. James P. Johnson, who recorded it in 1944, made no bones about his delight in it: 'Joplin was a great forerunner,' he wrote, 'fifty years ahead of his time. Even today, who understands *Euphonic Sounds*? It's really modern.' Rifkin found its 'increased registral and harmonic subtlety' remarkable, adopting a playing speed of around ♪120. Its remarkable C section

might have come out of a French ballet, contrasting well with the strong 'rondo' section. In performance it seems a remarkably rounded and satisfying work. (p. Seminary Music Co., New York) (CW:1; RP; PR:1)

55 *Paragon Rag* (1909). As if Joplin was consciously ringing all the possible changes at this time, *Paragon* steps back to harmonic simplicity and minstrel-influenced plantation melody. Lovers of early Joplin will rejoice at its flamboyant dance rhythms and catchy melodies. It has a strong first theme and a second which leans on the traditional melody *Bucket's Got A Hole In It* which, no doubt, Joplin heard many times in his career. The same strain has the right-hand breaks or lead-ins that were to become current in ragtime songs of the ensuing period, one of the hallmarks of much ragtime pastiche that was to follow, e.g. compositions by Zez Confrey and the like. The third song-like strain is clearly marked 'trio' and apes the typical band trio of the time. It seems to require a speed of around ♪138 to ♪144. (p. Seminary Music Co., New York) (CW:1; RP; PR:2)

56 *Stoptime Rag* (1910). The cover artist took this literally and put a drawing of a clock on the front in a style unlively enough to suggest that it had been stopped for many years. Joplin had in mind the foot-stamping emphasis that we first encountered in *The Ragtime Dance* – 'to get the desired effect of "stoptime" the pianist should stamp the heel of one foot upon the floor, wherever the word "Stamp" appears in the music'. It appears, to be exact, 173 times in the printed score so, with repeats, Joplin probably got a rake-off from the shoe repairers. With the stamps taking a prominent part and plenty of silent bars, the rag remains very much an exercise in folk dance, entirely gay and rhythmical, probably using some existing melodies which do not have the Joplinesque distinction about them. With unusual laxity the playing instruction is 'fast or slow'. It is an entirely free and zestful work and, again, in it one sees some of the ideas that were then whirling in his head as *Treemonisha* occupied so much of his writing time. (p. Joseph W. Stern, New York) (CW:1; GOR)

57 *Pine-apple Rag* – a song (w. Joe Snyder) (1910). It was eminently

suitable that the joyful *Pine-apple Rag* should be made into a song in the steps of *Maple Leaf* and others but we could regret that a Tin Pan Alley hack like Joe Snyder was brought in to do the job. The result, though pleasant enough musically, is a string of those unnecessary and phoney exhortations that were to become the hallmark of many future Alley ragtime songs: 'Hark to that music', 'that tune is certainly divine', 'isn't that a wonderful tune', 'hear me sigh, hear me cry . . . for that Pine-apple rag' – and so on, until one begins not to want to admire it. This was the last individual Joplin song to be published and it is sadly prophetic of the future world of ragtime that lacked the genius of Joplin to model its ways. (p. Joseph W. Stern, New York) (CW:2)

58 *Treemonisha* – an opera in three acts (w. Scott Joplin) (1911). The opera contains twenty-seven musical items which include an *Overture* and a *Prelude To Act 3*. Joplin's own preface gives the story:

The Scene of the Opera is laid on a plantation somewhere in the State of Arkansas, North-east of the Town of Texarkana and three or four miles from the Red River. The plantation being surrounded by a dense forest.

There were several negro families living on the plantation and other families back in the woods.

In order that the reader may better comprehend the story, I will give a few details regarding the Negroes of this plantation from the year 1866 to the year 1884.

The year 1866 finds them in dense ignorance, with no-one to guide them, as the white folks had moved away shortly after the Negroes were set free and had left the plantation in charge of a trustworthy negro servant named Ned.

All of the Negroes, but Ned and his wife Monisha, were superstitious, and believed in conjuring. Monisha, being a woman, was at times impressed by what the more expert conjurers would say.

Ned and Monisha had no children, and they had often prayed that their cabin home might one day be brightened by a child that would be a companion for Monisha when Ned was away from home. They had dreams, too, of educating the child so that when it grew up it could teach the people around them to aspire to something better and higher than superstition and conjuring.

The prayers of Ned and Monisha were answered in a remarkable manner. One morning in the middle of September 1866, Monisha found a baby under a tree that grew in front of her cabin. It proved to be a light-brown-skinned girl about two days old. Monisha took the baby into the cabin, and Ned and she adopted it as their own.

They wanted the child, while growing up, to love them as it would have loved its real parents, so they decided to keep it in ignorance of the manner in which it came to them until old enough to understand. They realized, too, that if the neighbors knew the facts, they would some day tell the child, so, to deceive them, Ned hitched up his mules and, with Monisha and the child, drove over to a family of old friends who lived twenty miles away and whom they had not seen for three years. They told their friends that the child was just a week old.

Ned gave these people six bushels of corn and forty pounds of meat to allow Monisha and the child to stay with them for eight weeks, which Ned thought would benefit the health of Monisha. The friends willingly consented to have her stay with them for that length of time.

Ned went back alone to the plantation and told his old neighbors that Monisha, while visiting some old friends, had become mother of a girl baby.

The neighbors were, of course, greatly surprised, but were compelled to believe that Ned's story was true.

At the end of the eight weeks Ned took Monisha and the child home and received the congratulations of his neighbors and friends and was delighted to find that his scheme had worked so well.

Monisha, at first, gave the child her own name; but, when the child was three years old she was so fond of playing under the tree where she was found that Monisha gave her the name of Tree-Monisha.

When Treemonisha was seven years old Monisha arranged with a white family that she would do their washing and ironing and Ned would chop their wood if the lady of the house would give Treemonisha an education, the schoolhouse being too far away for the child to attend. The lady consented and as a result Treemonisha was the only educated person in the neighborhood, the other children being still in ignorance on account of their inability to travel so far to school.

Zodzetrick, Luddud and Simon, three very old men, earned their living by going about the neighborhood practicing conjuring, selling little luck-bags and rabbits' feet, and confirming the people in their superstition.

The opera begins in September 1884. Treemonisha, being eighteen years old, now starts on her career as a teacher and leader.

SCOTT JOPLIN

As we know, *Treemonisha* failed to make the impression that Joplin had hoped for after its one disastrous rehearsal-standard production in Harlem in 1915. It was not entirely ignored. The *American Musician* went so far as to say that Joplin had 'created an entirely new phase of musical art and has produced a thoroughly American opera'. With hindsight we might justifiably say that he aimed too high. If he intended to show the musical hierarchy like Edward McDowell, then strongly denying that black American music had anything to offer American music as a whole, that ragtime could sustain an opera, he also lacked support from his own people. Had he aimed at the sphere where ragtime more naturally belonged – the musical comedy stage – he might well have had a roaring success on his hands. He would at least have supplied America with what it has lacked ever since – a really good musical in the ragtime vein; imagine its appeal today. Even Gershwin, with his added sophistication and musical ingenuity, only just succeeded in writing an opera in jazz idiom which the serious world of music could accept.

Treemonisha has been revived, with happy results, in Atlanta in 1972 – its first public performance after more than fifty years of lying neglected; but until we are more widely familiar with it on the stage, it must remain difficult to make a proper assessment. It appears to be a modest work, of not undue length, with Joplin's own libretto entirely in keeping with the music's mixture of genuine ragtime, minstrel song and American drawing-room ballad style. It avoids being a pastiche of Italian opera. Joplin outshines Delius and others who have tried to recreate the atmosphere of the Negro spiritual and plantation song simply by writing music so deeply embedded in the idiom, so simple in effect, that it has a folk quality about it. The *Cornhuskers* section takes us nearer to the authentic atmosphere than anything else in written form. *A Real Slow Drag* is in his hauntingly best ragtime vein. The whiter songs, never actually deserting their black quality, are intensely moving if sung by someone committed enough to overcome their occasional verbal naivety. In the end it is the music, as personal and sincere as anything that Joplin wrote, that carries us through the opera's self-imposed problems. Proper revival of it is essential. (CW:2)

59 *Felicity Rag* – a ragtime two-step (with Scott Hayden) (1911). The first two themes are probably by Hayden with Joplin adding a third strain, the only one that clearly shows his characteristics. The whole work seems unambitious and not particularly distinguished as though some remnants of earlier years had been reworked. (p. John Stark Music Printing & Publishing Co., New York & St Louis) (CW:1)

60 *Scott Joplin's New Rag* (1912). In the midst of his pre-occupation with *Treemonisha* Joplin turned out this last good rag in
the old vein. It is joyful, melodic and with a good stomping
bass that takes us back to *Original Rags* and *Swipesey Cakewalk* days. The rondo form is again used and the original
theme is used three times with two other themes interspersed.
It bears an unexpected instruction *allegro moderato* as if to
mark the work of one who was now a composer of opera, but
should clearly be taken at ♪152 or even faster. (p. Joseph W.
Stern, New York & Mexico) (CW:1; GOR; PR:1)

61 *Kismet Rag* (with Scott Hayden) (1913). Both this and *Felicity*
carry only the name of Joplin on the cover although Scott
Hayden is credited within. Again we find a three-theme rag
with a varied form of A rounding things off to make four
sections. As with the *Felicity Rag* it gives the impression of
using up old material but with considerably more success. Its
tunes have a vaudeville air about them, minstrel-type tunes
with one strain reminiscent of *The Preacher And The Bear*.
About ♪152. (p. Stark Music Co., St Louis) (CW:1)

62 *A Real Slow Drag* (1913). Revised version of item No. 27 from
the score of *Treemonisha* (q.v.) (p. Scott Joplin, New York)
(CW:2)

63 *Prelude To Act 3* (dated 1911) (1913) from *Treemonisha* (q.v.)
(p. Scott Joplin, New York) (CW:2)

64 *Magnetic Rag* (1914). With classical styled cover and marked
allegretto ma non troppo, *Magnetic Rag* is a beautiful, gentle
and entirely memorable rag that has something of the tranquil
air of *The Entertainer* about it. It has a distinction of form
that equals any of his earlier works, working from the simple
opening section, through a strange G minor based interlude, to
a heightened and complicated stomp, then through a curious
transitory passage marked *tempo l'istesso* in B♭ minor, returning most effectively to the original theme with an attractive coda added. Its range of moods, its natural momentum,
its searching character suggest, too late alas, a break-through
to a Chopinesque form of ragtime about to be made. Rifkin's
performance of this on his memorable first disc is the only

one where one feels that he has perhaps not grasped the work's full potential, perhaps taking it at too romping a gait. A tempo of about ♪116 is suggested. (p. Scott Joplin Music Publishing Co., New York) (CW:1; RP; PR:1)

65 *Frolic Of The Bears* (1915). Revised version of item No. 13 from the score of *Treemonisha* (q.v.) (p. Scott Joplin Music Publishing Co., New York) (CW:2)

66 *Reflection Rag* – syncopated musings (1917). This piece, obviously in the publisher's files, was published by Stark eight months after Joplin's death on 1 April of that year. It is so untypical of Joplin that its authenticity might be doubted. At best it suggests an experimental piece which he may have discarded. (p. Stark Music Co., St Louis) (CW:1)

67 *Silver Swan Rag* (p. 1971). Attr. Joplin. (p. Music Trust of Lottie Joplin Thomas) (CW:1)

Ragtime and Jazz

To evaluate ragtime's full contribution to jazz and to follow the thread of its influence through the years from 1917 to the present is beyond the capacity of this brief survey whose particular interest is, in any case, the work and life of Scott Joplin. The importance of ragtime is vastly overrated by its admirers and vastly underrated by many whose tastes are centred round later developments in jazz. An archaic music like ragtime is even actively disliked by many intelligent jazz experts who are not seduced by its period charm. Such opinions are perpetuated by the followers of jazz who feel obliged to defend one style or period; an attitude that has its roots in the days when jazz had to be staunchly defended to justify its existence. Perhaps no other branch of music has to live with such partisan and biased view-points. Speaking to a leading jazz record specialist the other day, a man of wide taste and influence, I was a little disheartened to have him respond to my fervent declaration of interest in ragtime with the sweeping assertion: 'I can't stand the stuff; a load of old rubbish.' I am naturally sorry that he misses its delights and I am certain that he is wrong; but I can see that anyone whose emotional tastes lie with modern jazz of the 1940s may well find it difficult to respond to a music whose spirit belongs to the 1890s and all that is therein implied.

We must be careful not to over-exaggerate the importance of ragtime. It was a side-shoot of jazz that blossomed for some twenty years a long time ago. If we knew more about the developing years of jazz that overlapped the ragtime era we would almost certainly discover that jazz on instruments other than the piano was already in existence, perhaps with other characteristics more apparent. And yet, our experience of early jazz bands, original and revived, suggests that the jazz music of New Orleans in the 1880s had something of the formal and ragged nature of ragtime about it. Certainly most of the pianists of the 1880s and 90s must have played in a style that approximates to ragtime as we now know it, a point that is emphasised by detecting ragtime strains in the playing of many important early jazz pianists.

A lot of ragtime's influence, as we have documented at length, was directed into the field of popular music and was most admirably caught in the song written by a composer who, not surprisingly, was also an accomplished ragtime pianist – *I'm Just Wild About Harry* by Eubie Blake. Ragtime, as we can see and feel in the later more experimental rags by Joplin and others, was always trying to break out into the smoother more swinging rhythms of jazz. As Charles Fox has neatly expressed it: 'that exhilarating moment when a tight discipline is being strained to accommodate new emotions and ideas'. But, of course, ragtime was not only the manifestation of a discipline but a music simply limited by its point in history.

Ragtime would have passed with much less notice if it had not thrown up composers like Joplin and Scott whose music can be admired and loved for its own sake. Within the limits of their experience and their period they created exquisite music; this music had its due influence on musicians and composers to follow, inspiring them to surpass it technically and to widen its bounds emotionally.

For the purpose of this chapter, all we need do is to mention two of the directions that ragtime took through the single or collective efforts of certain jazz musicians. The most obvious and satisfyingly fruitful link between ragtime piano and jazz piano was probably Ferdinand 'Jelly Roll' Morton who was born in Gulfport, Louisiana on 20 September 1885. Morton acknowledged many times his indebtedness to Joplin. He studied and admired his rags and from them developed his own equally individual style. His recording of Joplin's *Original Rags* has been faithfully transcribed by Richard Thompson and is printed in *The Art of Ragtime*. By studying the music and listening to Morton's recording we can see how he smoothed out Joplin's lines by dotting every other note in some of the phrases, a step towards the frequent use of the triplet that was to be a main characteristic of Morton's own music and of early jazz. The opening bars of Morton's early *Frog-i-more Rag* is a comprehensive lesson in making beautiful jazz on a ragtime basis. His introductory passage is richer than anything Joplin ever achieved. Morton did not give the name 'rag' to many of his compositions probably because he could already sense that the use of the word would suggest to unknowing ears the frivolous Tin Pan Alley kind of ragtime and Dixieland strains in jazz. Morton's ragtime-influenced jazz solos were often Joplinesque in their delicacy. *The Pearls* is one of his nearest approximations to a classic rag and yet one would never mistake its later period or its inimitable Morton styling. In the more extrovert mood *King Porter Stomp* and *Grandpa's Spells* have an obvious affinity with ragtime. And, of course, they also have an affinity with the Harlem stride piano of Johnson and Waller.[1]

You can detect a grain of ragtime in the playing of practically every jazz pianist you care to mention; instrumental jazz was a step nearer to Tin Pan Alley, in utilising the more superficial ragtime elements, the minstrel- and cakewalk-styled tunes and the ragged syncopations. The most obvious link here is found in the music of the Original Dixieland Jazz Band – specifically in the work of its composer pianists Henry Ragas and J. Russell Robinson. Buddy Bolden, Jack Laine, Bunk Johnson, King Oliver – most of the New Orleans bands had the ragtime strain in them; often perpetuating the name as in 'Jack Laine's Ragtime Band'. The music that such a band played was to become the staple diet of the Ragtime and Dixieland bands that followed : tunes like *Livery*

1 It is of interest to note that Morton, in a letter to Roy Carew, once confessed that he got out of the ragtime field and created his own kind of music because he felt unable to compete with the accomplished pianists performing ragtime. *(Pictorial History of Jazz.)*

Stable Blues, earlier known as *Meatball Blues*; *Tiger Rag* which started life as a quadrille and was adapted and played by every kind of band under the sun. The Laine band called their version *Praline* after the New Orleans candy. In the Laine band were musicians like Achille Baquet (clarinet), Lawrence Vega (cornet) and Dave Perkins (trombone) and, in his later Reliance Band, clarinettist Alcide Nunez, famed as one of the greatest exponents of ragtime on this instrument. Many of these musicians drifted into Brown's Dixieland Jazz Band which had its roots in a vaudeville orchestra. Larry Shields, Nick La Rocca and Eddie Edwards moved through these circles before coming together as the Original Dixieland Jazz Band, adding to *Livery Stable Blues* and *Tiger Rag* their own ragtime-based compositions like *Ostrich Walk*, *Sensation Rag*, *Original One-Step* and *Skeleton Jangle*. Through their pioneer recordings the gospel of early jazz travelled to Europe. If it was a kind of jazz later to fall out of favour with more sophisticated addicts, it always kept its following among the lovers of good-time jazz and was mainly the kind of music that sparked off the 1940s old-time jazz revival that followed the impact made by Muggsy Spanier's Ragtime Band, which played these old tunes in a nicely balanced contemporary/traditional style; and helped bring the name 'Ragtime' back into common usage.

The linking of ragtime and jazz and their interplay form the basis of a fascinating study that many people who become interested in ragtime will want to follow. This is an appropriate point to offer some reading guide-lines on these inter-related subjects and on the subject of ragtime itself.

Firstly, of course, there is the ragtime bible *They All Played Ragtime* by Rudi Blesh and Harriet Janis which is wholly and unapologetically committed to ragtime and its exponents and, apart from justifiable appreciation of people like Jelly Roll Morton and Tony Jackson, shows few signs of caring whether jazz was an outcome or not. It is quite simply the definitive book on ragtime and a magnificent piece of scholarship on a specific and well-defined area of music-making. Schafer and Riedel's *The Art* of *Ragtime* stands a little further back from its subject and relates it more to surrounding spheres of music. It wanders more explicitly into the subject of 'Ragtime Songs and Bands' (we will say a little more about the latter under the chapter on recordings) and takes a more dispassionate view of 'Ragtime Style and Performance'. Both these books are well documented and essential reading for anyone who wants to look into the subject beyond the bounds of our introductory survey. A purely factual documentation of ragtime recordings will be found in David A. Jasen's *Recorded Ragtime 1897–1958*. For those whose historical hunger is still unsatiated by the above, additional thoughts and directions for research will be found in two probing articles by Eric Thacker – 'Ragtime Roots' in issues of *Jazz & Blues* dated November and December 1973. Thacker goes as far as finding ragtime hints in Rameau, goes back to primitive African music and provides us with rich fields of speculation.

Many chapters devoted to ragtime and its emergence are to be found in books listed in Appendix 1(b) whose nature is self-explanatory. Jazz histories, with a proper sense of balance, generally slot ragtime into a few pages and are not particularly concerned to relate it to jazz. One of the best chapters in this respect is found in what is possibly one of the best introductions to jazz that we have readily available, Marshall Stearn's *The Story of Jazz* – which never lets anything go by without tidying up the ends and letting us know why it was worth a mention at all. In Martin Williams' anthology, *The Art of Jazz*, we are usefully served by two items by Guy Waterman – 'Ragtime – a Survey' and 'Joplin's Late Rags' which neatly precede a piece by William Russell called 'Jelly Roll Morton and the *Frog-i-more Rag*' – all adding up to a balanced helping of historical perspective. Others all add their share of fact and comment. Even the tentative assertions, half-truths and downright inaccuracies of books and chapters written prior to Blesh and Janis, add in an interesting way to understanding how the jazz world and the wider world have reacted to ragtime.

How to Play Ragtime

School of Ragtime

6

EXERCISES

FOR

PIANO

BY

SCOTT JOPLIN.

Composer of "MAPLE LEAF RAG" *etc.*

Price 50 cents.

NEW YORK
Published by SCOTT JOPLIN.

Key jazz musicians and popular composers influenced by ragtime
46 and 47 *Above:* The Original Dixieland Jazz Band *Left:* Jelly Roll Morton

49 *Above:* Irving Berlin

50 *Right:* Willie 'The Lion' Smith

48 *Left:* Duke Ellington 1927

51 James P. Johnson
1968

52 Fats Waller

53 From the film *Those Ragtime Years* 1960 *Left to right:* Ralph Sutton, Dick Wellstood, Eubie Blake and Hoagy Carmichael

54 *Above:* Scene from the ballet *The Prodigal Son* 1974

55 *Below:* The Band taking a curtain call, from the ballet *Elite Syncopations* 1974

56 *Above:* The film that started the ragtime revival, a scene from *The Sting* 1974

57 *Right:* The modern ragtime pianist Max Morath, with a picture of Percy Wenrich, 'The Joplin Kid', in the background

58 Joshua Rifkin, the musician who brought ragtime back to the concert hall
(*Photo: BBC Copyright Photograph. Joshua Rifkin records exclusively for Nonesuch
Records*)

Of course, Paul Kresh was absolutely right when he said, with such a graphic turn of phrase, that 'there are as many ways to play it as there are to skin a cat' – adding controversially 'some of them rather less interesting than others'.[1] We know there are that many ways to play ragtime because we have heard them. Yet it is also true to say that there is only one way to play ragtime correctly. We can qualify this even further by saying that, as in classical music, there is only one way to play each individual composition. The tempo of a musical work is vital to its character; and the tempo to be adopted, when not clearly marked in metronomic terms by the composer (who can sometimes be wrong) is dictated by the structure and density of the writing.

If we are thinking in terms of Joplin rags, and we accept that there are no other rags exactly like them, it soon becomes clear by trial and error that on the whole they gain from the composer's regularly repeated instruction 'Do not play this piece fast. It is never right to play Ragtime fast.' Joplin, Lamb and other classically-minded ragtime composers who made this frequent plea realised from practical experience that most pianists are unable to resist the temptation to exhibit their skill by playing everything as fast as possible. This happens in all music. How frequently we hear the opening of Mendelssohn's *Italian* symphony played at such high speed that the musicians can scarcely

1 *Stereo Review*, April 1974 – 'First Annual Ragtime Roundup.'

get the notes in and consequently are unable to phrase properly; quite incapable of rounding-off the cadences in a meaningful way.

If we take a clear example like *The Entertainer*, it is quite possible that we never had a chance to realise its true grace and charm because we had always heard it played at too great a speed. When Joshua Rifkin recorded it at a gravely measured tempo, playing the notes lightly, evenly and clearly, it suddenly came to life as a most distinctive and ingratiating musical work. We can be almost sure that he had achieved his effect by playing the piece at the speed that its nature indicated.

Now let us say right away that the way we heard Rifkin play *The Entertainer* was not unquestionably the way that many highly skilled professional jazz musicians would choose to play it. Rifkin simply played it as written and probably as many amateur musicians would have played it in its period and as a good classical pianist would play it if the score was put in front of him for the first time. The result, however, is undeniably effective. Paradoxically we have what claims to be Joplin's own piano roll version of the piece and he plays it about twice as fast and loses most of its charm. Joplin never made a gramophone record and rolls are not incontrovertible evidence because they can be altered, and we have no final evidence that those said to be made by Joplin were his for certain. Rolls can, in fact, be made without any live performer being involved. Nevertheless if we accept that Joplin did make his accredited version of *The Entertainer*, it is a puzzling contradiction to find him going against his own advice and playing it at a considerable speed.

Jelly Roll Morton was another composer who had much to say on the subject. Yet in spite of his oft-quoted dictum that 'jazz music is to be played sweet, softly, plenty rhythm' and his demonstration on the Library of Congress recordings that ragtime should not be hurried or accelerated, Morton was another composer who often played his own works excessively fast – for example, his band recording of *Black Bottom Stomp* and the trio recording of *Shreveport Stomp*. We might also point to Fats Waller's recording of his own classic *Handful Of Keys* where we admire the sheer dexterity and virtuosity but note that if he had taken it a fraction slower the result would have been cleaner, more poised and probably more effective.

On the whole we must fly in the face of recorded evidence and still insist that ragtime usually benefits from being played fairly slowly, certainly slower than most pianists are inclined to take it. We must come to the conclusion that a mixture of conceit and misjudgment is the main reason for speeding (it applies also to driving cars). There is a rooted belief that speed is synonymous with excitement and perhaps, in general, audiences are not sophisticated enough to appreciate the natural tempos and are partly to blame for urging musicians into excessive showmanship. Even the greatest can be blatantly wrong as demonstrated by Toscanini's incredible destruction of the minuet of Haydn's *Surprise* symphony, rattling through it as if it was background music for a Keystone Cops car chase.

But we must qualify matters even more by saying that there are natural slow rags, medium pace rags and even fast rags. For instance, one of Joplin's most ingenious and delightful compositions *The Cascades* is marked *tempo di marcia* and is ineffective at anything less than a brisk pace. In an interesting band performance on London's South Bank in August '74, André Previn chose to start it at a speed which just about lay within the capabilities of his dexterous fingers, manipulated a jarring deceleration in order to slow the middle section to a speed which the brass could manage, and then whipped up to full throttle again to achieve a whirlwind ending. Ragtime, like any other music, is there to be interpreted, but the more even and reasonable pace of Schuller's recording seems to be more satisfying.

The most famous of all the Joplin rags, *Maple Leaf*, is by nature a fast piece for the simple reason that the extremely mobile and telling left-hand part ceases to be effective if it is not accorded a speed that emphasises its own melodic pattern. Taken slowly it falls apart. On the other hand, taken too fast the melodic charm of the right hand ceases to have its effect. The right speed is probably around ♪ 192, give or take a little. *Original Rags*, which has a fast appearance on paper, benefits from a medium tempo approach; *The Ragtime Dance* definitely comes off best if Joplin's 'not too fast' instruction is obeyed and *Sunflower Slow Drag* should follow the suggestion inherent in the title.

It is not all a matter of speed, though all other considerations arise from it. Ragtime should maintain a strict and even tempo, at whatever chosen rate, and the notes should be given absolutely correct written value so that they flow in true legato style. The effect of giving Joplin's quaver-based phrases the benefit of evenly spaced notes is actually to achieve more impetus and flow than if one tries to force the pace by jazz-styled phrasing. The careful maintenance of absolute precision in the playing of classic rags gives them that delightful cliff-hanging quality which we sense in Rifkin's recordings. The maintenance of a strict tempo throughout allows the contrasts between the various sections which, we must grant to a skilled composer like Joplin, are deliberately and beautifully contrived, to have their own effect.

But, having demanded a degree of rigidity and an absence of jazz phrasing in the purest of pure classic ragtime, we must immediately knock down this particular sandcastle of argument by adding that such purity was probably a very rare and short-lived thing in the history of ragtime. The jazz instinct was always there in the majority of the black performers and probably Joplin himself was expected and prepared to 'swing it' in his off-the-cuff performances in the local establishments around St Louis and Sedalia. After a very short period when a number of classic ragtime rolls were cut, the virtuoso pianists began to investigate the various ways of 'skinning a cat' in no uncertain manner. One of the few to remain true to strictly orthodox ragtime was Joseph Lamb, paradoxically a white musician and composer, and probably for the reason that, like Joplin, he had a considerable amount of classical upbringing and appreciation in his musical background.

On record there is plenty of evidence of how material that had the basic ragtime characteristics began to be bent towards various jazz and popular music styles. The piece of ragtime that lays claim to be the first Negro composition in this vein to be printed (in 1897) – Thomas Turpin's *Harlem Rag* – is far nearer to a march in character than any of Joplin's more delicate pieces ever were. It has a four-square character and lacks melodic charm or sophistication. Its second section is a typical military band piece of writing with a trombone or tuba type melody in the bass in emulation of marches like *Under The Double-Eagle*. The march tradition, possibly adhered to with an eye to performance by a big money-making band like Sousa's, stayed strongly in later ragtime and in the Dixieland jazz repertoire. You can find it in pieces as disparate as James Reese Europe's *Castle House Rag* and Eubie Blake's *Fizz Water* which takes on an air of vaudevillian hilarity in the third strain. Luckey Roberts' pleasant *Junk Man Rag* has this same vaudeville-cum-Dixieland atmosphere without actually being a march, leading ragtime into popular song strains yet having the curious nature of a piece that might have been specially written to be made into a piano roll. James P. Johnson's *Daintiness Rag* and *Caprice Rag* have little of the jerkiness of the older rags, moving into the stride piano style that was to lead to the lighter world of Billy Mayerl and Charlie Kunz. Morton in his various pieces like *King Porter Stomp* wrote music that could also be played in the ragtime idiom, and demonstrated in his fascinating version of Joplin's *Original Rags* how he converted and led such music into the broader jazz stream. One of the most interesting rags ever recorded is Cow Cow Davenport's *Atlanta Rag* which manages successfully to combine almost pure ragtime in one strain with undiluted honky-tonk (almost boogie-woogie) characteristics in the next. It is also one of the few rags to compare in melodic distinction with Joplin's.

With all these, and countless more, examples in mind it would be presumptuous to deny that ragtime can be played in many ways. Which in no way invalidates the argument that only the pure and unbent classic ragtime has ragtime's special charm. To enjoy most of the other offshoots your musical palate has at least to adjust itself to other interesting and distinctive flavours.

For a final view of ragtime interpretation we can find it all neatly summed up in Wilfrid Meller's book *Music in a New Found Land* : 'Rag is the Negro's attempt at the buoyant optimism of the Sousa march and the brilliant elegance of the Gottschalk dance, and the mass feeling is depersonalized because personal feelings may be too much to bear. In this sense, rags are an *alternative* to the blues; and their use of the discipline of military music becomes equated with the disciplined non-humanity of a machine. This is literally true : for many rags were transferred to the pianola roll and, even if not played by a machine, should be played *like* a machine, with meticulous precision.'

But with delicacy and charm – let us add !

Ragtime on Record

Hullo, Ragtime!

on the "His Master's Voice" Gramophone with

His Master's Voice Records

The ultimate object of this chapter is to point to a few fairly easily obtainable LPs that will help in an appreciation of ragtime as well as providing entertainment. But while the average collector is unlikely to want or to be able to purchase many early cylinder and disc recordings (except where these have been reissued on LPs), so much of the fascination of ragtime, and all other branches of popular art that have been re-garnered in the current nostalgia boom, is in the quaint names and titles connected with it, that a look at early ragtime recording is worthwhile if only for the euphony.

Thomas A. Edison invented his phonograph in 1877, the sound being embossed on tinfoil round a cylinder. Chichester A. Bell and Charles Sumner Tainter introduced wax coated cardboard in 1885. In 1887 Emile Berliner announced the invention of the flat disc gramophone and in 1889 the first commercial machines were produced by a toy factory in Germany. In 1895 gramophones and discs were first made in the USA, Pathé Brothers set up in France in 1894, while Graphophone in America introduced the first spring-driven machine; the first shellac pressings came in 1897 and the Gramophone Company was established in London in 1898. In 1899 Eldridge Johnson introduced the means of cutting wax masters and in 1901 the first 10" discs arrived. Up till then they had ranged from 5" to the 14" Pathés (which played from the inside outwards). Gradually the 10" and 12" records became standard, 12" being established in 1903, and gradually playing speeds which had varied from 72rpm to 86rpm were established at 78rpm. Odeon issued the first double-sided record in 1904 while cylinders, which had made a break-through in 1908 with four-minutes playing time, and celluloid Blue Amberols of superior quality, continued to be issued by the Edison-Bell Company until 1913, then graciously gave in to the disc for good.

The American record companies exploited ragtime as soon as they were decently able to, the earliest ragtime recording being made by banjoist Sylvester Louis Ossman in 1897 for the Berliner Company. The Victor Company, incorporated in 1901, took a great interest in ragtime, as did the Columbia Graphophone Company founded in the same year. The Universal Talking Machine Company (later to become Zonophone) had been dabbling since 1899. Later entrants were Okeh (General Phonograph Corporation) from 1918; Brunswick – 1919, and Emerson – 1921. Ignoring the fact that ragtime was most correctly a piano music, the record companies, finding pianos difficult to record – the difficulty was to persist into the modern recording era – preferred the sharp and deep-cutting sound of the banjo. Mr Ossman found regular employment from 1897 onward and continued until 1917 including some records with the Ossman-Dudley banjo trio. Other banjoists who obliged with ragtime solos were Olly Oakley (real name Joseph Sharpe), Joe Morley, John Pidoux, Burt Earle and Parke Hunter; but the most popular of all was Fred van Eps who began recording on his five-string banjo from 1910 onwards, also with the Van Eps Trio. His last disc was made as late as 1952. Banjo and guitar playing was to have a spectacular revival in the 1920s and again in the 1950s.

Other instruments that contorted the ragtime idiom, with help from early recording techniques, were the saxophone, accordion, piccolo, guitar and xylophone; and there were numerous trombonists headed by the redoubtable Arthur Pryor. The great popularity of brass and military bands in America, including those headed by Pryor and Sousa, led to an enormous number of band recordings. The earliest band ragtime disc was made by the Metropolitan Orchestra for Berliner in 1897. Sousa was a great ragtime enthusiast and quickly followed. Pryor, then playing with the Sousa band, composed many rags especially for orchestra, and other bandleader/composers who came to the fore were Abe Holzmann, William H. Krell and J. Bodewalt Lampe. The Victor Military Band, the Zonophone Concert Band, Charles A. Prince's Band, and many others, crowded into the studios and attempted to direct their music down the tin horn.

This is an appropriate time to mention the increasing practice of publishing band arrangements of ragtime pieces soon after their initial publication. This was very often done for military bands by arrangers like Arthur Pryor. There were also innumerable orchestral scores as played by society bands such as John Robichaux's Orchestra in New Orleans (recently the New Orleans Ragtime Orchestra has recorded many of their original arrangements); arrangements for vaudeville use; dance-band arrangements (in constant demand); and eventually arrangements for jazz bands. The obvious need, with all these sources in mind, was for arrangements which could either combine all these resources or offer variants for smaller ensembles. With the orchestra pit mainly in mind Stark published the *Red-Backed Book of Rags* in 1912 with transcriptions of fifteen classic rags by Joplin, Scott, Lamb, Marshall and others, with parts for woodwind, brass and strings. These orchestrations have been particularly successful in recent recordings (some re-edited by Gunther Schuller) in reviving the palm-court sounds of the period with a spicing of Sousa and the piano there to add a touch of authenticity. The interesting point is that ragtime orchestrations of the period deviate strongly from jazz in following classical conventions; that is with first violin taking the melodic lead, other strings playing counter-melodies or guitar-type accompaniments; with woodwind playing harmony or occasional obbligato passages; cornet and clarinet occasionally given a lead part; trombone playing a semi-jazz-cum-military band role; and the drums with a scored part in true band style. It produced a charming sound and was very much the sort of band that the legendary Alexander presumably led. It was the nature of these ragtime bands as much as anything that differentiated between ragtime and jazz loyalties.

The first known piano rag recording is believed to be a

performance of *Creole Belles* by Charles H. Booth, studio pianist of the Victor Talking Machine Company, made in 1901. But piano ragtime recordings were rare until after 1912. By the 1920s there was a flood of piano recordings but by now in the hands of the novelty specialists like Zez Confrey and Billy Mayerl, Roy Bargy, Phil Ohman, Vee Lawnhurst, Fred Elizalde and Rube Bloom.

Companies like Saydisc and Vintage Jazz Music have in recent years (with considerable foresight considering the present ragtime revival was not then under full steam) collected together various LPs of early recordings which will be found listed in Appendix 3, Section 2.

It was sad that virtually none of the original ragtime pianists or composers, including Scott Joplin, went to the recording studios. For their interpretations we are reliant upon pianola rolls which are notoriously bad documentation, owing to the ease with which they could be edited and altered and casting doubts as to their true perpetrators. So while many of the classic ragtime names did make rolls, including Joplin, we can never feel really certain that this is a true representation of how they played. Better to listen through the hisses and scratches of an early recording for some glimpse of authenticity. Joplin's own renderings of his rags, whether through the limitations of piano roll technique or through his own shortcomings as a pianist, are not half as sensitive as one would expect from such a thoughtful composer. Nevertheless the acquisition of some of the piano roll recordings made by him and other pioneer ragtimers, as re-issued on Riverside, Biograph and other documentary labels, are essential to a study of ragtime – if only because there is no other way of hearing them.

By the 1920s recording was getting into its stride. One surviving name from the early days is that of Eubie Blake and it is interesting to follow his recordings from the earliest days to the present to discover a ragtime-cum-vaudeville-cum-jazz style that has more affinity with the Joplin rolls than with some recent exponents of ragtime. Perhaps this proves the point that Joplin and Co. took a less profound view of ragtime than many people do today. Two records that have great documentary interest are 'Black and White Ragtime' [Biograph BLP12047] which juxtaposes interpretations ranging from 1923 to 1943 with examples of Blake, James P. Johnson, Blythe, Rube Bloom, Morton, Zez Confrey and many others in what has been described as a 'post-ragtime anthology of ragtime'; and 'They All Played "Maple Leaf Rag" ' [Herwin 401] which contrasts performances ranging from 1907 to 1969, some of which have no traces of ragtime whatever in them, of Joplin's immortal classic.

Jelly Roll Morton has been amply recorded and certainly his Library of Congress recordings ought to be part of the experience of anyone at all interested in jazz and jazz piano history; as well as his classic *Red Hot Peppers* recordings. The later stride pianists such as Johnson, Waller and Willie 'The Lion' Smith have also been well documented. The gramophone managed to catch a few pioneer ragtime composers and pianists like Luckey Roberts and Brun Campbell (a pupil of Joplin's) who give us glimpses of the true flavour. The most important documentary in the ragtime field is the LP which Joseph Lamb made in 1959 just before he died, 'A Study in Classic Ragtime' [Folkways FG-3562] which forges an undying link between our age and Joplin's. The art of Euday Bowman and Dink Johnson has also been preserved on the same discs as we find Campbell.

Ragtime has had two distinct revivals. The first began in the early 1940s, along with the general jazz revival, and had its first impetus from the 1941-onwards recordings by the Lu Watters' Yerba Buena Jazz Band who knew and admired what they were reviving and had a ragtime orientated pianist Wally Rose in their ranks to add the authentic flavour. The Blesh and Janis book *They All Played Ragtime* added greatly to the impetus. But the 1940–50s revival was very different from the 1970s one which we are at present enjoying. It had neither the scholarly musicianship about it or such a keen sense of period that today colours our interest in the artistic activities of the late nineteenth and early twentieth centuries. On the one hand you had the commercialised honky-tonk kind of pianists and musicians who saw ragtime very much in the Dixieland-Yerba Buena vein as raz-ma-taz music of unrelenting jollity; pianists like Lou Busch, who recorded under the name of Joe 'Fingers' Carr, and Marvin Ash – to whom we are certainly indebted for making the world acutely conscious of ragtime again. In a similar vein ragtime achieved some best-selling hits in the 1940s, with Pee Wee Hunt's 1948 recording of *Twelfth Street Rag* selling over three million copies, and Winifred Atwell's *Black And White Rag* achieving comparable popularity. On the other hand there were the more serious pianists like Knocky Parker (who first put all the Joplin rags on to record), Ralph Sutton, Tony Parenti, Don Ewell and Ann Charters who admired ragtime and understood its more delicate potentials; who, even so, were nearly all playing in a jazz-orientated style to some degree. Thus in Sutton's versions of works like *Frog Legs Rag* and *Dill Pickles* we sense the proper flavour of ragtime in spite of the Wallerish overtones; the rhythms were always smoothed out as Morton dictated. In fact some of the English band performances, by such as Colyer and Barber, got just as near to having a genuine ragtime flavour.

The tremendous ragtime revival of the 1970s, given real substance by the New York Public Library's publication of Joplin's complete works which followed the tentative issue of other books of classic rags in less scholarly vein, and which was to lead to revivals of *Treemonisha* and the use of Joplin's music in all kinds of entertainment mediums, has had an entirely different flavour. It had, as to be expected, the almost reluctant blessing of much of the jazz fraternity who have always prefaced their printed appreciations with the bland assumption that ragtime will all die away again. This is unlikely in view of the fact that it has survived since the 1890s and because Joplin's work (and that of other composers) has such obvious strength, grace, beauty and other survivable qualities. Our general appreciation of the elements that went into ragtime, the Victorian mixture of coyness and honesty that we find in the works of Foster, Gottschalk, Sullivan, the drawing-room songs and the music-hall, is much more in sympathy with the music than ever before. An appreciation of ragtime is less in the hands of the jazz fellowship and open to the admiration of the general music lover, both popular and classical; and it is its pre-jazz character and flavour which have most successfully been brought out in the best recordings of late. But it is true, as Miles Kington wrote in a London *Times* roundup in October '74 that: 'We have been deluged with scholarly over-kill and rapidly pressed ragtime LPs designed to catch the revival while it lasts . . . all will be unobtainable in a couple of years and a few are worth getting.'

There have been several LPs that will certainly disappear but I feel certain that we shall long treasure the three Rifkin LPs [Nonesuch H-71248, H-71264 and H-71305] presenting Joplin's music with such convincing sincerity and charm without a trace of jazz influence, as well as the two Bolcom LPs that couch themselves in slightly freer terms yet with the same sense of style and period [Nonesuch H-71257 and H-71299]; also ranging beyond Joplin, the second LP is an invaluable guide to James Scott and Artie Matthews. The works of Joseph Lamb have been given due attention by John Jensen [Genesis GS1045] and Milton Kaye [London HSU5010]. Two wide-ranging discs by Keith Nichols [One Up OU2035] and Dick Wellstood [Chiaroscuro 109] take us beyond classic rags in an understanding and lasting way. Max Morath, who has done as much as anyone to promote ragtime in recent years, perhaps is nearest to ragtime as Joplin and his friends probably played it in Tom Turpin's back room and is not averse to a little instrumental accompaniment [Vanguard VSD39/40]. These and many other ragtime piano LPs are listed in Appendix 3 at the end of this book.

The flavour of ragtime has perhaps never been caught so richly as in the 'Red Book' orchestral recordings made by Gunther Schuller and the New England Conservatory Ragtime Ensemble, the best of these [EMI EMD5503] hitting at least five different musical strains of the turn of the century with uncanny accuracy. A similar but subtly different atmosphere is caught by the New Orleans Ragtime Orchestra. 'The Sting' soundtrack recordings kept a high degree of authenticity.

No, I remain convinced that with all these strands to explore, all the rich music that has been written and recorded, and a cohesive history covering a hundred years or more, that the reports of ragtime's death are vastly exaggerated. You cannot discard so much history nor can music of such strength and beauty ever be forgotten. Public interest is always likely to come and go but I happily predict that the name of Joplin, and others his near equal, will never ever be forgotten again.

Coda

Ragtime Roundup

'Someone is quoted as saying that "ragtime is the true American music". Anyone will admit that it is one of the many true, natural, and nowadays, conventional means of expression. It is an idiom, perhaps a "set or series of colloquialisms", similar to those that have added through the centuries and through natural means some beauty to all languages. Every language is but the evolution of slang, and possibly the broad "A" in Harvard may have come down from the "butcher of Southwark". To examine ragtime rhythms and the syncopations of Schumann and Brahms seems to the writer to show how much alike they are not. Ragtime, as we hear it, is, of course, more (but not much more) than a natural dogma of shifted accents. It is something like wearing a derby hat on the back of the head, a shuffling lilt of a happy soul just let out of a Baptist church in old Alabama. Ragtime has its possibilities. But it does not "represent the American nation" any more than some fine old senators represent it. Perhaps we know it now as an ore before it has been refined into a product. It may be one of nature's ways of giving art raw material. Time will throw its vices away and weld its virtues into the fabric of our music. It has its uses, as the cruet on the boarding-house table has, but to make a meal of tomato ketchup and horse-radish, to plant a whole farm with sunflowers, even to put a sunflower into every bouquet, would be calling nature something worse than a politician.'

Charles Ives from Essays Before a Sonata

At least in 1975 there is no need to be under any illusion as to what ragtime really was and in what forms it has survived. We all make our factual mistakes, individually and collectively, and quietly blush about them when reminded. But we can still take a gentle pleasure in the errors and half-truths that others have perpetuated. That temple of knowledge the *Oxford English Dictionary* offers the following basic definition: 'Ragtime. Orig. U.S. 1901. Music in which there is frequent syncopation as in many negro melodies.' The OED is so often wrong in its attributed dates in the musical field and popular mythology that we may be permitted to wonder how often its authoritative statements may be questioned – and that use of the word 'frequent' has the ring of a teetotaller writing about the pleasures of alcohol.

But the OED is not a musical authority. *The Oxford Companion to Music* presumably is. Its editor Percy A. Scholes was a great one for perpetrating myths. Even in the ninth edition of this bulky work we read: 'This phase in musical progress begins with the exploitation of Ragtime, i.e. the supplying of syncopation to music on a wholesale order. The father of published Ragtime was, it is said, Irving Berlin, and his first offspring to become widely recognized (1911) was *Alexander's Rag Time Band*. "Irving Berlin may be described without exaggeration as the Bach, Haydn, Mozart and Beethoven of Jazz – all the old masters in one" (H. O. Osgood, in *So this is Jazz!* 1926). However the world had ragtime before Berlin; indeed it was known in the 1880s. The tendency to ragtime is an African characteristic, brought to America by the slaves, used by them in their songs and, especially, in their dance music . . .', etc. In the 1935 *Radio Times Music Handbook*, the same author sums it up as: 'RAGTIME. A sort of music (usually dance music) that America made popular in the early 20th century, one in which the old and oft-used device of syncopation became the meal instead of the sauce.'

Another writer not much addicted to jazz and its relations but feeling compelled to nod in their direction was Eric Blom. In *Everyman's Dictionary of Music* he writes: 'Ragtime, an American form of syncopated dance music of Negro origin and coming into fashion c. 1910, the forerunner of Jazz and Swing.' The same hand is clearly indicated in his slight modification in *Grove's Dictionary of Music and Musicians*: 'RAGTIME. An American form of popular dance with strongly syncopated music coming into fashion about 1910, the forerunner of jazz and swing.' It is a relief to turn to that most reliable of sources *The Harvard Dictionary of Music* and to find there a balanced and informative entry on ragtime obviously written by somebody who knew what it was all about.

As one may fairly observe, there is a grain of truth in all these definitions but enough lop-sided distortion to make us aware that the writers were repeating what they had heard rather than what they understood or cared about. It is all very well sneering at other people's attempts to pen a definition, and perhaps we ought to try one for ourselves. On the grounds that the more important a subject becomes the longer its entry, we might sum ragtime up as follows: 'A style of American music of predominantly Afro-American origin with melodic and rhythmic roots in Negro folk song and dance and minstrel music, in form similar to the march. Adapting banjo characteristics for its syncopated melodies, it found its purest expression in the piano rags of composers such as Scott Joplin, James Scott and Joseph Lamb, though it was regularly instrumentated for band and orchestral use during its early vogue in the 1890s and early 1900s. The first Negro rag was published in 1897 and ragtime was first recorded in the same year. Ragtime songs were equally popular and after 1910 a modified version of ragtime was taken up by Tin Pan Alley composers and exploited into craze proportions both in popular song and dance in the theatre. Ragtime-styled melodies were an element of early jazz and the later Dixieland style. There was a strong revival of interest in ragtime in the 1940s and 1950s with the publication of the first authoritative book on the subject in 1950: and a further revival in the 1970s when ragtime fitted happily into the general cult of nostalgia for turn-of-the-century arts and crafts. The genius of Scott Joplin was acknowledged by the publication of his complete works in 1971 which led to their wide use in many entertainment fields.'

There is little doubt that Joplin deservedly became the acknowledged master of the ragtime idiom. But other composers of his time and after will eventually get their due recognition. The appreciation of classic ragtime as an elegant, charming and well-constructed music will, one hopes, lead to the appreciation of later developments of the style and will bring composers like Jelly Roll Morton, James P. Johnson and Fats Waller back into prominence.

Joplin has belatedly been put on a pedestal where he should always have been along with other popular composers such as Johann Strauss and John Philip Sousa, for his writings have the same immediacy, strength and durability as theirs. It is surprising that these memorable qualities have not been fully recognised before; the reason probably being inaccurate and unstylistic presentation hitherto and the fact that they are technically just beyond the reach of the average amateur performer. Being on a pedestal means that somebody is going to come along and try to knock you off it. Our viewpoint will in future teeter between what Dick Wellstood recently wrote on a record cover: 'There are ragtime freaks who would have you believe that ragtime is indeed quite complex, perhaps more significant than the stodgy old Beethoven sonatas. This is not so. Scott Joplin's rags are full of naive harmonizations, simple-assed bass progressions, mock-important interludes and 19th century salon cliché. That they are any good at all is attributable to the lyric gift of Joplin, for his song survives all the above-mentioned faults and many more'; and 'This dynamic quality of Joplin's musical personality is the true measure of his stature. Every outstanding composer of the Western world maintained a fresh outlook throughout his career – from Bach and Haydn to the twentieth century leaders, Schoenberg, Stravinsky, Hindemith. It is this quality more than the merits of *Maple Leaf Rag* or any other rag that sets Joplin above his contemporaries' – the more dedicated viewpoint of the discerning ragtime scholar Guy Waterman. Wellstood makes the usual hoary mistake of sneering at simple means towards an end and safely aligns himself with most music critics. Waterman puts no limit to the heights to which we may praise pure genius; and is also discerningly critical in his writings. He is careful to state elsewhere that we must not subject ragtime to 'the tyranny of jazz standards' and was discerningly predicting, back in the 1950s, that when we eventually remembered that ragtime was a written music and owed nothing to jazz improvisation and heard it played 'straight' (as, up to then, only Lee Stafford had done for many years) the difficulties of appreciating it would be overcome. This was the value of Rifkin's contribution, in removing the jazz element and playing ragtime as timeless music. Which, on the other hand, is not to say that ragtime cannot be jazzed or that its future development should never have gone in that direction. A brilliant rag like James Scott's *Frog Legs Rag* published in 1906 was one of the first to display, as Waterman also wrote, 'a vigor and brilliance not found in the placid two-beat of Turpin and Joplin. He gave the music richness and power, symbolized by his selection of the deeper flatted keys of the piano (A♭ and D♭ principally), with a crisper attack, sometimes built entirely on a one-bar splash of syncopation, as, for example, in the second theme of *Grace And Beauty*.' One could see from there that later pianists and composers like James P. Johnson and Morton would find no difficulty in 'progressing' (which doesn't simply mean adding more complex chords but also widening the expressive capabilities of a music by new rhythmic and melodic power) beyond Joplin's inspired but circumscribed efforts.

At this moment when Joplin is appreciated for his own sake we have tacitly learned that ragtime is not to be jazzed and Joplin is not to be Mortoned. Joplin's spiritual age is the 1890s and 1900s; Morton's is the 1920s and 1930s – a sea apart in the rapid evolution of popular music in the last one hundred years.

We have already discussed Joplin's various pieces at length and come to a collective attitude towards them. They were not all good. Some were misguided, some were weak and his sense of words was not gifted with great insight. It is the potential of his music that perhaps provides the most interesting speculation at this moment. We have heard contemporary orchestral realisations and the apt modern arrangements by Gunther Schuller and others – all of which have given Joplin's music another dimension beyond what it already offers to the discerning pianist. We have heard it used effectively as the background to a clever film. We have sat and watched Rifkin in tails, Previn in beach shirt surrounded by eminent musicians like Jack Brymer, Philip Jones, John Fletcher and the Cleveland Quartet, and Tom McIntosh and the City of London Chamber Orchestra play Joplin and others effectively in the same spirit as they play Mozart. We have heard the sympathetic orchestrations that Grant Hossack made when using Joplin's music for a successful ballet by the London Festival Ballet Company. The value of this score was not only in its use of Joplin's material beyond the more popular rags, showing us what attractive pieces some of his lesser-known waltzes and marches are, but in showing that the orchestral possibilities for their use are boundless. Hossack achieved a score which ideally coloured ragtime for those who find a long session of piano rags too black-and-white, using two distinct groups – a small ensemble and a full symphony orchestra, with piano to add a spice of the correct flavour. Some of the arrangements veer on light orchestral romanticism, sweeping strings and harp and all that, but the treatment of many of the pieces shows a real understanding of their nature. *Paragon Rag* was kept to the typical ragtime orchestration of the period; *Solace* was ravishingly used as a framework for saxophone and guitar solos; *Scott Joplin's New Rag* became an exciting flamboyant display; *March Majestic* was given true brass band treatment; *Maple Leaf*, *Swipesey* and *Pine-apple* wittily interchanged; *Rose-bud* became a period quadrille; and nobody could help but enjoy the high-spirited cakewalk character given to *The Cascades* and *Sunflower Slow Drag* in the dance hall scene. Some purists might recoil but they would merely be showing their reluctance to recognise the universal spirit of ragtime and its natural potential for exploitation in the wider fields of popular and light music as well as jazz. Something similar was done with slightly less tact and understanding by Philip Gammon for the Royal Ballet at Covent Garden – the fault here being the tendency to send-up the music and its associated dances. The Joplin pieces were treated with wit and period sense by the Frankfurt Ballet.

Joplin on a variety of unintended instruments has achieved

various results. Harpsichord recordings, for example, have been both good and very bad. Surprisingly, the Moog Synthesizer, although we may wonder at anyone going to such expense to produce a sound not so far removed from that of any Victorian barrel organ, has, when manipulated with taste – as it was at moments by the Eden Electronic Ensemble – managed to capture the elusive period atmosphere of ragtime. Something to do with the Moog's careful precision, and because its sound is very close to that of mechanical instruments of the turn of the century.

The pastiche that Debussy and Stravinsky and the other serious composers helpfully attempted has been overtaken and surpassed by the real thing being prised from its eggshell of obscurity and dressed up in bold colours for film and stage. If our military and brass bands miss the opportunity to revive some of Joplin's excellent marches they will be guilty of serious neglect. *Treemonisha* has been successfully revived in America, most recently by the Houston Grand Opera, directed by Frank Corsaro, and it may yet arrive with an anglicised libretto at the Coliseum in London.

To end on a personal note – I feel happily complacent when I see a composer who I have loved and valued for thirty-odd years being praised and exploited; and when I am asked by teenage sons – 'Have you seen *The Sting* – you'd like the music – it's great!' As ever, I feel equally sorry that a private pleasure has to be shared with those whose only end is to make money out of a good thing and to exploit it with frequent indifference to its real value. But Joplin will survive the exploitation, just as ragtime has survived Tin Pan Alley; he may well reap strength from it. Joplin will survive the well-meaning asides of *The Times*' intellectuals and the jazz eggheads. I don't even need to say that Joplin *will* survive. He *has* survived; there can be nothing lacking in a composer, sixty years in his grave, who is having such an impact in cynical times so remote in outlook from his own. The deepest sorrow is for Joplin himself who died insane with frustration – that he missed all this sweet and profitable success!

Appendix
Books

(a) **About Ragtime**

They All Played Ragtime: the True Story of an American Music by Rudi Blesh and Harriet Janis. Borzoi Books, Alfred A. Knopf, New York, 1950; 2nd Edition: Grove Press, New York, 1959; 3rd and 4th Editions: Oak Publications, New York, 1966 and 1971

English Ragtime: a Discography 1898–1920 by Edward S. Walker and Steven Walker. Edward S. Walker, Mastin Moor, 1971

Recorded Ragtime, 1897–1958 by David A. Jasen. Archon Books, Shoe String Press, Hamden, Conn., 1973

The Art of Ragtime: Form and Meaning of an Original Black American Art by William J. Schafer and Johannes Riedel. Louisiana State University Press, Baton Rouge, 1973

(b) **With Sections on and Reference to Ragtime**

Dinosaurs in the Morning by Whitney Balliett, ch. 'The Ragtime Game (Joseph Lamb)'. Lippincott, New York, 1962; Phoenix House, London, 1964; Jazz Book Club, London, 1965

Combo U.S.A.: Eight Lives in Jazz by Rudi Blesh, ch. 'Little Eubie (Eubie Blake)'. Chilton Book Co., New York, 1971

Jazz: A History of the New York Scene by Samuel B. Charters and Leonard Kunstadt, ch. 'Treemonisha'. Doubleday & Co., New York, 1962

America's Music from the Pilgrims to the Present by Gilbert

Chase, ch. 'The Rise of Ragtime'. McGraw-Hill, New York, 1955

Panorama of American Popular Music by David Ewen, ch. 'Ragtime, Blues, Jazz'. Prentice-Hall Inc., Englewood Cliffs, NJ, 1957

History of Popular Music by David Ewen, ch. 'Ragtime and Blues in Tin Pan Alley'. Barnes & Noble, Inc., New York, 1961

100 Years of the Negro in Show Business by Tom Fletcher. Burdge & Co. Ltd, New York, 1954

The Decca Book of Jazz ed. Peter Gammond, ch. 'Elite Syncopations (The Ragtime Years)' by Charles Wilford. Frederick Muller Ltd, London, 1958; Jazz Book Club, London, 1960

Jazz: from the Congo to the Metropolitan by Robert Goffin, ch. 'Between Tom-Tom and Ragtime'. Doubleday, Doran & Co., New York, 1944; Musicians Press Ltd, London, 1946

Tin Pan Alley: a Chronicle of the American Popular Music Racket by Isaac Goldberg, ch. 'The Rise of Tin Pan Alley : Ragtime'. John Day Co., New York, 1930; Frederick Ungar Publishing Co. Inc., New York, 1961; Constable & Co. Ltd, London, 1961

Ragtime Blues Guitarists by Stefan Grossman. Oak Publications, New York, 1965

Jazz by Rex Harris, ch. 'Ragtime and Early White Jazz'. Penguin Books Ltd, Harmondsworth, Middx., 1952; Grosset & Dunlap, New York, 1960

Jazz ed. Nat Hentoff and Albert McCarthy, ch. 'Ragtime' by Guy Waterman. Rinehart & Co., New York, 1959

Music in the United States: A Historical Introduction by H. Wiley Hitchcock, ch. 'Ragtime'. Prentice-Hall, Englewood Cliffs, NJ, 1969

Der Schlager: ein Panorama de leichten Musik, Vol. 1 by Heinz Peter Hofmann and Peter Czerny, ch. 'Cake Walk und Ragtime als Vorläufer der neuen Gesellschaftstänze'. VEB Lied der Zeit, East Berlin, 1968

From Jehova to Jazz by Helen L. Kaufman, ch. 'Ragtime'. Dodd-Mead, New York, 1937

Music in the Americas ed. George List and Juan Orrego-Salas, ch. 'Hot Rhythm in Ragtime' by Frank Gillis. Indiana University Publications, Bloomington, Ind., 1967

The Negro and his Music by Alain Locke, ch. 'Negro Culture and

History'. Associates in Negro Folk Education, 1936; Kennikat Press, Port Washington, NY, 1968. Ch. also in *Negro Art: Past and Present*. Arno Press, New York, 1969

PL Jazzbook 1947 ed. Albert McCarthy, chs. 'Ragtime – an Excavation' by Charles Wilford and 'Sedalia, Missouri, Cradle of Ragtime' by S. Brunson Campbell and R. J. Carew. Nicholson & Watson, London, 1946

Music in a New Found Land: Themes and Developments in the History of American Music by Wilfrid Mellers, ch. 'Orgy and Alienation : Country Blues, Barrelhouse Piano, and Piano Rag'. Barrie & Rockliff, London, 1964; Knopf, New York, 1965

The Negro in Music and Art ed. Lindsay Patterson, ch. 'Negro Producers of Ragtime' by Sterling Brown. International Library of Negro Life and History, Publishers Co., New York, 1967

Black American Music by Hildred Roach, various references in 'Part Two : the Awakening (1870s–1950s)'. Crescendo Publishing Co., Boston, 1973

Early Jazz: Roots and Musical Development by Gunther Schuller, chs. 'The Beginnings' and 'The First Great Composer (Jelly Roll Morton)'. Oxford University Press, New York & London, 1968

A History of Popular Music in America by Sigmund Spaeth, ch. 'Ragtime to Jazz'. Random House, New York, 1948; Phoenix House, London, 1960

The Music of Black Americans: a History by Eileen Southern, ch. 'Ragtime'. W. W. Norton, New York, 1971

The Story of Jazz by Marshall Stearns, ch. 'Ragtime'. Oxford University Press, New York & London, 1956; various reprints

After the Ball by Ian Whitcomb, ch. 'Ragtime'. Allen Lane, London, 1972; Penguin, London, 1973

The Art of Jazz ed. Martin T. Williams, chs. 'A Survey of Ragtime' and 'Joplin's Late Rags' by Guy Waterman and 'Jelly Roll Morton and the *Frog-i-more Rag*' by William Russell. Oxford University Press, New York & London, 1959

American Popular Song by Alec Wilder, ch. 'The Transition Era : 1885 to World War I'. Oxford University Press, New York & London, 1972

The Story of the House of Witmark: from Ragtime to Swing Time by Isadore Witmark. L. Furman, New York, 1939

(c) Books on Various Composers and Performers

Reminiscing with Sissle and Blake by Robert Kimbal and William Bolcom. Viking Press, New York, 1974

Mister Jelly Roll (Jelly Roll Morton) by Alan Lomax. Duell, Sloane & Pearce, New York, 1950; Cassell, London, 1952; Grove Press, New York, 1956; Jazz Book Club, London, 1956; Pan Books, London, 1959; California University Press, 1973

Jelly Roll Morton by Martin T. Williams. Cassell, London, 1962; Barnes, New York, 1963

Music on My Mind: the Memoirs of an American Pianist by Willie 'The Lion' Smith and George Hoefer. Doubleday, New York, 1964; MacGibbon & Kee, London, 1965; Jazz Book Club, London, 1966

Fats Waller by Charles Fox. Cassell, London, 1960; Barnes, New York, 1961

Ain't Misbehavin: The Story of Fats Waller by W. T. Ed. Kirkeby. Dodd, Mead, New York, 1966; Peter Davies, London, 1966; Jazz Book Club, London, 1967

(d) Other Books of Interest

Memory Lane 1890–1925: Ragtime, Jazz, Foxtrot and other Popular Music Covers ed. Max Wilk. Studioart, London, 1973

Minstrel Memories by Harry Reynolds. Alston Rivers, London, 1928. The standard book on 'black-face' minstrelsy in England from 1836–1927

Tambo and Bones: a History of the American Minstrel Stage by Carl Wittke. Duke University Press, Durham, N. Carolina, 1930

Gentlemen be Seated: a Parade of Old Time Minstrels by Sigmund Spaeth and Dailey Paskman. Doubleday, New York, 1928

The Story of the Original Dixieland Jazz Band by H. O. Brunn. Louisiana State University Press, Baton Rouge, 1960; Sidgwick & Jackson Ltd, London, 1961; Jazz Book Club, London, 1961

Slave Songs of the United States ed. William Francis Allen, Charles Pickard Ware and Lucy McKim Garrison. Simpson, New York, 1867 and 1925; Oak Publications, New York, 1965

Jazz Dance by Marshall Stearns and Jean Stearns. Macmillan, New York, 1968; Collier-Macmillan, London, 1968

Appendix
Music

Parenthetical entries refer to Appendix 4; entries in brackets indicate abbreviated titles.

(a) Joplin

The Collected Works of Scott Joplin 2 Vols. ed. Vera Brodsky Lawrence. Introduction by Rudi Blesh. The New York Public Library, New York, 1971. Vol. 1 is published separately as a paperback *The Collected Works of Scott Joplin for Piano*. Belwin/Mills Publishing Corps, Melville NY & Croydon. [CW: 1/2]

Scott Joplin: King of Ragtime (37 rags, marches, songs, etc.). Lewis Music Publishing Company Inc., Carlstadt, NJ, 1972. (1–20, 22–38) [KR]

The Best of Scott Joplin (with colour cover reproductions). ed. Bill Ryerson. Shattinger International Publications, Charles Hansen, New York, 1973. (7–10, 12, 15–17, 22, 23, 25–9, 36, 38) [BSJ]

Scott Joplin Piano Rags Books 1 & 2. Chappell & Co., London, 1973. (Book 1: 7, 17, 38, 41, 47, 54, 60, 64; Book 2: 16, 31, 35, 36, 43, 49, 51, 55) [PR: 1/2]

It's Easy to Play Ragtime ed. Frank Booth. Wise, London, 1973. (3, 4, 7, 12, 14, 15, 17, 18, 27, 29, 36, 38, 44, 70) [EPR]

Scott Joplin Classic Rags (arr. piano duet). Edward B. Marks Music Corporation, New York, 1973. [SJCR] (ditto, arr. organ)

The Sting (arr. Marvin Hamlisch). MCA/Mills Publications, Melville NY, 1974. (12, 17, 38, 41, 49, 51) (etc.) (S) (also: simplified, piano duet, organ, guitar, band, simplified band, stage band, marching band, orchestra, instrumental [various keys] versions available)

Music from *The Sting* arr. for band by John Cacavas. MCA/ Mills Publications, Melville, N.Y. 1974

Matt Dennis Plays Scott Joplin. Mel Bay Publications, Kirkwood, Mass., 1974. [MDPSJ]

Rags published separately: Nos 7, 17, 41, 49 and 60. Belwin/ Mills, 230 Purley Way, Croydon & USA. No. 7 (*The Entertainer*) also available in simplified, piano duet, organ, recorder, band, orchestral, vocal and choral versions. Also by Chappell

The Red Back Book ed. Gunther Schuller. Orchestral scores and parts of 7, 10, 12, 17, 28, 29, 38 and 48 – each published separately. Belwin/Mills, 230 Purley Way, Croydon & USA, 1973. [RBB]

Scott Joplin Rags (for brass quintet, arr. Frackenpohl). Belwin/ Mills, Croydon & USA. [SJR]

Treemonisha; opera in three acts ed. Vera Brodsky Lawrence and William Bolcom. Dramatic Pub. Co., Chicago, 1972

(b) Other Composers

Jelly Roll Morton's Famous Series of Blues & Stomps for Piano Vols 1–3. Melrose Music Corps, New York; Herman Darewski Music Publishing Co., London, nd. [JRM : 1/3]

Ragtime Treasures – Piano Solos by Joseph F. Lamb (13 recently discovered original solos). Foreword by Rudi Blesh. Belwin/ Mills Publishing Corps, Melville, NY, 1964. [RT]

Songs of Stephen Foster. Dover Publications Inc., New York. [SSF]

The Jazz Masters – Collection of Solos from the Golden Age of Jazz by Billy Mayerl. Keith Prowse, London, 1972 [JM]

Piano Music of Louis Moreau Gottschalk (26 pieces). ed. Richard Jackson. Dover Publications Inc., New York, 1973. [PMG]

Piano Works of Louis Moreau Gottschalk (112 pieces). Arno Press, New York, 1970. [PWG]

Rags published separately in modern editions include:
Barber Shop Rag (Krenz); *Black And White Rag* (Botsford); *Jazz Mag Rag* (Albam); *Mud Cat Rag* (Ramey); *Steamboat Rag* (Burnett); *Temptation Rag* (Lodge) – Belwin/Mills; *Leningrad Rag*

196

(Ramey); *Garden of Eden* – ragtime suite; *The Graceful Ghost Rag*; *Raggin' Rudi*; *Seabiscuits Rag* (all by William Bolcom) – Edward B. Marks; *Twelfth Street Rag* (Bowman); *Bugle Call Rag* (Pettis); etc.

Instrumental :
Ragtime Suite – for brass quintet (Frackenpohl); *Flute Rag* – band and trio (Frackenpohl) – Edward B. Marks.

(c) Ragtime Collections; etc.

Play Them Rags: a Piano Album of Authentic Rag-Time Solos. Mills Music, Inc., New York, 1961; UK : Belwin/Mills. (22, 48, 49) [PTR]

One Hundred Ragtime Classics ed. Max Morath. Donn Printing, Denver, 1963. [OHRC]

Ragtime Piano: a Collection of Standard Rags for Piano Solo. Mills Music Inc., New York, 1963; UK : Belwin/Mills. (53, 54, 55, 64) [RP]

Guide to Ragtime: a Collection of Ragtime Songs & Piano Solos ed. Max Morath. Hollis Music, New York, 1964; new and enlarged ed., *Ragtime Guide:* TRO Essex Music Ltd, UK, 1972 [GTR]

34 Ragtime Classics for Piano. Melrose Music Corp., New York, 1964. [TRC]

The Ragtime Songbook ed. (with historical notes concerning the songs and times) Ann Charters. Oak Publications, New York, 1965. [RS]

Giants of Ragtime ed. Max Morath. Edward B. Marks Music Corporation, New York, 1971; Belwin/Mills, UK. (41, 56, 60) [GOR]

Classic Piano Rags ed. Rudi Blesh (with an Introduction). Dover Publications, New York, 1973. [CPR]

Album of Rags Nos 1–3 ed. Winifred Atwell. Francis, Day & Hunter, London, nd. [AR : 1–3]

Original Ragtime Songs Nos 1–2. Francis, Day & Hunter, London, nd. [ORS : 1–2]

The Dixieland New Orleans: Famous Blues Stomps and Ragtime Books 1–3 ed. George Hoefer. Herman Darewski Music Publishing Co., London, nd; Melrose Music Corp., New York, 1958. [DNO : 1–3]

The Ragtime Book – a ragtime tutor. Schaum, New York, 1973. [RB]

Ragtime Piano Styles (simplified). Mel Bay Publications, Kirkwoods, Mass., 1973. [RPS]

The Joy of Ragtime, ed. Denes Agay. Yorktown Music Press, New York, 1974

Instrumental :

Ragtime Favourites for Strings. Belwin/Mills; *Ragtime Classics* – for clarinet and piano. Belwin/Mills; etc.

Appendix
LP Recordings

The following lists exclude 78rpm recordings, which are now the prerogative of the dedicated collector, but offer a selective list of titles now available on LP, either original or reissued. Jasen's *Recorded Ragtime 1897–1958* and *They All Played Ragtime* offer further guidance on 78s. The appearance of a record in the subsequent lists does not imply that it is currently or readily available. There has, however, been a generous flood of recent recordings which should satisfy the needs of the general collector and these can generally be identified by their current numbers.

(a) from Piano rolls

A comprehensive list of piano rolls will be found as an appendix to *They All Played Ragtime*. The following is a selection of LPs which reproduce piano roll transcriptions. Numbers in brackets refer (as elsewhere in the book) to the Joplin works (where known) which are included. See Appendix 4 for reference numbers.

'The Golden Age Of Ragtime' – USA: Riverside 12-110 (1902–13)

'Ragtime Piano Roll Classics' – USA: Riverside 12-126. Issued in UK as London 'Origins Of Jazz' AL3515 (6, 17, 47, 60), AL3523 (7, 28); AL3542 (64) and AL3563 (7) (from the original 10" Riverside issues RLP1006, RLP1025, RLP1049 and RLP1060)

'The Piano Roll' (ed. Rebor J. Tichnor) – USA: Folkways RBF-7

'Piano Roll Ragtime' – USA : Sounds 1201
'Pianola Ragtime' – UK : Saydisc SDL132 (available in USA)
'I'll Dance Till De Sun Breaks Through : Ragtime, Cakewalks &
    Stomps 1898–1917' – UK : Saydisc SDL210 (and USA)
'Pianola Jazz' – UK : Saydisc SDL117 (and USA)
'Ragged Piano Classics' – USA : Origin 16
'Ragtime – A Recorded Documentary' – USA : Piedmont 13158
'Scott Joplin : Ragtime Pioneer : 1899–1914' – USA : Riverside
    RLP8815 (6, 7, 10, 17, 22, 23, 28, 47, 49, 54, 56, 60, 64)
'Scott Joplin' Vol. 1 – USA : Biograph BLP1005Q; Vol. 2 – USA :
    Biograph BLP1008Q; Vol. 3 – USA : Biograph BLP1010Q; Vol.
    4 – USA : Biograph BLP1013Q; Vol. 5 – USA : Biograph BLP-
    1014Q
'Parlor Piano' (Historic piano rolls) – USA : Biograph BLP1001Q
'Jelly Roll Morton Solos' – USA : Riverside RLP140; UK : London
    AL3519
'Early Harlem Piano' (James P. Johnson) – USA : Riverside RLP-
    1046; UK : London AL3511 and 3540
'His Earliest Piano Rolls' (Eubie Blake) – USA : Biograph BLP-
    10112Q
'1917 Ragtime' (James P. Johnson) – USA : Biograph BLP100389

(b) Originals

Early recordings either made in the ragtime era or recordings
by pianists and composers who were active in the pioneering
days of ragtime and early jazz.

Collections

'A Programme Of Ragtime Music' Vol. 1 – UK : Vintage Jazz
    Music VLP1
'When Grandma Was A Teenager : A Programme Of Ragtime
    Music' Vol. 2 – UK : Vintage Jazz Music VLP2
'An Edison Memorabilia' (cylinder recordings), 2 Vols. – USA :
    Edison Foundation UR4S-1031/2
'Cylinder Jazz : 1897–1928' – UK : Saydisc SDL112
'Creative Ragtime' – USA : Euphonic CRS 1206
'Pioneers Of Boogie Woogie' Vol. 2 (contains Davenport's
    Atlanta Rag) – UK : London AL3537

'Red Onion Rag: Piano Ragtime of the Teens, Twenties & Thirties' – USA: Herwin 402

'Black And White Ragtime' – USA: Biograph BLP12047 (1923–43)

'They All Played "Maple Leaf Rag" ' – USA: Herwin 401

'Barrelhouse Piano' (Melrose, J. P. Johnson, Alex Hill) – UK: Vogue LRA10022 (1929–30)

Eubie Blake (b. 1883)

'The Wizard Of The Ragtime Piano' – USA: 20th Century Fox 3003; UK: Top Rank (EP) JKP2008 and JKP2014 (1958)

'The Marches I Played On The Old Ragtime Piano' – USA: 20th Century Fox 3039 (1959)

'Golden Reunion In Ragtime' – USA: Stereoddities (S) 1900 (1962)

'The Eighty-Six Years of Eubie Blake' – USA: Columbia (S) C2S-847; UK: CBS (S) 68250 (2 records) (1968–9)

'Eubie Blake With Ivan Harold Browning' – USA: Eubie Blake Music (S) EBM-1; UK: Side 1 only on London (S) SAH8474

'From Ragtime To Classics' – USA: Eubie Blake Music (S) EBM-2; UK: London (S) SH8463; (also cassette) (S) KSAC8463 (without *Rustle Of Spring*)

'Eubie Blake with Edith Wilson' – USA: Eubie Blake Music (S) EBM-3; UK: Side 2 only on London (S) SH8474

'Sissle And Blake' (early transcriptions) – USA: Eubie Blake Music EBM-4

'Eubie Blake – Live Concert' – USA: Eubie Blake Music (S) EBM-5. UK: London (S) SAH8476

'Eubie Blake Introduces Jim Hession' – USA: Eubie Blake Music (S) EBM-6

Jimmy Blythe (1899–1936)

'South Side Blues Piano' – USA: Riverside RLP1031; UK: London AL3527

'South Side Chicago Jazz' – USA: Riverside RLP1036; UK: London AL3536

Euday Bowman (1887–1949)

'The Professors' Vol. 2 – USA: Euphonic ESR-1202

Brun Campbell (1884–1953)

'The Professors' Vol. 1 – USA: Euphonic ESR-1201

'The Professors' Vol. 2 – USA : Euphonic ESR-1202
Bunk Johnson (1879–1949)
'Bunk Johnson' – UK : Columbia 33SX1015
Will Ezell
'Gin Mill Jazz' – USA : Riverside RLP1043; UK : London AL3539
Dink Johnson
'The Professors' Vol. 1 – USA : Euphonic ESR-1201
'The Professors' Vol. 2 – USA : Euphonic ESR-1202
'Dink Johnson's Good Time Music' – USA : Storyville (EP) SEP390
James P. Johnson (1891–1955)
'Father Of The Stride Piano' – USA : Columbia CL1780; UK : CBS BPG62090
'Yamekraw' – USA : Folkways 2842
'The Jazz Makers' – USA : Swaggie S-1211
'James P. Johnson' – USA : Xtra 1024; UK : Xtra 1024
'New York Jazz' – USA : Stinson 21
'Jazz Of The Forties' Vol. 1 – USA : Folkways 2841
'Harlem Party Piano' – USA : Circle 1027; UK : London HB-U1057 (1927)
'Daddy Of The Piano' – USA : Decca DL5190; UK : Brunswick LA8548 (1944)
'Farewell To James P. Johnson' – UK : HMV (EP) 7EG8164
'James P. Johnson' – USA : Blue Note BLP7011
'Favourites Fats Waller' – USA : Decca; UK : Brunswick LA8622
Joe Jordan (1882–1971)
'Golden Reunion In Ragtime' – USA : Stereoddities (S) 1900 (1962)
Joseph Lamb (1887–1960)
'A Study In Classic Ragtime' – USA : Folkways FG-3562 (1959)
Billy Mayerl (1902–59)
'The King Of Syncopation' – UK : World Records SH189
Jelly Roll Morton (1885–1941)
'Library Of Congress Recordings' – USA : Circle 14001-12; USA : Riverside RLP9001-12 (1938); Selection – USA : Riverside RLP12-132
'Piano Solos' – USA : Mainstream 56020, (S) 6020
'Jelly Roll Morton' – USA : Swaggie S-1213

'The Incomparable JRM' – USA: Riverside 128 and RLP8816; USA: Milestone MLP-2003 (1923–6)

'Classic Jazz Piano' – USA: Riverside RLP12-111; UK: London AL3534 and AL3559 (1923–4)

'Jelly Roll Morton' – USA: Gaps 010

'King Of New Orleans Jazz' Vol. 1 – USA: RCA LPM1649; UK: RCA RD-27113 (1926–8)

'King Of New Orleans Jazz' Vol. 2 – USA: RCA LPV-508; UK: RCA RD27184

'New Orleans Memories' – USA: Commodore 30000; UK: Fontana TL-5261 as 'Jelly Roll Morton Piano Solos'

'King Of The Piano' – USA: Brunswick 58003

'Stomps And Joys' – USA: RCA LPV508

'Hot Jazz, Pop Jazz, Hokum And Hilarity' – USA: RCA LPV524; UK: RCA RD-7807

'Mr Jelly Lord' – USA: RCA LPV546; UK: RCA RD-7914

'I Thought I Heard Buddy Bolden Say' – USA: RCA LPV559

'Classic Jazz Piano Styles' – USA: RCA LPV543; UK: RCA RD-7915

'Jelly Roll Morton' – USA: Commodore 30000; UK: Vogue LDE-080 (1936) (6)

'Morton's Sixes & Sevens' – UK: Fontana TL5415

'Red Hot Peppers' – UK: HMV DLP1016, DLP1044, DLP1071

Luckey Roberts (1893–1968)

'Harlem Piano' – USA: Good Time Jazz 12035; UK: Good Time Jazz LAG12256

'Harlem Party Piano' – USA: Circle 1027; UK: London HB-U1057

Willie 'The Lion' Smith (b. 1897)

'The Lion' – USA: Vogue 693-30

'Original Compositions' – USA: Commodore 30003

'Reminiscing The Piano Greats' – USA: Dial LP305; UK: Vogue LDE177 (7)

'The Legend' – USA: Grand Award 33–368; USA: Mainstream 56027; UK: Fontana TL5272

'The Lion Roars' – USA: Dot 3094; UK: London H-APB1017

'Harlem Piano' – USA: Good Time Jazz M12035; UK: Good Time Jazz LAG 12256

'Grand Piano' – USA: Exclusive (S) 501; UK: 77 (S) LEU 12/26

'The Memories Of ...' – USA: RCA (S) LSP-6016

'Live At Blues Alley' – USA: Halcyon (S) 104

'Jazz Piano – A Musical Exchange' – USA: RCA LPM-3499; UK: RCA RD7830

'The Swingin' Cub Men' – UK: Ace of Hearts AH-162

Charles Thompson (1891–1964)

'Golden Reunion In Ragtime' – USA: Stereoddities (S) 1900 (1962)

Thomas 'Fats' Waller (1904–43)

'Classic Jazz Piano Style' – USA: RCA LPV543; UK: RCA RD-7915

'Valentine Stomp' – USA: RCA LPV525; UK: RCA RD-7801

'Fractious Fingering' – USA: RCA LPV537; UK: RCA RD-7855

'Handful Of Keys' – USA: RCA LPM1502; UK: RCA RD-27185 (1934–49)

'One Never Knows Do One' – USA: RCA LPM1503; UK: RCA

'Young Fats Waller' – USA: Camden CAL3107; UK: HMV DLP-IIII

'Fats Waller And His Rhythm' – UK: HMV DLP1118

'34/35 Fats Waller' – USA: RCA LPV516; UK: RCA RD-7779 (1934–5)

'Fats On The Air, Vol. 1' – USA: RCA LPT6001; UK: RCA RD-7552

'Fats On The Air, Vol. 2' – USA: RCA LPT6002; UK: RCA RD-7553

'The Real Fats Waller' – USA: RCA Camden CAL-478; UK: Camden CDN131 (1929–43)

'Fats Waller Memorial Album' – UK: Encore ENC181

'Young Fats Waller' – USA: Riverside 12-103; USA: London AL-3507 (1923–6)

'The Amazing Mr Waller' – USA: Riverside 12-109; USA: London AL3522 and AL3521 (1939)

'Fats 1935–7' – USA: RCA LPM-1246; 'Ain't Misbehavin' – UK: RCA RD-27047 (1935–7)

'Fats 1938–42' – USA: RCA LPM-1502; UK: RCA-24004 (1938–42)

'Fats Waller In London, No. 1' – UK: HMV 7EG8304 (1938)

'Fats Waller In London, No. 2' – UK : HMV 7EG8341 (1938)
'Fats Waller' – USA : RCA EPA5005; UK : RCA RCX1010
'The Vocal Fats Waller' – UK : RCA LSA3112 (1934–43)
'African Ripples' – USA : RCA LPV-562
'Smashing Thirds' – USA : RCA LPV-550

(c) Ragtime Revivals

John Arpin
'Concert In Ragtime' – USA : Scroll 101
'The Other Side Of Ragtime' – USA : Scroll 103
'Ragtime Piano' – USA : Harmony (S) 6026
Marvin Ash (1914–74)
'Marvin Ash' – USA : Jazz Man 335
'Honky-Tonk Piano' – USA : Capitol T-188; UK : Capitol LC6544
Donald Ashwander
'The New View' – USA : Jazzology JCE-71
Winifred Atwell
'Winifred Atwell' – UK : Decca LF1075
'Black And White Magic' – UK : Decca LF1108
'Black And White Magic' Vol. 2 – UK : Decca LF1155 (above also
    DFE6098/9)
'Winifred Atwell' – UK : Philips BBR8020
'Double 7' – USA : London 1573
'The World Of Winifred Atwell' – UK : Decca PA51, (S) SPA51
Burt Bales (b. 1916)
'They Tore My Playhouse Down' – USA : Good Time Jazz GTJ-
    12025 (1950s)
'After Hours' – USA : Good Time Jazz; UK : Good Time Jazz
    LDG1316 (1949)
Chris Barber (b. 1930)
'Chris Barber Bandbox' Vol. 1 – UK : Columbia 33SX1158 (1959)
'Elite Syncopations' – UK : Columbia 33SX1245; Fr : Pathé CO62-
    9553
'New Orleans Joys' – UK : Decca LF1198 (1954)
E. Power Biggs
'Plays Scott Joplin' – USA : Columbia (S) M-32495

'Plays Scott Joplin – Vol. II' – USA : Columbia (S) M33205
Pete Bocage
'The Living Legends' – USA : Riverside 379
William Bolcom (b. 1938)
'Rags' – USA : Jazzology JCE-72
'Heliotrope Bouquet: Piano Rags 1900–1970' – USA : Nonesuch
　(S) H-71257; UK : Nonesuch (S) H-71257 (12, 44, 50) (1973)
'Pastimes And Piano Rags' (Artie Matthews and James Scott) –
　USA : Nonesuch (S) H-71299; UK : Nonesuch (S) H-71299 (1974)
Claude Bolling
'Original Ragtime' – USA : Philips 70.341
Lou Busch (Joe 'Fingers' Carr) (b. 1910)
'Honky Tonk Piano' – USA : Capitol T-188; UK : Capitol LC6544
　(1949)
Joe 'Fingers' Carr (b. 1910)
'Bar Room Piano' – USA : Capitol T-280; UK : Capitol LC6541
　(1951)
'Rough-House Piano' – USA : Capitol T-345; UK : Capitol LC6567
　(1952)
'And His Ragtime Band' – USA : Capitol T-443; UK : Capitol LC-
　6612 (1953)
'Plays The Classics' – USA : Capitol T-649; UK : Capitol T-649
'Mister Ragtime' – USA : Capitol T-760; UK : Capitol T-760
'Honky Tonk Street Parade' – USA : Capitol T-809; UK : Capitol
　T-809
'The Hits Of Joe "Fingers" Carr' – USA : Capitol T-2019; UK :
　Capitol T-2019
'The World's Greatest Ragtime Piano Player' – USA : Warner
　Bros (S) 1386; UK : Warner WM4018, (S) WS8018
'Brassy Piano' – USA : Warner Bros 1456
'Joe "Fingers" Carr' – UK : Capitol LCG572
'Fireman's Ball' – UK : Capitol LC6686
Ann Charters
'Essay In Ragtime' – USA : Folkways 3563
'A Joplin Bouquet' – USA : Portents 1; UK : Sonet SNTF631
　(1950s)
'Treemonisha' – USA : Portents 3
'The Genius of Scott Joplin' – USA : GNP Crescendo 9032; UK :
　(S) Sonet SNTF 661

Ken Colyer (b. 1928)
'New Orleans To London' – UK : Decca LF1152 (1954)
'They All Played Ragtime' – UK : Decca (EP) DFE6466
Bob Darch
'Ragtime Piano' – USA : United Artists 3120
'Gold Rush Daze' – USA : Stereoddities (S) 1901
'Evening In A Fine Saloon' (with Eubie Blake and Joe Jordan) –
  – USA : Maple Leaf Club, 1 Jan.
Rev. Gary Davies
'Ragtime Guitar' – USA, UK : Transatlantic (S) TRA244
Pete Davis
'Ragtime Piano' – UK : Saydisc SDL-118 (7) (also USA)
Lois Delano
'The Music Of Joe Jordan' – USA : Arpeggio 1205
Neville Dickie (b. 1937)
'Ragtime Piano' – UK : Saydisc SDL-118 (6, 25, 38, 55) (also USA)
'Creative Ragtime' – USA : Euphonic 1206
'Introducing Neville Dickie' – USA : Major Minor (S) 5039
'I Love A Piano' – USA : Major Minor (S) 5054
'Piano Rags' – USA : Piano Contour (S) 287190
Al 'Spider' Dugan
'Please Don't Put Your Empties On The Piano' – USA : Warner
  Bros 1329
The Dukes of Dixieland
'Piano Ragtime' – USA : Audio Fidelity 1928, (S) 5928
Hank Duncan
'Hot Piano' – USA : Ri-Disc 4
Eden Electronic Ensemble
'Eden Electronic Ensemble Plays Joplin' – UK : Pye (S) NSPL41037
  (10, 16, 17, 18, 19, 28, 29) (1974)
Lee Erwin (pipe-organ)
'Rosebud' – USA : Angel (S) S-36075 (6, 29, 34, 36, 51, 56)
  (etc.)
Don Ewell (b. 1916)
'Pianist' – USA : Winding Ball 101
'Music To Listen To Don Ewell By' – USA : Good Time Jazz GTJ-
  12021; UK : Vogue LAG12131 (1956)
'Grand Piano' – USA : Exclusive (S) M501; UK : 77 LEU12/26
Ray Foxley (b. 1929)

'Ray Foxley Trio' – UK : Tempo EXA 24 (44)
Joe Glover
'That Ragtime Sound' – USA : Epic 3581
Marvin Hamlisch
'The Sting' (original soundtrack) – USA : MCA (S) 390; UK : MCA
  (S) MCF2537 (12, 17, 38, 41, 49, 51) (1973)
'The Entertainer' – USA : MCA (S) MCA-2115 (7, 17, 31, 56) (1974)
Paul Hersh and David Montgomery
'Ragtime : The Great Classics' – USA : RCA (S) ARLI-0364
Grant Hossack
'Prodigal Son' – a ballet – USA : Columbia (S) S73363; UK : CBS
  (S) S73363 (1974) (5, 6, 7, 8, 10, 11, 14, 17, 20, 28, 31, 34, 35, 38,
  41, 47, 49, 51, 55, 60)
'The Entertainer' – a ballet – USA : Columbia (S) M-33185
Armand Hug (b. 1910)
'Plays Rags And Blues' – USA : Golden Crest 3064, (S) 3064
Dick Hyman
'Scott Joplin : The Complete Works for Piano' (5 Vols.) – USA :
  RCA (S) CRL-1106
Cliff Jackson
'Hot Piano' – USA : Ri-Disc 5
David A. Jasen
'Creative Ragtime' – USA : Euphonic 1206
'Piano Rags' – USA : Blue Goose (S) 3001
'Rompin' Stompin' Ragtime' – USA : Blue Goose (S) 3002
John Jensen
'James Scott Piano Rags' – USA : Genesis (S) GS1044
'Joseph Lamb Piano Rags' – USA : Genesis (S) GS1045
Hank Jones (b. 1918)
'This Is Ragtime Now' – USA : ABC Paramount 496
Milton Kaye
'The Classic Rags Of Joe Lamb' – USA : Golden Crest (S) CRS-
  4127; UK : London (S) HSU-5010
'Ragtime At The Rosebud' – USA : Golden Crest (S) CRS-31032
  (11, 12, 23, 28, 34) (etc.)
Stephen Kovacs
'Tiger On The Keys' – USA : Elektra 111
Bill Krenz
'Oh Willie, Play That Thing' – USA : MGM E-184

David Laibman and Eric Schoenberg
'New Ragtime Guitar' – USA: Asch (S) S-3528; UK: Transatlantic
    (S) TRA253 (5, 56)
Paul Lingle (b. 1902)
'Vintage Piano' – USA: Euphonic 1203
'They Tore My Playhouse Down' – USA: Good Time Jazz
    12025
Johnny Maddox
'Authentic Ragtime' – USA: Dot 102
'The World's Greatest Piano Rolls' Vols 1–4 – USA: Dot (S) 24321,
    25476/7/8
Bill Mitchell
'Vintage Piano' – USA: Euphonic 1203
Max Morath
'A Scintillating Program' – USA: Epic LN-24066
'Oh, Play That Thing' – USA: Epic (S) 26106
'The Entertainer' – USA: Arpeggio (S) 1204S
'At The Turn Of The Century' – USA: RCA (S) LSO-1159
'The World Of Scott Joplin' – USA: Vanguard (S) VSQ30031,
    (S) SRV3105D
'The Best Of Scott Joplin And Other Rag Classics' – USA: Van-
    guard (S) VSD39/40; UK: Vanguard (S) VSD39/40
'Ragtime Favourites' (with Wally Rose) – UK: CBS EMB31059
Russ Morgan and Eddie Wilser
'Kitten On The Keys' – USA: Decca 8746
Turk Murphy (b. 1915)
'The Music Of Jelly Roll Morton' – USA: Columbia 559
'The Many Faces Of Ragtime' – USA: Atlantic (S) SD1613
The New Orleans Ragtime Orchestra
'The New Orleans Ragtime Orchestra' – USA: Pearl 7
'The New Orleans Ragtime Orchestra' – USA: Vanguard 69/70
'Grace And Beauty' – USA: Delmark (S) DS-214
'The New Orleans Ragtime Orchestra' – USA: Arhoolie (S) 1058;
    UK: Sonet (S) SNTF632 (16, 52, 60)
'That Teasin' Rag' – USA: Delmark (S) DS-214
New Sunshine Jazz Band
'Old Rags' – USA: Flying Dutchman (S) BDL1-0549 (60) (etc.)
Keith Nichols
'Plays Scott Joplin And The Classic Rag Masters' – UK: One Up
    (S) OU2035 (12, 23, 28, 29, 41, 42, 52)

Red Nichols (b. 1905)
'Blues And Old-Time Rags' – USA : Capitol (S) 2065
Knuckles O'Toole
'The Greatest All Time Ragtime Hits' – USA : Grand Award 373
Tony Parenti (1900–72)
'Ragtime' – USA : Jazzology 15; USA : Riverside 205; UK : London LTZ-U15072 (8, 10) (etc.) (1947–8)
'Ragtime Jubilee' – USA : Jazzology 21
Knocky Parker
'Knocky Parker Trio' – USA : Dixie 101; UK : London H-BU1044
'Professor's Progress' – USA : Dixie 102/3; UK : London HA-U2008 (7, 49, 51, 52)
'Complete Works Of Scott Joplin' – USA : Audiophile AP-71/2
'Complete Works Of James Scott' – USA : Audiophile AP-76/7
'Complete Works Of Jelly Roll Morton' – USA : Audiophile AP102/5
'Golden Treasury Of Ragtime' – USA : Audiophile AP89/92
'Old Rags' – USA : Audiophile AP-49
Itzhak Perlman & André Previn
'The Easy Winners' – USA : Angel (S) 37113; UK : EMI (S) ASD 3075
Brooke Pemberton
'The Ragtime Kid' – USA : Warner Bros 1235
E. Power Biggs
'Plays Scott Joplin On The Pedal Harpsichord' – USA : Columbia (S) M32495; UK : CBS (S) 61478 (6, 7, 9, 10, 12, 14, 16, 18, 33, 49)
Ronnie Price
'The Scott Joplin Ragtime Album' – UK : CBS Embassy (S) EMB-31043 (6, 7, 10, 12, 14, 16, 17, 38, 41, 49, 51, 60)
The Ragtimers
'Music From "The Sting"' – USA : RCA Camden ACLI-0599, (S) ACSI-0599
'Ragtime Special' (with Max Morath and Muggy Spanier) – USA : Camden ADLZ-0778
Charlie Rasch
'Ragtime Down The Line' – USA : Ragtime Society 4
Joshua Rifkin (b. 1944)
'Piano Rags By Scott Joplin' Vol. 1 – USA : Nonesuch (S) H-71248; UK : Nonesuch (S) H-71248 (7, 17, 19, 41, 47, 54, 60, 64)

'Piano Rags By Scott Joplin' Vol. 2 – USA : Nonesuch (S) H-71264;
   UK: Nonesuch (S) H-71264 (16, 31, 35, 36, 43, 49, 51, 55)
'Piano Rags By Scott Joplin' Vol. 3 – USA : Nonesuch (S) H-71305;
   UK: Nonesuch (S) H-71305 (6, 23, 28, 29, 45, 48, 53, 56)
William Neil Roberts
'Great Scott! Ragtime On The Harpsichord' – USA: Klavier (S)
   KS-510 (5, 7, 8, 9, 10, 12, 16, 31, 44, 49, 56)
'Great Scott . . . Music Of Scott Joplin' – UK : Decca (S) PFS4292;
   USA : London (S) SPC21105 (5, 7, 8, 31, 49, 51, 55, 60, 64)
Alan Rogers
'From Rags To Riches' – UK: Polydor (S) 2400 227 (7, 10, 51) (etc.)
Eric Rogers
'Great Scott . . . The Music Of Scott Joplin' – UK : Decca (S)
   PFS4292; USA: London (S) SPC21105 (5, 7, 8, 31, 49, 51, 55, 60,
Wally Rose (b. 1913)
'Ragtime Classics' – USA : Good Time Jazz L-3
'Ragtime Piano Masterpieces' – USA : Columbia CL6260
'Ragtime Classics' – USA : Good Time Jazz 12034
'Ragtime Favorites' (with Max Morath) – UK : CBS (S) EMB31059
'Cakewalk Lindy Hop' – USA : Columbia 782
'The Music Of Jelly Roll Morton' – USA : Columbia 559
'Rose On Piano' – USA : Blackbird 12007
Slugger Ryan
'Plays Honky Tonk Piano' – USA – Judson 3015
St Louis Ragtimers
'St Louis Ragtimers' Vol. 1 – USA : Audiophile 75
'St Louis Ragtimers' Vol. 2 – USA : Audiophile 81
San Francisco Harry
'30 Barbary Coast Favorites' – USA : Fantasy 3270
Gunther Schuller: New England Conservatory Ragtime Ensemble
'Ragtime Classics' – USA : Angel (S) S-36060 (S); 'The Red Back
   Book' – UK : EMI (S) EMD5503 (7, 10, 12, 17, 28, 29, 38, 48)
'More Scott Joplin Rags' – USA : Golden Crest (S) CR531031; UK :
   London (S) HSU5009 (6, 9, 16, 25, 31, 41, 49, 50, 51, 54, 60,
   64)
'The Road from Rags to Jazz' – USA : Golden Crest CRS-31042
Tom Shea
'Classic And Modern Rags' – USA : Ragtime Society 1
'Prairie Ragtime' – USA : Ragtime Society 2

Frank Signorelli (b. 1901)
'Ragtime Duo' – USA : Kapp 1005
The Southland Stingers (cond. George Sponhaltz)
'Palm Leaf Rag' (Scott Joplin) – USA: Angel (S) 536074; UK:
   EMI (S) EMD5517 (15, 25, 26, 31, 41, 49, 50, 51, 52, 56)
'Magnetic Rag' (Scott Joplin) – USA: Angel (S) 536078; UK:
   EMI (S) EMD5522 (16, 18, 22, 27, 33, 36, 42, 44, 45, 64)
Sammy Spear
'Authentic Ragtime Music' – USA: Mercury 20116
Chris Stone (Moog Synthesizer)
'Gatsby's World – Turned-on Joplin' – USA: ABC (S) ABCX-823
   (3, 7, 10, 12, 16, 17, 28, 29, 44)
Ralph Sutton (b. 1922)
'Piano Solos' – USA: Riverside 212
'Backroom Piano' – USA: Verve MGV-1004; UK: Columbia
   33CX10061 (7) (etc.)
'Piano Solos' – USA: Commodore 30,001
'A Salute To Fats' – USA: Harmony HL7019
'Ralph Sutton Piano' – USA: Ace of Hearts 39
'Ragtime U.S.A.' – USA: Roulette 25232
'Knocked-Out Nocturne' – USA: Project 3 (S) PR-5040
Butch Thompson
'Plays Jelly Roll Morton' Vols 1 & 2 – USA: Center 4 and 9
Trebor Jay Tichenor
'Mississippi Valley Ragtime' – USA: Scroll LSCR-102
'St Louis Ragtimers' – USA: Audiophile
'King Of Folk Ragtime' – USA: Dirty Shame (S) 2001
Ray Turner
'Honky Tonk Piano' – USA: Capitol T-188; UK: Capitol LC6544
'Kitten On The Keys' – USA: Capitol H-306
Lu Watters (b. 1911) *and The Yerba Buena Jazz Band*
'Yerba Buena Jazz Band' – USA: Good Time Jazz LP-8
'1942 Series' – USA: Good Time Jazz GTJ12007
'San Francisco Style' Vols 1–3 – USA: Good Time Jazz GTJ12001/
   2/3; UK: Good Time Jazz LAG12025 (6, 12, 49), LAG12030
'Dixieland Jamboree' – USA: Verve MGV1008
'Blues Over Bodega' – USA: Fantasy 5016
Ron Weatherburn

'Ragtime Piano' – UK: Redifussion (S) 0100170 (6, 7, 17, 44, 47)
Dick Wellstood (b. 1927)
'From Ragtime On' – UK: Chiaroscuro (S) 109
'Joplin Rags' – USA: Pickwick (S) SPC-3376 (7, 10, 12, 17, 28, 29, 38, 41, 47, 49, 51, 60)
Albert White
'Your Father's Moustache' – USA: Barbary Coast 33008
'Your Father's Moustache' Vol. 2 – USA: Fantasy (S) 8040
Quentin Williams
'Ragtime Piano' – UK: Saydisc SDL-118
Zinn's Ragtime String Quartet
'Zinn's Ragtime String Quartet' – USA: Music Minus One (S) CJ13 (7, 12, 44, 45, 56, 60) (etc.) (1974)
Collections:
'They All Played Ragtime' – USA: Jazzology JCE52
'An Evening With Scott Joplin' – USA: New York Public Library (S) NYPL-SJ (7, 16, 31, 38, 49, 51, 52, 58-excerpts, 64)
'They All Played "Maple Leaf Rag"' – USA: Herwin 401 (7)
'Picture Rags' (guitar) – UK: Transatlantic (S) TRA SAM 26 (6, 7)
'Ragtime Special' – USA: RCA Camden ADL2-0778

(d) Classical

A selective list of classical works influenced by ragtime and jazz with records listed where available
Paul Abraham (1892–1960)
'Viktoria Und Ihr Husar' (1930) – Telefunken (S) NT516
John Alden Carpenter (1876–1951)
'Krazy Kat' – a jazz pantomime (1922)
'Skyscrapers' (1926) – USA: Desto (S) 6407
Aaron Copland (b. 1900)
'Music For The Theatre' – a dance (1925) – USA: Columbia (S) MS-6698; UK: CBS (S) 72074
'Rodeo' – a ballet (1942) – USA: Columbia (S) M-30114; UK: CBS (S) 72888; USA: Columbia MS-6175; UK: CBS (S) 72411; UK: Classics for Pleasure (S) CFP40060; etc.
'Old American Songs' (1950–2) – USA: Columbia (S) MS-6497; UK: CBS (S) SBRG72218

'Clarinet Concerto' (1948) – USA: Columbia (S) MS-6805; UK: CBS (S) 72469

Claude Debussy (1862–1918)

'Children's Corner Suite' – Golliwog's Cakewalk (1908) – USA: Turnabout (S) TV34166; UK: Turnabout (S) TV37024S; USA: DG (S) 2530 196; UK: DG 2530 196

'Préludes Book 1' – Minstrels (1910) – UK: HMV (S) SLS803; UK: Turnabout (S) TV37027S

'Préludes Book 2' – General Lavine – eccentric (1913) – UK: HMV (S) SLS803; USA: Turnabout (S) 34166; UK: Turnabout (S) TV37027S

George Gershwin (1898–1937)

'Rhapsody In Blue' (1924) – USA: Angel (S) S-36810; UK: HMV (S) ASD2754

'Piano Concerto In F' (1925) – USA: Angel (S) S-36810; UK: HMV (S) ASD2754

'Piano Music' – USA: Nonesuch (S) H-71284; UK: Nonesuch (S) H-71284

Louis Moreau Gottschalk (1829–69)

'40 Piano Works' (Mandel) – USA: Desco 6470/3

'Piano Works' (Pennario) – USA: Angel (S) S-36077

'Piano Works' (various) – USA: Vanguard (S) S-275; UK: Vanguard (S) SRV275S; USA: Turnabout (S) TV3440/2; UK: Turnabout TV37036S and TV37084S; USA: Vanguard (S) 485

'Cakewalk' – a ballet suite (arr. Hershy Kay) – excerpts – USA: RCA (S) VI CS1053; UK: RCA (S) VICS1053

Louis Gruenberg (1884–1964)

'Polychromatics' (1922)

'Daniel Jazz' (1923)

'Jazz Suite' (1924)

'Jazzettes For Violin And Piano' (1925)

'Jazzberries' (1925)

Karel Hába (1898–1972)

'Four Dances' (Shimmy Blues, Blue, Boston, Tango)

Paul Hindemith (1895–1963)

'Kammermusic No. 1' – (1922) – USA; Telefunken (S)-43110/2

'Klaviersuite' (1922)

Arthur Honegger (1892–1955)
'Concertino For Piano & Orchestra' (1925) – USA : Turnabout (S) TV34130S; UK : Turnabout (S) TV34130S
Joseph Horovitz (b. 1920)
'Music Hall' – a suite for brass – UK : Pye (S) GSGC14114
Jerome Kern (1885–1945)
'Jazz Symphony'
Ernest Krenek (b. 1900)
'Jonny Spielt Auf' (1927) – UK : Philips (S) SAL3498; USA : Mace (S) S-9094
'Sprüng Uber Den Schatten' (1924)
Constant Lambert (1905–51)
'Rio Grande' (1927) – UK : HMV (S) ASD2990
'Elegiac Blues' (1927)/'Piano Sonata' (1929) – UK : Argo (S) ZRG-786
Darius Milhaud (1892–1974)
'La Création du Monde' (1923) – USA : Angel (S) S-35932; UK : HMV (S) ASD2316
'Three Rag Caprices' (1923)
'Le Boeuf Sur Le Toit' (1919) – UK : Philips (S) SAL3637
Francis Poulenc (1899–1963)
'Les Biches' (1923) – USA : Angel (S) S-35932; UK : HMV (S) ASD2989
Maurice Ravel (1875–1937)
'L'Enfant et les Sortilèges' (1925) – a foxtrot – USA : Richmond (S) 33086; UK : Decca (S) SDD168
'Piano Concerto In G' (1931) – USA : Columbia (S) MS-6043; UK : CBS (S) 72170
'Violin Sonata' (1920) – UK : Decca (S) SDD352
Erik Satie (1866–1925)
'Parade' (1917) – Ragtime de Paquebot – UK : Philips (S) SAL3637
Schulhoff, Erwin (1894–1942)
'Partita'
'Hot Music'
'Etudes de Jazz'
'Esquisses de Jazz'
'HMS Royal Oak' – a jazz oratorio (1930); etc.

Leo Sowerby (1895–1968)

'Monotony' – a symphony for jazz orchestra and metronome (1929)

'Synconata For Jazz Orchestra'

Igor Stravinsky (1882–1971)

'Ragtime For Eleven Instruments' (1918) – UK: Decca (S) PFS4280; USA: Columbia (S) M-30597; UK: Supraphon (S) SUAST50968

'Piano Rag Music' (1919) – USA: Nonesuch (S) H-71212; UK: Nonesuch (S) H-71212

'Ebony Concerto' (1945) – USA: Columbia (S) MS-68805; UK: CBS (S) 72469

'L'Histoire du Soldat' (1918) – USA: Columbia (S) MS-7093; UK: CBS (S) 72007

Virgil Thomson (b. 1896)

'Ten Études For Piano' (1943) – No. 10 – Ragtime bass – USA: Decca DL4083; UK: Brunswick AXL2009

Sir William Walton (b. 1902)

'Façade' (1923) – UK: HMV (S) ASD2786

Kurt Weill (1900–50)

'Aufstieg Und Fall Der Stadt Mahagonny' (1927) – UK: CBS (S) 77341

'Die Dreigroschenoper' (1928) – USA: Columbia (S) 02S-201; UK: CBS (S) 77268

Additions to the above Listings

'Ragtime 1 – The City' – USA: RBF17

'Ragtime 2 – The Country' – USA: RBF18

Ragtime Rheingold: 'Ragtime' – USA: Regent 6009

'Ragtime Entertainment' – USA: Folkways (S) 22

Appendix
Checklist of Music by Scott Joplin

+ = piano roll made
p = published

The numbers are used as a quick reference throughout the book
1   *Please Say You Will* – a song (w. Joplin) – p. 20.2.1895
2   *A Picture Of Her Face* – a song (w. Joplin) – p. 3.7.1895
3   *The Crush Collision March* (*Great Crush Collision* – a march) – p. 15.10.1896
4   *Combination March* – p. 16.11.1896
5   *Harmony Club Waltz* – p. 16.11.1896
6   +*Original Rags* (arr. Charles N. Daniels) – p. 15.3.1899
7   +*Maple Leaf Rag* – p. 18.9.1899
8   +*Swipesey Cake Walk* (with Arthur Marshall) – p. 21.7.1900
9   +*Peacherine Rag* – p. 18.3.1901
10 +*Sunflower Slow Drag* – a ragtime two-step (with Scott Hayden) – p. 18.3.1901
11 *The Augustan Club Waltzes* – p. 25.3.1901
12 *The Easy Winners* – a ragtime two-step – p. 10.10.1901
13 *I Am Thinking Of My Pickanniny Days* – a song (w. Henry Jackson) – p. 9.4.1902
14 *Cleopha* – a march and two-step – p. 19.5.1902
15 *A Breeze From Alabama* – a ragtime two-step – p. 29.12.1902
16 *Elite Syncopations* – p. 29.12.1902
17 +*The Entertainer* – a ragtime two-step – p. 29.12.1902
18 +*The Strenuous Life* – a ragtime two-step – p. 1902
19 *The Ragtime Dance* – a song (w. Joplin) – p. 29.12.1902
20 *March Majestic* – a march and two-step – p. 1902
21 *A Guest of Honor* – a ragtime opera (w. Joplin) – p. 18.2.1903

22 +*Something Doing* – a cakewalk march (with Scott Hayden) – p. 24.2.1903
23 +*Weeping Willow* – a ragtime two-step – p. 6.6.1903
24 *Little Black Baby* – a song (w. Louise Armstrong Bristol) – p. 7.10.1903
25 +*Palm Leaf Rag* – a slow drag – p. 14.11.1903
26 +*The Favorite* – a ragtime two-step – p. 23.6.1904
27 +*The Sycamore* – a concert rag – p. 22.8.1904
28 +*The Cascades* – a rag – p. 22.8.1904
29 +*The Chrysanthemum* – an Afro-intermezzo – p. 22.8.1904
30 *Maple Leaf Rag* – a song (w. Sydney Brown) – p. 22.8.1904
31 *Bethena* – a concert waltz – p. 6.3.1905
32 *Sarah Dear* – a song (w. Henry Jackson) – p. 11.8.1905
33 *Bink's Waltz* – p. 11.8.1905
34 *Rose-bud (The Rose-bud March)* a two-step – p. 1905
35 *Leola* – a two-step – p. 1905
36 *Eugenia* – p. 26.2.1906 (copyright notice and in Canada 1905)
37 *Antoinette* – a march and two-step – p. 12.12.1906
38 +*The Ragtime Dance (Rag-time Dance)* – a stop-time two-step – p. 21.12.1906
39 +*Searchlight Rag (Search-light Rag)* – a syncopated march and two-step – p. 12.8.1907
40 *When Your Hair Is Like The Snow* – a song (w. Owen Spendthrift) – p. 18.5.1907
41 +*Gladiolus Rag* – p. 24.9.1907
42 *Lily Queen* – a ragtime two-step (with Arthur Marshall) – p. 8.11.1907
43 +*Rose Leaf Rag* – a ragtime two-step – p. 15.11.1907
44 *Heliotrope Bouquet* – a slow drag two-step (with Louis Chauvin) – p. 23.12.1907
45 +*Nonpareil (None To Equal) (The Nonpareil)* – a ragtime two-step – p. 1907
46 *School Of Ragtime* – 6 exercises for piano – p. 29.1.1908
47 +*Fig Leaf Rag* – a high-class rag – p. 24.2.1908
48 +*Sugar Cane* – a ragtime classic two-step – p. 21.4.1908
49 +*Pine-apple Rag* – p. 12.10.1908
50 +*Wall Street Rag* – p. 23.2.1909

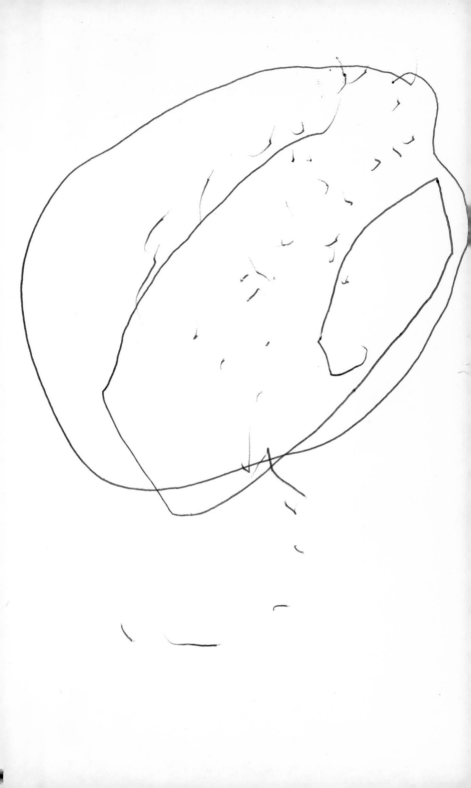